DATE DUE

PAUL BEW is Professor of Irish Politics at Queen's University, Belfast; his numerous books include *Conflict and Conciliation in Irish Nationalism 1890–1910*, a best-selling biography of Parnell and *Ideology and the Irish Question, 1912–16*. He co-authorered *Sean Lemass and the Making of Modern Ireland* and *The British State and the Ulster Crisis* with Henry Patterson.

PETER GIBBON is Senior Researcher at the Centre for Development Research, Copenhagen. He is author of *The Origins of Ulster Unionism* and joint author of *Thurcroft: A Village and the Miners' Strike*; he is also the editor of *Social Change and Economic Reform in Africa* and joint editor of *Adjustment, Authoritarianism and Democracy*.

HENRY PATTERSON is Professor of Politics at the University of Ulster and the author of many books and articles on modern Irish history including *The Politics of Illusion: A Political History of the IRA* and *Class Conflict and Sectarianism*. With Paul Bew and Ellen Hazelkorn, he is also the co-author of *The Dynamics of Irish Politics*.

Northern Ireland
1921–2001

Political Forces and Social Classes

Paul Bew
Peter Gibbon
Henry Patterson

Serif
London

First published, in slightly different form,
as *Northern Ireland 1921-1994*, in 1995,
and republished, as *Northern Ireland 1921-1996*, in 1996,
by Serif
47 Strahan Road
London E3 5DA

This revised and updated edition first published 2002

British Library Cataloguing in Publication Data.
A catalogue record for this book is available from the British Library.

Library of Congress Cataloging-in-Publication Data.
A catalog record for this book is available from the Library of Congress.

ISBN 1 897959 38 9

Designed by Ralph Barnby.
Typeset in Liverpool by Derek Doyle & Associates.
Printed and bound in Ireland by ColourBooks, Dublin.

Contents

Abbreviations

CDC	Citizens' Defence Committee
CDU	Campaign for Democracy in Ulster
CGIA	Capital Grants to Industry Act
CPRS	Central Policy Review Staff
CSJNI	Campaign for Social Justice in Northern Ireland
DORA	Defence of the Realm Act
DUP	Democratic Unionist Party
GOC	General Officer Commanding
IDA	Industries Development Act
IRA	Irish Republican Army
ITGWU	Irish Transport and General Workers' Union
LGA	Loans Guarantee Act
NICS	Northern Ireland Civil Service
NIHC	Northern Ireland House of Commons Debates (*Hansard*)
NIHT	Northern Ireland Housing Trust
NILP	Northern Ireland Labour Party
NIO	Northern Ireland Office
OUP	Official Unionist Party
PRO	Public Record Office (London)
PRONI	Public Record Office of Northern Ireland (Belfast)
PUP	Progressive Unionist Party
RIC	Royal Irish Constabulary
RUC	Royal Ulster Constabulary
SDLP	Social Democratic and Labour Party
SPO	State Paper Office (Dublin)
UDA	Ulster Defence Association
UDP	Ulster Democratic Party
UDR	Ulster Defence Regiment
UIDA	Ulster Industries Development Association
UIL	United Irish League
UUC	Ulster Unionist Council
UULA	Ulster Unionist Labour Association
UVF	Ulster Volunteer Force
UWC	Ulster Workers' Council
VUPP	Vanguard Unionist Progressive Party

Preface

From its creation in 1921 until its destruction in 1972 the Northern Ireland state was ruled by a single party, the Ulster Unionists. This party was supported for all purposes exclusively by Protestants, who comprised two-thirds of the local population. In the course of its rule it departed in a number of notable ways from the normal forms of parliamentary democracy.

These three facts – whose truth is indisputable – pose a number of important questions. How was a party able to remain in power for over half a century? Why should its overthrow have coincided with the destruction of the state itself? What was the relationship of the Unionist Party to the Protestant population? How did it rule this population, and that of Northern Ireland as a whole? Which social forces did the party represent? What did the modifications to parliamentary democracy really signify? On what bases, in short, were Ulster Unionism and the state in Northern Ireland organised?

These questions have been posed and answered before, though perhaps not exactly in this form. Readers will want to know why they should be expected to find the answers offered in this book any more illuminating than those given elsewhere. The reason is very simple. The present authors are the first to have had at their disposal the archives of the Northern Ireland state itself, which were made available through the Public Record Office of Northern Ireland in January 1977 (at least for the period until 1947).

In its preparation we have incurred debts which we wish to acknowledge, chiefly to a number of fellow researchers whose co-operation proved indispensable: Michael Farrell, J.H. Whyte, Breda Howard, Rosamund Goldie, Denis

Norman, Patrick Maume, Sharon McClenaghan and Philip McVicker. In addition, the assistance of those responsible for making available specific sources should be mentioned. The trustees of the Spender papers gave permission to quote from Wilfrid Spender's *Financial Diary*. John McColgan gave uspermission to quote from his PhD thesis, while the help of Trevor Parkhill, Peter Smythe and Sean McMenamin of the Public Record Office of Northern Ireland was most valuable. Of course, none of these individuals shares any responsibility for the positions or interpretations of the authors.

It should be noted that as a result of changes in the PRONI classification scheme the source referred to as Cab. 7 is now Cab. 9.

As we were finishing our work on the first edition of this book, the Provisional IRA announced on 31 August 1994 a 'complete cessation' of military operations, a ceasefire that was to last for almost eighteen months. The second edition was published shortly after the ending of that ceasefire with the bombing of Canary Wharf in February 1996. This edition goes to press after a period that has seen a new IRA ceasefire, the negotiation of the Good Friday Agreement and the IRA's historic decision to begin the process of decommissioning its weapons. Although paramilitary violence continues, we hope that it is not being foolishly optimistic to believe that the major source of violence over the thirty years of the Troubles, the armed struggle of the Provisional IRA, has ended for good. However, nearly four years after the Good Friday Agreement, Northern Ireland remains deeply divided and this new edition provides an analysis of a society that oscillates between progress towards political stabilisation and continuing inter-community polarisation.

P.B.   P.G.   H.P.

Introduction

The most obvious characteristic [of the Northern Ireland state] was continual one-party rule and the complete exclusion of the main opposition party, the Nationalists, from all offices beyond the level of a chairman of an urban district council ... In Derry City there was still a Unionist majority on the council, although there were more Nationalist voters in one ward than Unionists in the entire city ... All these features indicated a type of political system that in many respects differed from the British model. In no respect, however, did Northern Ireland stand out as much as in the area of security, through the existence of an armed Special constabulary, exclusively recruited from the Protestant population, and two pieces of legislation, the Special Powers Act (1922) and the Public Order Act (1951) ... It authorised the 'civil authority' (the Minister of Home Affairs) to take all such steps and issue all such orders as may be necessary for preserving peace and maintaining order. Under the Act, the Minister was authorised to issue internment orders against anyone suspected of subversion or helping subversion.[1]

This book is a radically revised version of an earlier work, *The State in Northern Ireland, 1921-72*, first published in 1979 and based primarily on the massive release of archive material in the mid-1970s. A change in the law allowed government papers to be released after 30 rather than 50 years, so suddenly two decades of official records were released for historical evaluation, although some of those studied here were later withdrawn from the scrutiny of historians. This change of policy made available not only the archives of the by then defunct Stormont regime but also many of the documents in London which deal with Irish affairs. This new work takes into account the principal elements of the documents released since then and also

1

draws attention to the implications of more recent scholarly research. A more substantial historical dimension has been provided with the addition of a new introduction and new chapters covering the two decades from 1972 to 1993 and the subsequent beginning of the 'peace process'.

There have been a number of important monographs and articles which supplement some of the arguments in *The State in Northern Ireland*; in particular, the work of Brian Barton[2] and Graham Walker[3] have valuably expanded our interpretation of the 1930s and 1940s without materially altering it. Michael Farrell's *Northern Ireland: The Orange State* appeared in 1975, written without the benefit of access to the archives of this state which were opened after publication and, therefore, failing to convey in a rounded way the full dynamic of the system. In 1983 Farrell published his *Arming the Protestants*,[4] a very much more impressive, detailed work based on the newly released papers. This substantive analysis of security policy in the period 1920-27 nevertheless seems to us to exaggerate the degree of London's support for the Unionist security apparatus. Indeed, episodes which were clearly marked by serious tension between London and Belfast are presented by Farrell as areas of unproblematic agreement between the two sides.[5] At the end of the day, however, Britain did reluctantly pay for the Northern Ireland security forces. The question remains: why? Surely the logic here is a simple one; the alternative was to ditch Sir James Craig and his government and to become directly involved again in the affairs of Ireland. This ran counter to the principal objective of British policy, which was to hold Ireland (and Irish affairs) at arm's length, the bitter lesson learned after two generations of aggravation following the Fenian rising of 1867 and the growth of Parnellism.

The most important new book to have appeared since 1979 is not, in fact, directly about the North; this is Dennis Kennedy's *The Widening Gulf*, published in Belfast in 1988, which dealt with northern attitudes towards the Irish Free State between 1920 and 1939. Kennedy clearly demonstrates – more decisively than any other writer – that Unionist attitudes in the North were seriously affected not only by the nationalist violence directed against southern Protestants in the period 1920-22 but also by their general treatment thereafter as Dublin moved even more explicitly towards the adoption of a Catholic constitution in 1937. It remains the case that northern nationalism is neglected by scholars, but important new work by Eamon Phoenix in *Northern Nationalism* has thrown much sympathetic light on Northern nationalist responses from 1912 to 1940.

Many readers will be familiar with James Connolly's prediction of how partition would actually work: 'a carnival of reaction'. We have, however, forgotten that there was also a benign theory of how it might work; this was expressed by those who, as the bitterness of the Home Rule crisis intensified in the period 1912-14, desperately sought to achieve a compromise. Leading constitutional nationalists like Redmond, Dillon and Devlin came very reluctantly to the conclusion between 1914 and 1918 that the logic of the general opposition to coercion in Anglo-Irish relations implied an acceptance of some form of partition, if only because the alternative was to present a new Irish parliament with insurmountable problems of public order. But for these constitutionalists their hope was for a continued form of direct rule which would be subject to a degree of nationalist supervision – it should be remembered that under the Home Rule scheme nationalist MPs would remain at Westminster.

The 1918 election result swept away the parliamentary nationalists – except in the North where, for example, Joe Devlin easily defeated Eamon de Valera in West Belfast. The Sinn Fein victory effectively destroyed the Home Rulers' project for mitigating partition whilst creating a context – political violence and the collapse of the administrative order in much of Ireland – which helped propel even pro-direct rule Unionists towards support for a northern parliament and state machine. Although Sinn Fein won the majority of nationalist votes in 1918, it was still opposed by a large segment of Irish opinion. Sinn Fein's President, Eamon de Valera, stood in 1918 (though not later in his career) for the principle of coercion of northern Unionists, but the leadership of both the Irish Party and the Unionists (and indeed Sinn Fein's Vice-President Father Michael O'Flanagan) resolutely rejected this policy and, instead, insisted on a policy of consent. Some form of partition was clearly inevitable – but what form would it take?

Even those who advocated a parliament in Belfast and another in Dublin assumed that the rights of minorities would be protected. The theory was a simple one. There were very large numbers of Catholics and of Protestants on the 'wrong' side of the border; both governments would, therefore, have to treat their respective minorities fairly, otherwise retribution would fall on 'their people' on the other side of the partition line. It did not work out this way, hence the greater accuracy of Connolly's prediction. But why? In the first place, because it was clear by the end of the 1920s that Protestant numbers in the Free State were falling markedly. This removed a key constraint from James Craig and his northern Cabinet; in the 1930s, as Dr Kennedy's book shows, Craig ignored complaints about unfair treatment from southern Protestants as easily as those from northern Catholics. A man whose political skills in his early days had been organisational rather than imaginative, Craig in his fifties – and even more in his sixties – settled into a rut in which *cuius regio, euius religio* appeared to be the simple solution of the Irish question. His 'after good dinner appearance' and 'lack of charm', to use George Buchanan's telling phrases, became more marked.[6] In consequence Craig, who had spoken in support of 'broad views' and 'tolerant ideas' in February 1921 (admittedly when the spotlight of British public opinion was on him, but also when he faced a daily threat of assassination), moved towards a much more systematised adoption of anti-Catholic sectarian rhetoric, both on his own part and that of other members of his government.

In many respects this was a rather paradoxical development. After 1925 it was clear that the threat represented by the Boundary Commission to the stability, at any rate, of the territorial extent of the Northern Ireland government, had evaporated. The eventual report of that body left the 'six counties' intact. Sir Wilfrid Spender later recalled a meeting between Sir James Craig and the Irish Free State Premier, W. T. Cosgrave, at which 'Mr Cosgrave burst into tears and said that Lord Craigavon had won all down the line and begged and entreated him not to make things more difficult for him.'[7] In fact, however, Craig was at first anxious to establish a much better north-south relationship. A new era had, in principle, opened up: as Stephen Gwynn pointed out, the fact that Lord Londonderry was believed to have twice turned down the offer of a post in the British Cabinet to stay in the Northern Irish government was an indication of the seriousness of the potential for instability between 1921 and 1925; equally, the fact that Londonderry felt free to leave in 1925 revealed the measure of 'relief'.[8] As far as the economically straitened Irish government was concerned, the North was anyway a potential burden – *vide* the decision to stop paying the salaries of nationalist teachers who refused to recognise the Craig government revealed even before the end of 1922. It was enormously important that the tripartite boundary agreement signed in London on 3 December 1925 released the Irish government from significant financial liabilities. More broadly, throughout 1926, and indeed until the assassination of Kevin O'Higgins, the Cabinet's most impressive personality, on 10 July 1927, the Dublin regime seemed to give a primacy to reaching some kind of accommodation with Anglophile forces in Ireland. This is a point, for example, which is much stressed in the analysis prepared for the Rockefeller Foundation.[9] Craig, in turn, armed by what he felt to be firm Dublin recognition of his own government, was prepared to offer a new deal:

> I have always taken the view that the illustration that I have used with regard to the two friendly neighbours holds equally strong when one considers that for future time the North and South have got to live together as neighbours and the prosperity of Northern Ireland does undoubtedly affect the prosperity of Southern Ireland and a peaceful and prosperous Southern Ireland reflects on the North ...
> Therefore, a man is shortsighted indeed and no patriot to his country who would see one portion standing out prosperous, rich, happy and content if, on the other side, he was to see despondency, poverty and going down the hill instead of going up. So it is for the government of the South and the government of the North to turn their hands rather from the matters which may have divided them in the past to concentrate on the matters which really affect the welfare of the people in their own area with a view that the whole of Ireland, and not one part of it alone, may be prosperous.[10]

Internally, Craig offered a 'fair deal' to nationalists and George Leeke, the Derry Nationalist MP, announced that he intended to enter the Northern Irish parliament and put

Craig to the test without conferring any legitimacy on partition. It all appeared to be very promising, yet things turned sour. In part, the subsequent deterioration was due to the effect of applying the logic of a devolved system of competitive party government to a divided society, especially as pressures on the government increased. As Lord Charlemont, the regime's relatively liberal Minister of Education, wrote to General Hugh Montgomery on 5 February 1936, sectarian speeches by the Unionist leadership had become much more commonplace 'in the last years or so'.

> It's not entirely religious fervour – it's the gradual increase of pressure from independent organisations, leagues, socialism, all the political expressions of Ulster individualism. For the first ten years of self-government, the hurrah boys and their friends kept Unionist MPs in their seats. But we're used to self-government now ... this is the trend of present politics, and unless the Herodianism of the Protestant League can be out-Heroded, I, a supporter of the government, will lose my seat to a jackanapes, and with it, any chances of preferment.[11]

Of course, Charlemont's comment avoids the issue of the regime's responsibility for the emergence of sectarian pressure groups. General Hugh Montgomery, probably the most liberal figure to emerge from within the Unionist establishment, wrote to R. Dawson Bates, the Minister of Home Affairs and probably the least liberal figure to emerge from the same quarter, that, 'Their growth [the Ulster Protestant League] does not surprise me, after the encouragement the extreme section have received from most of our political leaders, not to mention the smaller fry.' Referring to a celebrated speech in favour of sectarian discrimination in employment by Sir Basil Brooke, Minister for Agriculture, Montgomery added:

> Basil's bloomers were bad enough but I don't think they would have counted for much if the other members of the government had not allowed themselves to be publicly identified with the boycott policy. Can you wonder then when this was closely followed by the 'Protestant government for a Protestant people' these rogues and their 'cut throat' friends from Glasgow should have taken the government at their word and tried to go one better?[12]

Interestingly, Craig, who had spoken of a 'Protestant parliament for a Protestant people' in 1934, went on immediately to say that he now saw north-south relations in terms precisely of that competitive model which he had himself so explicitly rejected in 1926. Of course the evolution of the Irish government towards an explicitly 'Catholic constitution'[13] containing a 'claim' on the North, as southern Protestants left in droves, played an important role here, as was to emerge in a later correspondence between General Montgomery and John Andrews, Craig's successor as Prime Minister in 1941.

Montgomery argued that the world war had clearly strengthened the Union but that a future Labour government was sure to hold a commission of enquiry to investigate the treatment of Northern Irish Catholics. Any far-sighted local regime had two obvious courses of action open to it. The first was to establish the most 'neighbourly relations which circumstances permit' between Ulster and 'our next-door neighbours across the border'. It was no use asking Dublin to abandon its claim on the North; this was 'equivalent to saying "I am quite prepared to make friends – if you would change your views and agree to mine"'. Secondly, it was to remove 'any reasonable cause of complaint from our Roman Catholic fellow subjects in the six counties'. Montgomery asked explicitly:

How is the fact to be explained that in Fermanagh some 25,000 Unionist have 17 seats in the County Council, while some 35,000 Nationalists get only 7; and that in Tyrone, some 60,000 Unionist get 16 seats while some 75,000 Nationalists have only 11? Is the fact that although the average percentage of Catholics in the six counties of Northern Ireland (excluding Belfast and Derry) is approximately 40, the average %age of salary received by RCs as officials is about 10%.[14]

Andrews would hardly deny discrimination. Indeed, he was himself convinced of the need for it. He therefore offered a rather different line of defence. He agreed that both parts of Ireland should act as 'good neighbours' though 'not as co-partners'.

The fact remains, however, that so long as those in authority [in Dublin] demand Ulster, improved relationships could be difficult to establish, because this demand cuts at our nerve centre ... You also refer to certain injustices under which you argue the Roman Catholics suffer. If you compare their position with that of the Protestants in Eire you will see how much better their position is, both as regards appointments and freedom from coercion such as the Protestants of Eire suffer by being compelled to learn Irish which, I understand, in connection with government and other appointments, is marked higher than English, I fear with a sinister object ...[15]

In March 1943 John Andrews told Sir Wilfrid Spender, who was coming near the end of his stint as head of the Northern Ireland Civil Service:

... we could only take into our service those who were loyal. He then went on to refer to the position of the Ministry of Agriculture, where he said there was a large number of Roman Catholic inspectors. This caused a great deal of difficulty. In fact, he knew a case in Comber where it was shown conclusively that unfair discrimination had been made by one of these inspectors. He knew a branch of the Ministry of Agriculture in which practically the whole staff were Roman Catholics. I said that I thought he must be referring to the slaughterhouse branch, in which Protestants refused to work because of the conditions of employment. This was the case.

Spender commented:

Personally I am of opinion that the Prime Minister is making a mistake in going into this matter at all ... he would find it a source of embarrassment if he produced any statistics or defended himself in this matter. Offence would be caused in Great Britain if he took a bigoted point of view, and he would also further exacerbate the difficulties between the British government and Eire: on the other hand it was a mistake to encourage representations which showed any intolerance amongst his followers.[16]

The requirement in the Unionist political leadership to win elections within the framework established in 1921 should never be forgotten. Craig, in particular, had acquired in early electoral forays on his own account and on his brother's a strong sense of the potentially fissile nature of the Protestant bloc at a time when the nationalist threat was in abeyance, as it was after 1925. In the 1900s the threat came from the politics of land 'reform' or 'Russellism'; in the interwar period, it came from Labour or Unionist splits. Craig seems to have developed an exaggerated concern for the need to preserve the unity of the Protestant bloc. His views were not always shared by other prominent Unionists. There are many documents in this book outlining the criticisms of senior Unionist Cabinet members and officials of Craig's 'populist' style. With the benefit of hindsight, their concern both about Catholic alienation and British anger at the growing cost of Northern Ireland seems to be justified.

In the 1930s Craig certainly appears to have fallen in love with a devolved system only reluctantly accepted in the 1920s, whilst at the same time occluding the realities of growing financial dependence on London from the eyes of his supporters in the country at large. Yet Craig's patriarchal Protestant style – emphasising the unity of that community to the exclusion of the minority – was the answer to one key problem: how to win elections for the Northern Ireland parliament. His willingness to flout London Treasury expenditure guidelines and his general desire to maintain some kind of social parity with the Britain – even when Northern Ireland itself could not afford it – made perfect short-term political sense and even, at times, materially benefited the Catholic community, as when proportionate places appear to have been reserved for it on outdoor relief schemes.[17] These problems dogged all later Unionist premiers.

Craig's successor, John Andrews, as we point out, was forced to make incautious promises of social expenditure which in effect, helped to terminate his premiership in 1943. Andrew's successor, Basil Brooke, for many years thrived on his decision to force through the 'socialist' welfare state against the opposition of his more conservative colleagues, but in a way he was the victim of his own success – and, it should be noted, the collapse of the IRA's 1956 campaign – and he had lost large parts of Belfast Protestant working-class opinion to the Northern Ireland Labour Party before his retirement in 1963. The project of winning back this lost support – and not the civil rights grievances of the

Catholic population – dominated the relatively liberal Terence O'Neill's early years as premier. Again with the benefit of hindsight, this appears to be absurd, as O'Neill himself was to acknowledge in later life.[18] Nevertheless, the recently released Cabinet papers amply confirm this interpretation – the reduction of unemployment as the government's grand obsession – whilst also showing that the Belfast government understandably felt that the new Lemass government in the Republic had broken decisively with traditional nationalist ideology in many respects, thus opening up the possibility of a new era of pragmatic co-operation.

This book aspires to be a serious historical attempt to deal with the specificity of the Northern Ireland state, and most of its analyses of key questions have never been challenged; in the context of efforts made either to demonise the system rather than understand it (the labelling of Northern Ireland as an 'apartheid state'), or alternatively to whitewash it, we present this extended interpretation which, unlike so many others, at least has the merit of a substantial acquaintance with the archives.

Notes

1. Cornelius O'Leary, 'Northern Ireland, 1921-72, Misshapen Constitutional Development and Scholarly Silence' in R.J. Hill and M. Marsh (eds), *Modern Irish Democracy*, Dublin 1993.

2. Brian Barton, 'Relations between Westminster and Stormont during the Attlee Premiership', *Irish Political Studies*, Vol. 7, 1992. See also his *Brookeborough: The Making of a Prime Minister*, Belfast 1988.

3. Graham Walker, 'The Commonwealth Labour Party in Northern Ireland 1942-47', *Irish Historical Studies*, Vol. XXIV, No. 93, May 1984; for the 1930s, see his 'Protestantism before Party! The Ulster Protestant League in the 1930s', *Historical Journal*, Vol. 28, No. 4 (1985). See also his biography, *The Politics of Frustration: Harry Midgely and the Failure of Labour in Northern Ireland*, Manchester 1985.

4. Michael Farrell, *Arming the Protestants: The Formation of the Ulster Special Constabulary and the Royal Ulster Constabulary, 1920-27*, London 1983.

5. For example, our view of General Archibald Montgomery's War Office enquiry in 1922 is rather different from Farrell's.

6. *Morning Papers*, London 1965, p. 49.

7. PRONI D715. Sir Wilfrid Spender's Financial Diary, 24-29 May 1943.

8. Stephen Gwynn's *Observer* article on this topic is reprinted in the *Derry Standard*, 26 February 1926.

9. Dr Gregg to Dr Pearse, 19 August 1927, Tarrytown, Rockefeller Foundation, New York, Series 1.1. Sub Series, Ireland 403A/1/6/1.7. The Rockefeller Foundation was asked by the Irish government for financial help with a series of expensive social and medical projects, hence the existence of these detailed reports on Irish political life.

10. *Derry Standard*, 19 February 1926.

11. P. Bew, K. Darwin and G. Gillespie, *Passion and Prejudice*, Belfast 1993, p. 50.

12. PRONI D2661/C/1/M/1/1. Hugh Montgomery to Sir Dawson Bates, 27 April 1936.

13. For the sectarian tone of some Dublin parliamentary discussions, see D. O'Sullivan, *The Irish Free State and its Senate*, London 1940, pp. 415-8.

14. PRONI D2662/C/A/1/18. Hugh Montgomery to John Andrews, 29 July 1941.

15. D2661/C/1/A/1 20. John Andrews to Montgomery, 30 July 1941.

16. PRONI, D715. Financial Diaries of Sir Wilfrid Spender, 29 March 1943.

17. Bew, Darwin and Gillespie, *Passion and Prejudice*, p. 54.

18. We owe this point to the research of Dr Alan Grattan of the University of Surrey.

1   The Formation of the State, 1921–1925

The subject of this study, the Northern Ireland state, was born in 1921 – or, more precisely, between that date and 1925, when the report of the Boundary Commission left the border as it was. While the circumstances of its conception, gestation and birth did not wholly prefigure its later development, they made a profound contribution to it. It is only right, then, that they should be examined in detail. The year 1918-19 will be taken as a starting point.[1] Three sets of events together began to dominate the stage of Irish politics in that year. Their conjuncture amounted to a crisis which set the parameters for the formation of both states in Ireland.

Firstly, and most importantly, British political and military domination of Ireland was broken by the IRA. In response, a shift took place in political relations within the Unionist bloc, a shift which was to have a decisive effect on the spontaneous process of state formation in the north of Ireland. Thirdly, the British political elite devised a series of new Irish strategies aimed at coping with the new situation and ensuring an outcome that would do least injury to British interests. These strategies determined the nature of the external modifications to the spontaneous process of state formation, and in some degree further modified political relations between Protestants.

Most of this chapter will be concerned with the second and, more particularly, the third of these events. Although an analysis falls outside the scope of this work, some prefatory remarks are necessary about the first of them.[2]

The Loss of British Dominance in Ireland

While it could be argued that any moral hegemony had been

dead since the Famine, or at least since the Land War, British political hegemony in Ireland remained effectively undisturbed until 1918. Parnell, Dillon and Redmond were by no means its spokesmen, but after 1886 they allowed the British, for all their vacillation, to establish a form of *pax Hibernica* and to dictate the nature of the Irish question.

From 1913 to 1918 the essence of the *pax Hibernica* was devolution plus partition. The formula proved resilient because it succeeded in minimising a serious conflict in Britain as well as one in Ireland and became a relatively stable reference point for all parties. Equilibrium was disrupted temporarily in 1916 and permanently in 1918-19 by the onset of popular guerrilla warfare, the electoral destruction of the United Irish League (UIL), constitution of the first Dail and other associated changes.

Just as the waning of British rule led to the decomposition of *pax Hibernica*, it led also to a weakening of the Irish middle class's influence in favour of the 'tyranny of the dead'. Like the loss of British hegemony, this accelerated as the military struggle gained ground in 1920. Before 1919 the principal source of the nationalist bloc's disunity had been conflict between constitutional nationalism and the 'physical force' party. By 1920 the latter grouping was itself in disarray. Like Parnell's party, Sinn Fein and the IRA possessed leaders of strong moral authority; unlike it, they had no strong bureaucratic centres to dictate local policy.

In Belfast, however, the Catholic middle class largely retained its leadership over local nationalistic politics, as the membership figures for the different nationalist and republican organisations in the city in 1920 make clear.

Table 1　*Membership of Nationalist and Republican Organisations in Belfast, 1920*

Nationalist		Republican	
United Irish League	6,533	Sinn Fein	980
National Volunteers	1,300	Irish Volunteers	500

Source: H. Patterson, *Class Conflict and Sectarianism*, Belfast 1980, p. 185, n. 5.

Even though Joseph Devlin's* supporters far outnumbered the membership of other organisations, his influence was diminished by the changing national balance of forces. The faltering of his control over both northern Catholics and southerners who came to fight in the North was discerned by the Unionist leadership, and in a probably more exaggerated way by the British Colonial Secretary, Winston Churchill.[3]

The essence of all these changes was that the traditional nationalist stance of political bargaining and readiness to compromise on partition, which had won grudging acceptance from both the British and the Unionists, now appeared to be suffering eclipse. A resolute determination to destroy British administration forcibly throughout Ireland was now to the fore. Equally significantly, all but those in the British armed forces believed that little could ultimately be done to resist it. The exception was, of course, the Unionists.

The Unionist Bloc, 1913-1921

The Unionist bloc had been constituted in its contemporaneous form during the opposition to the third Home Rule Bill in the period 1911-13. Previously, while there had been a bloc, it was far from inclusive of Ulster Protestants and even further from being unified.

The basic source of disunity was not the tradition of liberalism among Ulster Presbyterians, as has often been maintained, but the much stronger tradition of autonomous political activity by the Protestant labour aristocracy, shopkeepers and small employers. Dating back at least to 1868,[4] it was complex and heterogeneous in its origins, but possessed a clear and distinct ideology combining militant anti-Catholicism with democratic, anti-landlord and anti-oligarchic sentiment.[5] While its political expressions tended to be episodic, they nevertheless modified the development of both conservative politics and the labour movement in the Six Counties.

Independent Orangeism, as it was known, proved most influential in periods when British governments were following conciliatory Irish policies, for example between 1900 and 1905.[6] Partly in order to circumvent this, the local

* See Biographical Note on p. 255.

middle class in 1905 reorganised itself politically into a force independent of the Conservative Party at Westminster. The setting up of the Ulster Unionist Council was a decisive step which neutralised independent Orangeism's rhetoric and the orthodox Orange Order began to expand rapidly soon after.[7] Independent Orangeism's decline was complete by 1913, when the forces it had represented became integrated into a bloc with Protestant landlords and business leaders, exemplified in the paramilitary Ulster Volunteer Force (UVF). This provided an irresistible focus of popular Unionist opposition to a united Ireland.

There were two consequences of the new integration. The more obvious was that the politics and ideology of the Protestant working class were stripped of their progressive elements. These remained only residually, in the form of a militant lack of deference to traditional authority. While the new ideology occasionally accommodated reformist labour views, it found its main expression in a stronger version of loyalism of the middle classes. The other was that with the establishment of large-scale political and military organisations there emerged a professional political leadership possessing its own relative autonomy from the Unionist elite. This was popularly known, after its headquarters, as the Old Town Hall circle. Here the situation rested until 1918.

1918 and 1919 were the years not only of the crushing of the UIL and the development of a militant Sinn Fein challenge to British rule, but also of intense class conflict throughout Britain, manifested in a large increase in trade union membership and a series of strikes. Locally, the longest and most militant stoppage was a three-week strike of Belfast shipyard and engineering workers. Traditionally well organised, and predominantly Protestant, they defied the national leadership of the Confederation of Shipbuilding and Engineering Unions in demanding a ten-hour reduction in the working week. The strike spread to involve municipal, gas and electricity workers and closed down large sections of industry and commerce. A General Strike Committee assumed powers to issue permits allowing 'necessary' production, published a daily newspaper and generally adopted the attributes of a local soviet. Its activities instilled fears in a section of the Unionist leadership, particularly

Edward Carson* and R. Dawson Bates,† that the class alliance embodied in the old UVF was under threat of dissolution.

Carson in particular appears to have been predisposed to exaggerate the danger of a Bolshevik outbreak in Britain. This notion afflicted right-wing conservatives generally and achieved institutional expression in the activities and publications of the British Empire Union, of which Carson became president in 1918. In Belfast the Unionist leadership had – in the recently created Ulster Unionist Labour Association (UULA) – a means of initiating a purge from the local trade union movement of 'Bolsheviks' and (what it saw as the same thing) republicans. Based on some of the most traditionally fervent working-class Unionists in the shipyards, the UULA was first intended as an instrument of Carson's 'New Unionism', i.e. a more 'socially conscious' and 'democratic' Unionist party, designed to stave off electoral losses to Belfast Labour in the city. In this role it made little progress. 'New Unionism' was opposed by sections of the local middle class and left the working class cold. The organisation's subsequent history was to prove more congenial to all concerned. Effectively it involved sounding the counter-revolutionary alarm to 'loyal workers' against the twin threats of socialism and republicanism.

By the beginning of 1920 growing unemployment in the engineering and linen industries and the large numbers of demobilised soldiers still out of work were creating friction within the Protestant bloc. The ex-servicemen, who were comparatively well organised, were a particular thorn in the side of the local middle class. With the latter's encouragement the UULA succeeded in giving the conflict a sectarian twist. It identified the unemployment problem, especially that of Protestant ex-servicemen, with the alleged 'peaceful penetration' of Belfast industry during the war by 'tens of thousands' of Catholics from the south and west.

As the guerrilla campaign in those regions intensified, the Unionist leadership increasingly 'exposed' the connection between socialism and republicanism, a process in which it was assisted by the British labour movement's (verbal)

---

* See Biographical Note on p. 250.
† See Biographical Note on p. 249.

support for the national struggle. In the spring and summer of 1920, as the Old Town Hall circle demanded more repression from the British state, its working-class appendage held 'indignation' meetings in Belfast to attack the unions on the other side of the Irish Sea for their 'pro-republicanism' and 'Bolshevism'. The meetings also pledged support for the police and demanded more vigorous counter-insurgency measures. After one such gathering in the shipyards in July, attacks began on Catholics and workers identified as Belfast Labour members and socialists. They spread throughout the engineering and some sections of the linen industry to result in over 8,000 expulsions within a week.

Perceiving themselves to be increasingly vulnerable, the employers and leading Unionists not only acquiesced in such events but justified them – in sharp contrast to their attitude to previous expulsions, for example in 1893 and 1912. To the Unionist leadership the reserves of the British government seemed weak, and as a result they were willing to endorse practices which served to consolidate their class alliance and guarantee the social basis for a more authoritarian response to Sinn Fein.

Subsequently in the shipyards, large engineering works and railways, Vigilance Committees were set up to ensure that no 'disloyalist' was re-employed. Most Protestant employers looked on with tacit approval. For the remainder of 1920 popular Protestant domination of Belfast workplaces was ritually celebrated in a series of Union Jack unfurlings and parades, often addressed by members of the UULA. Soon the first signs of Catholic retaliation emerged. Trains carrying shipyard workers were subjected to sniping and bomb attacks. Reprisals were inevitable and in East Belfast there followed widespread looting and burning of Catholic-owned spirit groceries and fatal clashes between the British army, guarding Catholic property, and Protestant crowds. Leading members of the UULA became involved in creating an unofficial special constabulary, drawn mainly from shipyard workers, with the task of 'policing' Protestant areas.

A shift in political relations had taken place within the Protestant community. In its anxiety to re-establish a militant basis for resistance to republicanism which could operate independently of the British, the Unionist leadership had been obliged to concede a portion of its power to the Orange section of the working class. Having done so, it strove to confer institutional and official status on the arrangement. Popular Protestant practices of workplace exclusivism became linked to efforts by Carson and Craig* to reconstitute the UVF and secure British government approval and funds for it and UULA-based constabularies in Belfast.

One Unionist argument in trying to persuade the British to finance the constabularies was that, unless such organisations were officially sanctioned, wild and enraged Protestants would take the law into their own hands. Since 'the younger and wilder the better' was in some areas a criterion for membership, this was ironic.[8] Although the granting of official status to these bodies had Lloyd George's approval from the beginning, such characteristics ensured that his approbation was not shared by other important figures in the Irish administration. In particular, approval was withheld by the commander-in-chief of the British army in Ireland, Sir Neville Macready. Macready was even accused of sending enthusiastically nationalist members of the Royal Irish Constabulary north to lead the UVF into ambushes.[9] In the event he and his supporters were overriden and official status was conferred upon the B Specials in November 1920.[10]

The formation of the state had been anticipated by the formation of one of its most critical apparatuses – an independent paramilitary force whose populist flavour of Protestant self-assertiveness was not to be diminished by its new status. The official endorsement of this spirit was to shape both state formation and Catholic attitudes to it.

The British State and its Strategies, 1921-1925

At the onset of the Anglo-Irish war the strategy of the British political establishment became once more a subject of dissension. Three main positions emerged. There were those who advocated a new *pax Hibernica*, involving a predisposition to unity and capitulation to the IRA; opponents of capitulation, who favoured a pragmatic adaptation of the old

* See Biographical Note on p. 251.

pax Hibernica; and the rump of the old British Unionists, whose motto was 'govern or get out'.[11] These camps were fluid in membership and were spread right across the relevant British state institutions.[12] The result was a degree of incoherence and unpredictability in British policy which increased at least until 1921.

It is evident that until this date efforts were made by successive Cabinets to keep all options open. For long periods temporary restrictions were repeatedly placed upon the Ulster Unionists' political freedom. It was insisted, for example, that after the treaty the B Specials be stood down, generally for three months and for a considerably longer period in specific areas.[13] More fundamentally, Lloyd George was still making periodic efforts as late as November 1921 to get Craig to go into a united Ireland as the easiest route to a general dominion settlement.[14]

Nevertheless, during 1921 two major areas of strategic agreement were reached within the British political elite. First, the doctrine that Ulster could not be coerced into a united Ireland by force was finally acknowledged. Lloyd George told Griffith, 'The instrument [the army] would break in our hands if we tried.'[15] It is important to recognise that this did not imply a unanimous endorsement of partition. 'We are pledged not to coerce Ulster,' Tom Jones, Assistant Secretary to the Cabinet, wrote on 10 November 1921, adding, significantly, that 'some would confine that to physical force'.[16]

The reason why a united Ireland was still favoured in some quarters related to the second measure of broad strategic agreement that had been reached, as to which of the likely outcomes of the Anglo-Irish war was the most desirable. There was a consensus that the setting up in Dublin of an Irish republic under de Valera* should be prevented, and it was now commonly understood that this meant the promotion and installation of the Free State party. Be that as it may, a serious tactical difference arose on how the objective should be attained.

The Prime Minister, Lloyd George, and his immediate associates (in particular Tom Jones) took the view that successful installation of the Free State party depended upon

---

* See Biographical Note on p. 254.

a hard line being pursued against the Unionists. Only by showing that they could make the British rap the Unionists knuckles could the Free Staters gain sufficient credibility in the South to persuade people that they could bring about Irish unity. It mattered not whether the Free Staters had this power, nor whether they would ever indeed unite the country. It was important only that the impression be given. To that extent the fate of the Unionists was a subordinate concern.

This prognosis was contested by the Colonial Office and its Secretary of State, Winston Churchill. Churchill's position was even more complex than Lloyd George's. In the long run he felt that the best opportunity for the success of a stable settlement in Ireland was an ultimate unity between the most conservative elements, north and south.[17] But for this to be secured, he reasoned, the Unionists had to be convinced of the conservative *bona fides* of 'Cosgrave, Mulcahy and the others'. It followed that the Free Staters should be encouraged to draw 'a clear line between [themselves] and the Republicans'.[18] On this basis Sir Alfred Cope, Churchill's link man in Dublin, 'gave them [the Free Staters] hope of the north coming in on terms provided the Provisional Government won through the present troubles'.[19] While Churchill therefore strongly agreed on excluding de Valera and the republicans from power, he reversed the order of tactical imperatives formulated by Lloyd George. While he hoped the Free Staters would be installed in power (preferably by civil war[20]) this did not have priority over support for the Unionists.

From December 1921 what differences (as a former Liberal Home Ruler) Churchill had with the Ulster Unionists began to evaporate. Craig's wife recorded that her husband found him the most reliable ally in the British Cabinet.[21] Churchill reciprocated the feeling.[22] He could find the Unionists irritating, believing that they were slow to reach sensible arrangements with Collins,* the Free Staters' leader.[23] He was also anxious that they remain within the law and seems to have been sensitive to the plight of Belfast Catholics,[24] but in the last resort he was Ulster Unionism's implacable supporter. It was predictable that Sir Henry

* See Biographical Note on p. 251.

Wilson, the pro-Unionist Chief of Imperial General Staff, should have noted in February 1922 that Churchill's committee had agreed to 'reinforce Ulster as much as she wanted'.[25]

Inevitably, the level of British support for Ulster soon became a matter of contention between the Lloyd George group and the Colonial Office. On 17 March 1922 Tom Jones told the Prime Minister:

> We are departing from the spirit of the treaty and will be charged by the world of one more breach of faith if we continue in the present policy of paying for the Special Constables ... cloaking military force under the guise of a police force.[26]

Churchill cheerfully ignored such warnings and continued to offer Unionism wholehearted support. On 29 April his aide, Sir James Masterson Smith, wrote to Lord Londonderry:

> Sir James Craig was evidently pleased with the talk he had with Winston, and realises that Winston appreciates to the full the difficulties that confront the northern government at the present time and the heavy burden that Sir James Craig and his colleagues are carrying. Early next week Winston hopes to be able to have a meeting at his home with Lord Cavan [Commander-in-chief, Aldershot] and others to explore with care and in detail the requirements for which the northern government press. I think you will find that Winston will be able to go a long way towards meeting Sir James Craig ...[27]

It is no surprise to find Craig informing the Ulster Cabinet on 12 May 1922 that the loyalist position was now receiving a much more sympathetic hearing in England.[28] It is hardly surprising, either, to find him reporting that, as far as Irish affairs were concerned, Churchill 'undeniably had the predominating voice where the wider interests clashed with the costs involved'.[29]

The differences between Churchill and Lloyd George came to a head in May, when an unexpected *rapprochement* between Collins and de Valera suddenly appeared likely. Churchill's tactics would have been nullified by such an event. Never a stable man, he now became almost hysterical. He spoke of 'social deterioration going on in many parts which Collins was doing nothing to arrest' and of the need to reconvert the 'English capital' (Dublin) into a new Pale.[30] Meanwhile he transferred troops from Cork to the Six Counties to reassure the Ulster government.[31] Masterson Smith thought him in need of a holiday.[32]

The Lloyd George circle realised the extent to which the situation was slipping from their control. They continued to believe that Churchill's conciliation of the Unionists was undermining the Free Staters. There is some evidence that this was indeed the case.[33] Lloyd George further believed that if the northern state continued to be strengthened while Collins and de Valera reached agreement there would be war between north and south. In his view, for this *rapprochement* to be undermined at de Valera's expense it was imperative to weaken the position of the Unionists immediately. He responded to increasing southern complaints about unofficial Protestant violence and breaches of the Craig-Collins pact signed the previous March.[34] With strong support from the Treasury, he informed the northern government of his intention to hold a judicial enquiry into its affairs.

The Treasury's hostility to the Unionists centred on their 'profligacy' with public funds. It viewed the likely consequence of Churchill's policies as indefinite and unlimited British subvention of forces over which it had no control.[35] 'Of course he does,' scrawled the Treasury controller, Otto Niemeyer, in the margin of a letter from Masterson Smith informing him that Craig preferred to work through Churchill.[36] Niemeyer was a virulent critic of the northern regime who detested Craig's manoeuvrings and retained a lifelong contempt for him. Like Lloyd George, he saw Ulster Protestants as spongers and described Craig's financial demands as 'incredible if they were not in black and white'.[37] Above all, the Treasury deeply resented the setting up of a Joint Exchequer Board to arbitrate conflicts between Belfast and the Treasury, since its very existence constituted a blow to the principle of strict Treasury accountability. Its findings were to make the Treasury powerless to resist what O'Nuallain has called,

> a consistent line of policy pursued by Sir James Craig and his Ministers ... to extract the maximum, financially, economically and politically, from their connection with Britain,

while at the same time endeavouring to whittle down their obligations.[38]

Had the Treasury objections been sustained in full, life would have been made almost impossible for the Belfast regime. Since this would have run counter to the objectives of both the Churchill and the Lloyd George factions, it was not seriously contemplated. A more interesting question is why a united front of both the Lloyd George circle and the Treasury failed to have any practical effect on the Belfast government's security policies. Craig seems to have attributed it to the strength of Churchill's resolution on the matter, but his strategic position as chairman of the Cabinet committee on the Irish Provisional government was also of great help.[39] Yet it is unlikely that the Colonial Office could have sustained its position for much longer had not a dramatic turn of events occurred in the south.

On 28 June 1922 battle was joined in the Four Courts in Dublin, marking the start of the Civil War in the South, and the conflict soon reached the point of no return in its intensity. The whole nature of London-Dublin-Belfast relations was transformed. There was no longer a political constraint on British policy towards the North, in other words the need to maintain Collins's credibility. Subsequent attempts to interfere with the development of the northern security forces were fitful and individualistic rather than the product of concerted government effort. Internal division had prevented such action at precisely the time when it would have counted for most.

Already, though, Lloyd George had shown signs of retreat from an uncompromisingly critical stance towards the Unionists. This is evident from the sequel to the proposal for a judicial enquiry. When the Northern Irish Cabinet first discussed the British government's proposal at the end of May it immediately threatened to resign *en masse*.[40] Bates, now Minister of Home Affairs, was particularly infuriated. On 15 June he wrote to Lloyd George,

> … it would be impossible to give any explanation as to why, if the occurrences in Northern Ireland were to be judicially enquired into, those in the South and West were left unchallenged. In truth the suggested Commission is

impossible. You cannot try a Government responsible to a Parliament by a Commission of judges ...[41]

The Ulster Prime Minister resolved to travel to London, there to challenge this turn in British policy at its source. A crucial meeting was held at 10 Downing Street on 16 June. Craig argued that a public enquiry could be justified on only two grounds. Either there had to be a strong outcry in Britain against the Ulster government, or the British government must feel the money spent financing security was not justified. Neither of these conditions applied, he claimed. Craig therefore sought instead an inquiry by a British government official.

The pressure on Craig began to show in his exaggerated statements and needless provocations. He said a judicial enquiry would destroy the operation of intelligence work in Ulster, but this was not accepted. When Lloyd George muttered a few homilies on the mixture of parties and creeds that made up the British Empire, Craig could not resist a characteristic interjection – 'there was no advantage in that' – to which Lloyd George replied that, 'there was every advantage'.[42] Lloyd George made it clear that he was anxious not to endanger his relations with the southern leaders – 'It was most important that we should not appear indifferent to the fate of the [Ulster] RCs.'[43]

Nevertheless, Lloyd George gave way on the decisive point. He accepted Craig's proposal that the enquiry should be secret and be carried out by a public official. The name of S.G. Tallents was agreed upon. It was hardly a controversial choice – Tallents was attached to Churchill's Irish committee. Balfour was unhappy about this proposal as the meeting ended. 'A report from Tallents, if public, would have little effect in counteracting propaganda,' he told Lloyd George. Lloyd George replied, 'Sir James [Craig] had to carry his colleagues with him. A report from Mr Tallents making it quite clear there was a ground for a public enquiry would enable him to do this.'[44]

The decision to appoint Tallents was made at a moment of great importance. Craig had staved off a judicial enquiry which in all likelihood would have destroyed his government. *Either* it would have had to acquiesce in the commission, in which case its relation with the Protestant working class would have been undermined, *or* it would have had to oppose the commission and declare unilateral independence. The decisive factor seems to have been Lloyd George's appreciation that Craig's Cabinet was solidly united behind him. Nevertheless the situation was still unresolved in an important sense. Craig had agreed to accept a recommendation – if Tallents should feel it necessary – to create a judicial commission. Tallents's report would apparently be of great moment.

Tallents arrived in Belfast towards the end of June 1922 and began making enquiries. He quickly made up his mind. Look, for example, at his unflattering portraits of the Unionist leadership. But note his crucial conclusion. Craig he described (somewhat generously) as having 'a great desire to do the right and important thing: not a clever man, but one of sound judgement and can realise a big issue'.[45] Pollock, Minister of Finance, was better informed and 'more intellectual than his colleagues. On any question but politics his word would be taken absolutely.'[46] Bates, on the other hand, was 'a weak man and a political hack. His two chief assistants are also violent partisans.'[47] In general, 'Ministers are too close to their followers and cannot treat their supporters as from a distance.'[48] However, any move against Craig would not strengthen a relative moderate like Pollock – rather it would play into the hands of loyalist extremists. The implication was clear. For better or for worse, the British government was going to have to work with Craig.

Tallents placed most of the blame for the failure of the Craig-Collins pact on the IRA: 'I have no doubt that the failure to give effect to Clause 6 of the agreement, which provided for the cessation of IRA activity in the Six Counties, was the major cause of its failure ...'[49] Given the level of republican violence at the time, this conclusion had plenty of evidence to support it.[50]

His recommendation was clear. There was no need for a judicial enquiry. 'Inadvertently it would encourage Northern Catholics in their refusal to recognise the Northern government.' He added that if he had to choose a precise wish for immediate fulfilment it would be the kindly removal of the present Minister of Home Affairs to a less responsible post.[51]

Tallents had undoubtedly produced an essentially Unionist analysis. Whatever its conclusions, they would, however, have been strategically redundant by the time the Cabinet came to read them. The political and military miscalculations of the Free Staters and republicans had seen to that.

The Security Forces

The strategy of class alliance pursued by the Unionist middle class, together with the diplomatic strategies of the British government, were responsible for the establishment of a Northern Ireland state with a sectarian-populist flavour. It is time now to examine the effects of this pedigree on the general form of the state, which was to acquire its outlines in this period.

If there is one field which exemplifies the specific characteristics of state formation in Northern Ireland it is the constitution of the security forces. The most important – and the most revealing – event within this area in this period was the Solly-Flood affair, a complex of events which have hitherto been kept secret.

Major-General Sir Arthur Solly-Flood was appointed Military Adviser to the Northern Ireland government on 7 April 1922, at the height of the IRA offensive and of official and unofficial Protestant counter-offensives in the North.[52] He was the nominee of Sir Henry Wilson, Chief of the Imperial General Staff and one of the leading Irish Unionists within the British political elite. Wilson, who Craig saw as an important ally, had unofficially been advising the Ulster Cabinet on security for some time. In the spring of 1922 he retired from his military posts to become Unionist MP for North Down at Westminster. It was not simply the establishment of a sectarian Protestant force, the B Specials, as an integral part of the security system of the new state which is worthy of note, although this was remarkable enough, but the issues of control which logically followed. It is indeed most unusual to find a regional government in possession of a paramilitary police force over which the central government had so little direct influence, and even more remarkable to find that efforts to establish a certain professionalism in the force were constantly blocked.

Neither Solly-Flood nor Wilson was in any sense a supporter of the Lloyd George position. Neither had the slightest idea of ever temporising in the Unionist cause,

which Wilson at least saw as a key imperial issue. Even
Churchill was obliged to exaggerate the reactionary nature
of his position to gain credibility with Wilson.[53] Nevertheless,
Solly-Flood was soon to find himself ostracised as a
subversive.

Craig presumably requested military advice, through
Churchill, because of the incapacity of his own forces to deal
with the intensification of the IRA campaign. As Farrell
points out, the appointment itself must have been a victory
for the Northern Irish government, since under the
Government of Ireland Act the Belfast regime was
prohibited from raising or controlling a military force.[54]

On the other hand there can be no doubt whose idea the
original conception of the Military Adviser was, or what it
entailed. In correspondence in September 1920 both Sir
Neville Macready and Wilson had agreed that the notion of
a special constabulary was a dangerous one. 'To arm those
"Black men" in the north without putting them under
discipline is to invite trouble,' Wilson wrote.[55] An earlier
note in his diary was more specific:

> Winston suggested arming 20,000 Orangemen to relieve the
> troops from the North. I told him that this would mean
> 'taking sides', would mean civil war and savage reprisals,
> would mean, at the very least, great tension with America and
> open rupture with the Pope. Winston does not realise these
> things in the least and is a perfect idiot as a statesman.[56]

Both Wilson and Macready saw a need for a new scheme for
the organisation and control of the Ulster security forces.
Macready was later to explain further how the new appointment of Military Adviser was to play a key role in this
reorganisation. It was to be backed by a competent staff loaned
by the British government and by a thoroughly effective CID
staffed by officers 'unbiased towards those political and
religious currents which run so strongly in the North'.[57]

It was this role which Solly-Flood set out to play. He threw
himself into his work with perhaps rather too much gusto. It
is clear that in the eyes of the British government he became
linked with various grandiose and highly expensive
schemes.[58] As the nominee of a politician famous for his
imperialist and reactionary views, he was bound to be

unpopular in certain circles. Tallents quite reasonably requested that a close eye should be kept on his activities.[59] Unionist apologists have suggested that his eventual removal was purely an 'economic' decision.[60] In fact, it is certain that Solly-Flood was encouraged by Craig himself to believe in the existence of massive financial backing.[61]

Solly-Flood was given to dramatic gestures. 'He came from explaining to a meeting a scheme for handing out six to eight revolvers per factory *for use by tried men under the owner's control*,' Tallents reported after one encounter.[62] He did not even win the trust of three B Special commandants who had resigned and approached Tallents with harrowing tales of unpunished murders and other indications of religious bias in their force.[63] None of this should be any particular cause for surprise. Sir Henry Wilson's nominee was likely to pursue the task of defeating the IRA with enthusiasm and, to some, an irritating flamboyancy.

But it must be insisted that despite his demagogy Flood's course was a complex and contradictory one. It had a genuinely cutting edge with respect to certain organs of the newly formed northern security forces. He was a forceful critic of the B Specials' style of work. He was amazed to find that they had, as far as he could see, no disciplinary code. He drew up a number of critical documents on the force. 'The B Special Constabulary ... are not only a sedentary force but their ability is greatly impaired by their lack of commanders, discipline and training,' is a typical comment.[64] There is clear evidence that he became an object of fear and suspicion to B Special commanders.

He was also capable of winning a limited degree of Catholic approval. Father Murray, one of the 'front-line' Belfast priests, declared at a meeting in which Solly-Flood expressed his determination to crack down on Protestant terrorism, 'I wish we had the military in charge; we would be all right comparatively.'[65]

Gradually tensions grew between Solly-Flood and the Unionist establishment. At the end of June 1922 his position was greatly weakened by the assassination of his sponsor, Wilson, by the IRA. By 12 September the Cabinet conclusions record the Unionist leadership's determination to centralise the command of security forces in Northern Ireland under one man, the RUC Inspector-General,

Charles Wickham. Solly-Flood offered his resignation almost immediately, but his staff carried on until the end of the year.

In this period Solly-Flood and his staff fought a rearguard action against their opponents. In September the English staff of the CID submitted evidence critical of the RUC and the B Specials to a secret British enquiry under Barrington Ward, KC, into the murder of three Catholics in Cushendall in June 1922.[66] As the permanent officials of the Ministry of Home Affairs expected, the subsequent report strongly condemned the Ulster branches of the security forces and was suppressed.[67] His staff also sought to leak embarrassing material concerning the judicial flogging of IRA suspects – a major concern to both British and Irish governments at this time.[68]

But Solly-Flood had few allies. His other major sponsor besides Wilson, Macready, was regarded with general suspicion because of his suspected sympathy for moderate nationalism. Solly-Flood was believed in Unionist circles to have passed on his criticism of the B Specials to the War Office, and certainly Lord Derby who, having taken over at the War Office following a change of government, became his most important supporter.

Macready complained bitterly about Solly-Flood's removal:

> Major-General Solly-Flood and the staff he took with him to reorganise the Police Force in Ulster have without doubt made a very great improvement and the CID branch under Col. Haldane has been mainly instrumental in bringing about the present lull in activities of both Sinn Feiners and Orangemen. It is due to this Department also that they have been very instrumental in stopping reprisals because both officers and agents were entirely unbiased.
>
> The officers of this Department, I understand, refuse to serve under Col. Wickham who, I am given to understand, is not imbued with the necessity for a strong CID Department, which in my opinion should be maintained even at the expense of the executive police. In addition to this I am quite satisfied that Col. Wickham is quite incapable of organising and commanding a police force such as is required at the present time in Ulster. This was also the opinion of Sir Henry Wilson when he suggested to the Northern government that

the command of the RUC was the limit of Col. Wickham's capacity.[69]

Tallents 'replied' in a letter to Masterson Smith on 6 December 1922:

There is, I know, though I have not been directly involved in it, a considerable row on about the CID here. This has hitherto been under Solly-Flood who, I understand privately, is now about to leave. He has for many weeks now been a mere ornament, and otherwise than perhaps socially will not be a practical loss. About a fortnight ago the Minister of Home Affairs gave Wickham orders to take the CID over. This much upset GHQ, whom I happened to see the same day. This implied that the CID had Imperial interests in their keeping and they would have physically to prevent the transfer after due notice ...

I have kept outside the discussions, but my sympathies are, I must say, with Wickham and the Northern government. If one twentieth of what I have heard about the CID is true, the sooner it goes the better. I do not see how one can defend an arrangement which makes it difficult in principle for the Military Adviser, an employee of the Northern government, to give control of the police to the same government. And if it be true that it also had military and other work outside the scope of the Northern government, I presume that its fruits on that particular branch appear on the reports which used to be circulated to the Lord Lieutenant, and which seemed to be always a proof of wasted money. I hear that Derby has written to Craig, and that Craig has refused to reconsider the change of control. Macready, as you know, always had a low opinion of Wickham and was, in my opinion, wrong about this as some other Northern questions.[70]

What is significant about Tallents's response is not so much his area of explicit disagreement with Macready – in the assessment of Wickham and the work of the CID – as the problems he did not mention. These included the original conception of the post of Military Adviser, his unpopularity with the B Specials, the Cushendall enquiry, differing attitudes on flogging and so on. It is impossible to regard his letter as anything but a cover-up.

The true significance – it must be emphasised – is that the Military Adviser and his staff were intended in part at least as a curb on the 'natural' sectarianism of the repressive apparatuses in the North. Macready more than hints that their impartial action against Orange extremists had brought them into disrepute with the regime. It is surely also worthy of note that Solly-Flood's staff refused to serve under Wickham. With the departure of the Military Adviser a curb on the partisanship of the security forces was removed.

It should not be thought that Wickham was blind to the defects of the B Specials. His private and public comments on the subject do not admit of such a reading.[71] However, his personal authority and career were closely linked with the fortunes of the B Specials at this point. He therefore took full advantage of Solly-Flood's discomfiture.

The Solly-Flood affair left a legacy in the shape of War Office proposals to reorganise the Special Constabulary which plagued the Ulster government as late as 1925. In 1924 the War Office seemed to have returned to the idea of a new Military Adviser. Wickham resisted any erosion of his position in a letter to Spender: 'Any scheme which would place a B man under the control of the police and a military organiser would be liable to friction.'[72] In 1923 General Sir Archibald Montgomery carried out an enquiry for the War Office. The Loughgall commandant of the B Specials wrote to Spender* on 14 December 1925 in response to this visit:

> We have been bothered again with rumours about scrapping the 'B' force or turning it into something else which have disturbed our men. We have traced the trouble to General Montgomery's visit, and as far as I can gather, the expressions used by him in person. We saw the Inspector-General last week and found him in absolute agreement with us on the necessity of keeping up night patrols under the present organisations – and on the type of work. There was a flavour of the late Military Adviser's opinions in General Montgomery we did not like. Any voluntary force like the 'B' force is a delicate instrument needing to be played skilfully not banged on, and whatever their shortcomings, they don't like to be told they are no good and must either be swept or completely reorganised, officers and all![73]

The Solly-Flood affair illustrates some basic tendencies in the new state which were to be of the utmost importance.

Firstly, there is the fact that the Unionist leadership

* See Biographical Note on p. 264.

regarded as its principal objective the retention of a military force responsible to it alone, and which the British could never use independently. Had Solly-Flood's proposals been implemented it is probable that the IRA offensive would have been blunted sooner, since the B Specials were notoriously ineffective militarily. In the long run, however, military effectiveness was not the point. Rather, it was that the Unionist elite's military independence should receive permanent institutional recognition. The maintenance of such an institution was crucial. Its meaning was clear – a signal that Ulster could not be coerced. Because of all this the B Specials were to occupy a position of the greatest importance in the new security forces.

Secondly, the affair shows what the Unionist leadership understood as the local condition of maintaining the viability of the B Specials. It was no more and no less than retaining the force's essentially 'populist' character. This amounted to a propensity to sectarianism, to a kind of democracy in which unpopular officers were squeezed out of the force and to a voracious appetite for public funds. The primacy accorded to the objective of having such a force therefore required as a strategic imperative the retention of a special relationship between the Unionist leadership and the Protestant working class. Not only were the B Specials to occupy a significant position within the security forces, but the latter as a whole were to acquire a decidedly populist character.

Thirdly, the affair shows the external condition for establishing such a situation – the acquisition of a large degree of autonomy from Westminster as far as law and order was concerned. Wilson and Solly-Flood were enthusiastic Unionists but were not 'Ulstermen'. They failed to understand that the best allies were not those who tendered Unionism advice, or even apologised for it, but those who shut up. Northern Ireland's viability required not 'good' government but its own government, with as much administrative discretion as possible. Over the years, safeguarding this discretion was effectually to become Unionism's 'foreign policy'.

Conclusion

There are two main trends in the polemical literature on the construction of the northern state. In the nationalist or republican version British imperialism divided Ireland with the objective of weakening Irish nationalism or even creating a bridgehead for the eventual reconquest of the whole island. No doubt this was made easier by Unionist popular support for partition, but primacy is given to the role played by the British state. It is sometimes argued in defence of this position that there was even a section of the Belfast middle class which favoured unity and remained cool towards partition. According to George Dangerfield, for example, there was still a viable opposition to Sir James Craig among the Belfast business community in 1921-22.[74] There is reason to believe that this may have been the view of the Lloyd George circle until Tallents's visit.[75] Such views had little foundation, however. The evidence they were apparently based on suggests only that some Belfast business circles saw themselves as moderates and were worried by what they saw as Craig's excessive reliance on the working class.

Craig acknowledged this in a major speech when he asked for 'closer liaison' with businessmen and requested a greater, even if 'nominal', participation in the B Specials from them.[76] He admitted that business support had been much greater for the old UVF. The premier asked local business leaders for £100,000 for propaganda purposes. The response was less than rapturous, as Lord Londonderry explained to Tallents:

> In the old days Carson and the Old Town Hall circle had propandised the shipyard workers. The business community were not wholeheartedly with them. Craig recently appealed for £100,000 as a minimum propaganda fund, result £13,000, £1,000 from me.[77]

The Chamber of Commerce continued to press vigorously for 'an end to outrages from whatever quarter'.[78] A clear difference of emphasis is noticeable. Certain sections of the Unionist middle class undoubtedly felt that the political leadership cultivated unnecessarily close links with the working class.[79] Here is the seed of the division between the populists and anti-populists which – once the threat to the state's very foundation had been removed – was to appear within the government. As we shall see, this division was to

prove crucially important in the history of Northern Ireland.
At this stage, however, the conflict remained muted and
subordinate, and was to remain so for some time.

In the Unionist version the critical aspect is the determination of the Ulster Protestants not to accept a united
Ireland. At best, many British political leaders were seen as
unreliable allies. In this account the role of the British state
is of secondary importance compared to the weight of
pressure within Ireland itself. As for the shape of the state,
this was dictated by Catholic nationalist hostility, north and
south.

The last of these propositions needs to be heavily qualified.
It is now possible to reconstruct the attitude of the key
nationalist political elements towards the northern regime.
The anti-Treaty forces under de Valera were, of course,
uncompromising opponents of the Craig regime. They had
little influence in Ulster, however, and were regarded with
contempt by the more representative northern leaders.[80]
This did not, of course, mean that they were unable to
maintain a certain capacity for both aggressive and protective
violence – as the pro-Treaty IRA did. The two most important
northern leaders were Joseph Devlin, the constitutional
Nationalist MP, who still retained the support of most of
Belfast's Catholics, and Bishop Joseph MacRory,* a supporter
of Michael Collins and Sinn Fein, who spoke for the militant
Sinn Fein spirit to be found in the Catholic areas closer to the
border. Throughout the spring and summer of 1922 Devlin's
prominent supporters (particularly in the Belfast Catholic
business – as opposed to professional – community)
contrived to give the impression that they favoured
immediate recognition of the regime.[81] MacRory was torn
between accepting this view and listening to the more
aggressive councils of Michael Collins.[82] Collins told him in
January that Southern non-recognition of the Northern
parliament was necessary, 'otherwise they would have
nothing to bargain with Sir James Craig'.[83] He committed
himself to the support of schoolteachers and local bodies
who refused to recognise the Ulster regime. MacRory noted
that, 'If the policy of non-recognition was adopted, the
people of the North would have to fight alone.'[84] The bishop

* See Biographical Note on p. 259.

was caught on the horns of a dilemma. He sought to follow Collins but he seems to have been pulled in the direction of support for Devlin. In May, for example, with a show of reluctance he conveyed Devlinite pressure on the subject to Collins.[85] At the end of June he told Tallents that he favoured an 'absolutely free Ireland' but saw it was 'not practical politics'.[86] He offered recognition of the Northern regime if it agreed to co-operate with the South on certain broad general questions.

During this period Michael Collins, as the leader of the Provisional government, was the decisive figure around whom the others were dancing. Throughout 1922 the Cabinet records report him as being committed to a 'peace policy'[87] towards the Unionists, but the term covered a wide variety of practices – some of which were not exactly peaceful. He supported northerners who refused to recognise the state. He reminded his Cabinet when – perhaps symptomatically – it appeared to be forgetful of the necessity of drawing up schemes of non-co-operation with the loyalists.[88] In early March he was to be found arguing that the Sinn Fein line should be insistence on confronting uncompromising Unionists with a boundary commission followed by a tariff war against those portions which still remained outside the Free State.[89]

By the end of March 1922 such militancy was also compromised by the pact with Craig, which obviously involved a degree of *de facto* recognition. The paramount obsession of Belfast Catholics was a reversal of the expulsions and evictions, and this had undoubtedly been conveyed to the Free State government in strong terms. By the end of May Collins was furious that Craig had failed – in his view – to keep the terms of their personal agreement. He warned the British government that its support for loyalism was endangering its broad agreement with him. He continued to send arms to the North, and it is certain that broad groupings in the IRA continued to have confidence in him.

By June, however, the militancy of the Free State government had weaned somewhat. The anti-Treaty IRA's offensive in the Belleek triangle of County Fermanagh was reversed early in the month by British troops. The affair seems to have greatly alarmed the Free State regime, which reaffirmed its commitment to a 'policy of peaceful obstruction' on the North and resolved 'that no troops from the Twenty-Six Counties, either those under official control or attached to the executive, should be permitted to invade the Six Counties'.[90] This commitment undeniably helped to spark off the subsequent civil war in the South. At the end of June Collins publicly stated the new position:

> I think any attitude towards Ulster which is the attitude of the government is not understood. There can be no question of forcing Ulster into union with the Twenty-Six Counties. I am absolutely against coercion of this kind. If Ulster is going to join us it must be voluntary. Union is our final goal, that is all.[91]

The beginning of the Civil War was soon followed by further indications of a slackening of interest in reunification. Early in July Cabinet hints were already being dropped that the policy of paying the salaries of northern nationalist teachers who refused to recognise the regime should be abandoned.[92]

Collins, however, retained a strong if inconsistent personal involvement in Ulster. On 2 August, as commander-in-chief, he called a meeting with the northern leaders of the pro-Treaty IRA. According to Seamus Woods, the Officer Commanding of the 3rd Northern Battalion (Belfast):

> The late Commander-in-Chief [Collins] outlined the policy we were to adopt – the non-recognition of the Northern government and passive resistance to its functioning. At the same time from the military point of view we were to avoid as far as possible coming into direct conflict with the armed forces of the Northern government; any action on our part would be purely protective. The late Commander-in-Chief made it clear to us that the Government in Dublin intended to deal with the Ulster situation in a very definite way, and so far as the Division was concerned, every officer present felt greatly encouraged to carry on the work which we had policy to pursue and an assurance that the Government would stand by them.[93]

A few days later he seemed to give a different impression in a letter to Churchill when he noted, 'The Nationalists of the North-East stood out *for the time being* to prevent the carving up of their country.'[94] Nevertheless on 22 August, when Collins was killed in the course of the Civil War, militant northern nationalists felt they had lost their most significant supporter on the Free State side. Seamus Woods wrote at the end of September pointing out that the Free State government now appeared to favour recognition of the Unionist state. 'Owing to the position that has arisen in the rest of Ireland [the Civil War] I take it the Government feel that they are not equal to the task of overcoming the Treaty position with regard to Ulster.'[95]

In November, accepting the logic of its position, the Free State withdrew financial support for those Northern teachers it had previously supported.[96] Some months later Cosgrave told Craig that for the Southern leader the only significance of the Boundary Commission was the need 'for a political cry etc. ... at the coming elections'.[97]

Such collusion seems to date from 12 September 1922. On that date Craig wrote to Churchill:

I am delighted to see that the Provisional Government really seems to be taking a firm line and I have received unofficial representations from them that we should assist in rounding up certain agitators who make a practice of crossing the border into Northern Ireland whenever the pursuit in the South of Ireland becomes too hot. This forms an additional reason that we should maintain our force at a high state of efficiency.[98]

The matter of nationalist attitudes towards the foundation of Unionist government is therefore of some complexity. As far as the Free State faction in government was concerned, the summer and autumn of 1922 appear to have marked phases of retreat from support for even peaceful forms of resistance in the North. Key Ulster Catholic leaders seem to have favoured some form of recognition of Craig's regime. On the other hand, in certain moods Collins had been sufficiently belligerent to create genuine loyalist fears as to what the real meaning of the 'peace' policy was. Moreover, Catholic opposition in border areas where there was a nationalist majority tended to be strong.[99] On balance it seems difficult to suggest that the nationalist pressure was sufficiently coherent or united to explain *ipso facto* the form of the state. For example, there is no evidence to suggest that

Belfast Catholic non-recognition of the regime was automatic.

The history of the Belfast Catholic Recruiting Committee, set up to investigate the possibility of recruiting Catholics into the B Specials, is instructive in this respect. It has been pointed out that two of its members were arrested, while three others were put on the 'wanted' list.[100] Even so, the committee continued to meet and to discuss the principle of Catholic involvement in the security forces. There was no question of outright Catholic rejection of the idea. Father Laverty, the most important 'political' Catholic priest in Belfast and a supporter of Collins, claimed to have prevented personally the resignation of 50 Catholic members of the RUC. The overwhelming impression that emerges is that Catholic involvement in the B Specials depended on a cessation and reversal of the expulsions of Belfast Catholics from their jobs and homes.[101] In other words, the Belfast Catholic attitude to the Northern Ireland state was a product of a specific conjuncture of events rather than simply the expression of a deep-seated ideological attitude.

The major strand in the Unionist viewpoint has the merit of stressing the dominant importance of forces inside Ireland. That of the nationalists has the value, on the other hand, of stressing the role of an important external force – even if British policy is accorded a unity it did not always possess. However, a persuasive analysis of the situation cannot be produced simply by supplementing these strands. For in fact both Unionist and nationalist accounts share a common deficiency. They do not pose the connection between the formation of the Northern Irish state and the class relations inside either the Unionist or the nationalist blocs. In this chapter primacy has been given to the analysis of these relations. The action of external forces was effective only in so far as it fused with forces thrown up by these relations.

In particular, the expulsions of the summer of 1920 marked a critical phase within the Unionist bloc, a crisis which permitted the development of the B Specials and gave the Unionist security forces a particularly repressive aspect from the Catholic point of view. Yet although the Unionist political leadership's dependence on the B Specials (which worried at least some sections of the middle classes) was already marked in the period 1920-22, it did require external British support – and here the nationalist account is correct – to underwrite this relationship.[102]

British policy vacillated and was subject to internal divisions, but in the outcome the pressure on the Ulster security forces evaporated.[103] The combination of developments inside the Unionist bloc with the principal strategy within the British state produced a particular form of state in Northern Ireland. Subsequent personal attempts to reduce its sectarian paramilitary aspect were easily thwarted. Full Catholic recognition, which in the first instance had been negotiable, receded into the distance.

The result was, of course, disastrous for the Catholic community. They did not contest the gerrymandering of the local government election boundaries by the electoral commission under the control of Bates's nominee, Sir John Leech, KC. The 1924 election revealed the vital importance of the committee's work. As Farrell notes, 'Some of the results were bizarre. In the Omagh Rural Council area with a 61.5 per cent Catholic majority, the nationalists had won the council in 1920 with 26 seats to 13. After Leech's endeavours the Unionists held it with 21 seats to 18.'[104] The nationalist boycott of the Leech commission gave the Unionists a ready-made excuse. In the course of a British government investigation Tallents told Sir Alexander Maxwell:

> The Northern Ireland government will no doubt contend that they have every desire to be fair and that if any unfairness in the distribution of districts has taken place, it is due to the fact that the nationalists did not appear before the Commission.[105]

In fact, in later years, the Home Office itself – to the irritation of the Dominions Office – offered precisely this explanation for what had happened.[106] The gerrymandering naturally increased opportunities for discrimination in local government employment. As one official admitted, 'There can be little doubt that in those areas where there was a Protestant majority in the councils, in practice posts do not often go to Catholics.'[107]

The Unionist leadership, perhaps significantly, was not totally united on this issue. Sir Wilfrid Spender hoped (and claimed that Sir James Craig did so too) that it would be possible to induce some of the councils to use their powers of co-option for the purpose of securing a better representation of minorities.[108] Spender also opposed discrimination against Catholics by local government agencies.[109] But such doubts and reservations within the Unionist bloc were to prove of little significance in the absence of a systematic Catholic attempt to utilise them.

It was not that nationalists were unaware of these divisions – they simply lacked a strategy for exploiting them. Seamus Woods, commanding the Belfast Battalion of the IRA, pointed out how intra-Unionist conflicts had led to shooting incidents between different sections of the security forces. In the summer of 1922 he noted that, 'A desire for peace became popular amongst the better classes and the Northern government took up the task of restoring order in good faith.'[110] This led to violent conflict with the extremist District Inspector Nixon's followers – whom Woods compared with the irregulars in the South. (Woods ought to have been well informed: the IRA had stolen all the files from the RUC headquarters and from Solly-Flood's office!) Woods, however, merely noted these developments and made no comment on their implications, if any, from a nationalist point of view. Some months later Collins's intelligent assistant legal adviser, Kevin O'Shiels, commented on a mid-November speech of Craig's:

> It will be noted that he is now suffering from the danger of unlawful and irregular action among his own disappointed supporters ... behind the veneer of calmness ... There are grave rumblings of discontent which may do much to drive the Northern premier to seek accommodation with us.[111]

Again, beyond the expression of pious hope there is nothing here in the way of a political strategy.

In 1940 'Ultach' published in the *Capuchin Annual* a paper entitled 'The Persecution of Catholics in Northern Ireland'. Arguably, it is still the most eloquent and concise condemnation of the discriminatory and oppressive features of the Unionist regime. Stormont paid the author the compliment of banning his sequel. In the storm it provoked one crucial feature has been ignored: 'Ultach' did not argue, as so many nationalists have done, that the oppression of

Catholics was an inevitable product of partition. He wrote: 'I do not regard the present intolerable position of Catholics in the partitioned area as being a necessary consequence of *partition as such*, but rather the result of a *particular form of administration.*'[112] This chapter has sought to detail the processes, at the level of the British state, the Dublin government and, most important of all, relations within Ulster itself, that determined this outcome, the outlines of this 'particular form of administration'.

Notes

1. The most important works covering the genesis of Unionism are P. Buckland, *Irish Unionism*, Vol. II, *Ulster Unionism and the Origins of Northern Ireland, 1886-1922*, Dublin 1973, P. Gibbon, *The Origins of Ulster Unionism*, Manchester 1975, and H. Patterson, *Class Conflict and Sectarianism*, Belfast 1980.

2. Two major works on this subject are F.S.L. Lyons, *Ireland Since the Famine*, London 1971, and E. Rumpf and A.C. Hepburn, *Nationalism and Socialism in Twentieth-Century Ireland*, Liverpool 1977.

3. PRONI Cab. 4/14/11; PRO C.O. 906/25 (meeting of Churchill and Belfast Catholic businessmen, 2 June 1922).

4. cf. Gibbon, *Origins*, pp. 87-111.

5. cf. H. Patterson, 'Independent Orangeism and Class Conflict in Edwardian Belfast: A Reinterpretation', *Proceedings of the Royal Irish Academy*, Vol. 80, C, No. 1.

6. H. Patterson, 'Refining the Debate on Ulster', *Political Studies*, XXIV (1976).

7. Between 1908 and 1913 the Order's membership in Belfast more than doubled, rising from 8,834 (Patterson, *Class Conflict and Sectarianism*, p. 158, n. 5.) to 18,800 (S. Baker, 'Orange and Green' in H. Dyos and M. Wolff (eds), *The Victorian City*, London 1973, Vol. II, p. 808). It was to remain around this figure in the 1920s – an estimate of 20,000 was given in the *Belfast Newsletter*, 7 January 1924.

8. W. Clark, *Guns in Ulster*, Belfast 1967, p. 9.

9. Spender, *Financial Diary*, October 1943, PRONI D715.

10. P.J. Buckland (ed.), *Irish Unionism, 1885-1923: A Documentary History*, Belfast 1973, p. 442.

11. For an analysis of the leading figure in this group see K. Jeffrey, 'Sir Henry Wilson and the Defence of the Empire', *Journal of Imperial and Commonwealth History*, V (1977).

12. The Irish Office concentrated these divisions. In 1919 Haldane spoke of 'some 36 departments, many of them hardly on speaking terms with each other'. T.J. Jones, *Whitehall Diary*, Vol. III, *Ireland*, London 1971, p. 12.

13. They remained excluded from the Bone area of Belfast in January 1922 (*Belfast Newsletter*, 21 January 1922).

14. St.J. Ervine, *Craigavon: Ulsterman*, London 1949, p. 444.

15. Quoted in N. Mansergh, *The Irish Question, 1840-1921*, London 1975, p.31.

16. Jones, *Whitehall Diary*, p. 160.

17. Churchill to his wife, 14 August 1922, in M. Gilbert, *Winston S. Churchill*, Companion Vol. IV, Part 3, London 1977, p. 1957. (All other references are to Part 3 of this volume unless otherwise stated.)

18. Churchill to Cope, 24 August 1922, in ibid., p. 1964.

19. Cope to Masterson Smith, 4 August 1922, PRO C.O. 31.

20. Gilbert, *Churchill*, pp. 1891 (PRO Cab. 23/30), 1947-8.

21. Ervine, *Craigavon*, p. 473.

22. Churchill to his wife, 10 February 1922, in Gilbert, *Churchill*, p. 1766.

23. Uncirculated draft Cabinet memo, 11 February 1922, in ibid., p. 1847.

24. PRO C.O.906/25.

25. Diary of Sir Henry Wilson, in Gilbert, *Churchill*, p. 1774.

26. Jones, *Whitehall Diary*, p. 194.

27. Churchill Papers, 22/12, in Gilbert, *Churchill*, pp. 1879-80.

28. PRONI Cab. 4/41/10.

29. Craig to Baldwin, 28 November 1922, PRO T. 160/150/5814/1.

30. Jones, *Whitehall Diary*, p. 201.

31. Cab. 23/30, in Gilbert, *Churchill*, p.1893.

32. Jones, *Whitehall Diary*, p. 200.

33. Lyons, *Ireland*, pp. 454-5.

34. The pact was signed in view of the growing 'anarchy' north and south. Its formal objective was co-operation in pursuit of peace. The significant clause of the pact concerned security. An advisory committee of Catholics was set up to recruit Catholic specials to patrol Catholic areas. Many Unionists feared that if such provisions were implemented the force would be destroyed.

35. 'Sir James Craig rather humorously says that the last thing in his mind is to escape the obligations of the 1920 Act. But under that Act the *whole* obligation for the Specials is on the Ulster exchequer.' (Niemeyer's note, 26 May 1922, PRO T. 163/6; g 256/049.)

36. PRO T. 163/6; g 256/049 (9 May 1922).

37. Niemeyer to the Chancellor, 22 November 1922, PRO T. 160/150/5814/1.

38. L. O'Nuallain, *Ireland: The Finances of Partition*, Dublin 1952, p. 44.

39. Gilbert, *Churchill*, p. 1706.

40. PRONI Cab. 4/46/2.

41. PRO C.O. 906/29.

42. PRO C.O. 906/26. Minutes of Downing Street meeting.

43. Ibid.

44. Ibid.

45. PRO C.O. 906/24. The Tallents papers are to be published in full by Kevin Boyle.

46. Pollock had quite a reputation as an intellectual. He had lectured an amazed Irish Convention in 1917 on Parnell's views on economics. Lord Charlemont, a Cabinet colleague, regarded his opinions on education as 'close to those of the leaders of the Soviet Union' (Ervine, *Craigavon*, p. 524).

47. PRO CO. 906/24.

48. Ibid.

49. PRO C.O. 906/30.

50. M. Farrell, *Northern Ireland: The Orange State*, London 1975, p. 57.

51. Tallents to Masterson Smith, 4 July 1922, PRO C.O. 906/30.

52. For details, see Farrell, *Orange State*, pp. 39-65.

53. C.P. Scott, Diary, quoted in Gilbert, *Churchill*, p. 1681.

54. Farrell, *Orange State*, p. 54.

55. G.F.N. Macready, *Annals of an Active Life*, London 1924, Vol. II, p. 488.

56. Wilson papers, 26 July 1920, in Gilbert, *Churchill*, Companion Vol. IV, Part 2, p. 1150.

57. Macready, *Annals*, Vol. II, p. 629.

58. Jones, *Whitehall Diary*, p. 198.

59. Tallents to Masterson Smith, 4 July 1922, PRO CO. 906/30.

60. A. Hezlett, *The 'B' Specials*, London 1973, p. 102.

61. cf. Craig to Churchill, 19 September 1922, PRO T. 160/150/5814/1.

62. Documents of June 1922, PRO C.O. 906/27. See also Ricardo's notes.

63. Undated document, probably early July 1922, PRO C.O. 906/27.

64. Guiding lines of plans for the defence of Ulster, 20 September 1922, p. 17, PRONI 7G/25.

65. Belfast Catholic Recruiting Committee, 31 March 1922, PRO C.O. 906/25.

66. Sir Arthur Hezlett has written, 'Cushendall was the ambush of A Specials on 23 June in which four IRA were killed' (*B Specials*, p. 92). The report of Barrington Ward reads a little differently: 'My conclusion is that no one except the police and the military even fired at all ... I am unable to accept the evidence of the Special Constabulary from Ballymena. I am satisfied that they did not tell me all they knew about the circumstances in which three men died, and in view of the reports made by the military officers at the time and the evidence given by them before me, I do not believe that none of the police entered any of the houses ... Major Ross-Blundell was ready to assume responsibility for the acts of the Special Constabulary under his temporary command: but I am bound to say that I do not see how any steps could be taken to prevent what happened (Secret report of Barrington Ward, Cab. 24/138 CP 4193.)

67. Megaw to Craig, 4 September 1922, PRONI Cab. 7B/47/1.

68. Megaw to Craig, 1 September 1922, ibid.

69. Secret S.F.B. 69, 2 September 1922, PRO Cab. 43/2.

70. PRO C.O. 739/1.

71. Macready, *Annals*, Vol. II, p. 609. In a passing-out parade speech at a Specials training camp, Wickham 'asked them, and the others with whom they worked and lived, to maintain control over themselves and put a stop finally to the outrages which had occurred in the past' (*Belfast Newsletter*, 30 September 1922).

72. Wickham to Spender, 19 November 1924, PRONI Cab. 7A/4/3.

73. PRONI 7G/26.

74. G. Dangerfield, *The Damnable Question: A Study in Anglo-Irish Relations*, London 1977, p. 347.

75. cf. the reports from Cecil Litchfield (a senior Ulster civil servant) that Belfast businessmen were prepared to hold a joint economic conference with the south (Jones, *Whitehall Diary*, p. 195).

76. Speech, 3 April 1922, PRO C.O. 906/23.

77. PRO C.O. 906/24.

78. *Belfast Newsletter*, 4 April 1922.

79. cf. recollections of Sir W. Hungerford, first secretary of the Unionist party, in Buckland (ed.), *Unionism*, pp. 441-2.

80. S.G. Tallents, memorandum on talk with Bishop MacRory, 1 July 1922, PRO C.O. 906/26.

81. Tallents to Masterson Smith, 4 July 1922, PRO C.O. 906/30.

82. See the tone of his letter to Collins, 7 May 1922, in SPO S1801a.

83. SPO, Cabinet conclusions, Vol. 1, meeting of the Provisional Government, 30 January 1922, North East Ulster Policy. (Hereafter PG.)

84. Ibid.

85. MacRory to Collins, 7 May 1922, SPO S180 1a.

86. Talk with Bishop MacRory, 1 July 1922, PRO C.O. 906/26.

87. SPO, Provisional Government Cabinet conclusions, 1 February, 3 June 1922, etc., 19 August 1922, p. 1.2. 1922.

88. SPO, Provisional Government Cabinet conclusions, PG12, 4 May 1922; see also PG17.

89. SPO, Provisional Government Cabinet conclusions, 6 March 1922.

90. SPO PG27, 3 June 1922.

91. *Belfast Newsletter*, 30 June 1922.

92. SPO PG56, 30 June 1922.

93. S. Woods to Commander-in-chief in the South, 29 September 1922, SPO S1801a.

94. PRO C.O. 906/31. Emphasis added. Collins to Churchill.

95. S. Woods to Commander-in-chief in the South, 29 September 1922, SPO S1801a.

96. SPO PG57a, 8 November 1922.

97. PRONI Cab. 4/84/9, 30 July 1923.

98. PRONI Fin. 30/FC/9. We are indebted to Philip McVicker for this reference.

99. This problem might have been reduced by a different boundary line.

100. Farrell, *Orange State*, p. 54.

101. Minutes of meeting, 31 May 1922, PRO C.O. 906/23.

102. To the tune of £6.78 million of a total cost of £7.5 million in the period 192 1-25 (Farrell, *Orange State*, p. 79).

103. Cab. 23/30, 3 August 1922, in Gilbert, *Churchill*, Companion Vol. IV, p. 1948. Here the decision not to prune Belfast's paramilitary forces is explicit.

104. Farrell, *Orange State*, p. 84.

105. 'The local elections in Northern Ireland', 25 April 1924, Sir A. Maxwell, PRO D.O. 35/893.

106. Dominions Office comment on Home Office views, Sir Harry

Batterbee, 18 November 1938, PRO D.O. 35/893.

107. Ibid.

108. Tallents told this to Maxwell ('Local Elections in Northern Ireland'), PRO D.O. 35/893.

109. *Financial Diary*, latter half of October 1934.

110. He claimed that Nixon was currently threatening to shoot Wickham. For this matter see his document in SPO 81801a.

111. Notes in SPO S1801/C.

112.. 'The Persecution of Catholics in Northern Ireland', *Capuchin Annual*, 1940, p. 161, emphasis added.

2   Political Forces and Social Classes, 1925–1943

Existing characterisations of the Northern Ireland state, whether they derive from nationalist or Unionist standpoints or from political science textbooks, have shown a common tendency to adopt what might be called a 'check-list' approach. Various institutions have been listed and described and then compared with abstract types of parliamentary democracy, fascism or 'divided regimes'. The state itself has been evaluated accordingly. Like the method, the consequent characterisations have been highly abstract, moralistic and all too often uninformative.

As a result of this concern with classification the question of *why* the state took its peculiar form has been ignored. Why, for example, did Sir James Craig feel compelled to continue to insist upon its 'Protestant' character long after any republican military threat had receded? Why did it seem to remain so remote from the British model? Why was no effort made to build a consensus upon which it could rest? These are the real questions that need to be asked about the inter-war period in Northern Ireland.

There are a number of ways of answering questions of this kind: in terms of the political and psychological make-up of the principal protagonists, for example, or in terms of common 'ideological survivals', whose effects were the same. These will be considered in the course of this analysis. The route chosen here is different, however. It will involve seeking to trace and identify the connections between class relations in the dominant social bloc and their effects upon the state.

The Cabinet 1925-1943

An examination of the public records of the inter-war period generates an unexpected picture of Ulster politics. While the Northern Ireland state presented a basic unity in 1925, this was not to last long. Significantly, in a greater or lesser degree the various branches of the state were all to become arenas of conflict between two clearly identifiable groups striving to effect very different sorts of procedures and decisions. The opposition between these groups leaps out from almost every file in the archives.

One group centred Sir James Craig, John Andrews,* the Minister of Labour, and R. Dawson Bates, the Minister of Home Affairs. Broadly speaking, this group sought to generalise to the state as a whole the relation between Protestant classes epitomised in the B Specials. This relationship was characterised by a combination of sectarian and 'democratic' practices, and by a high consumption of public funds. As a matter of shorthand, it will here be called 'populist'. Another group, centred on two Ministers of Finance, Hugh Pollock† and John Milne Barbour,‡ and the head of the Northern Ireland Civil Service, Sir Wilfrid Spender, opposed this tendency. They strove instead to press the state along a *via Britannica* of a pre-Keynesian kind and we shall refer to them as 'anti-populists'.

Particularly instructive were the tensions between these forces in four major areas: the construction and composition of the Northern Ireland Civil Service, the role of the Ministry of Finance, the question of social service expenditure and, most importantly, the status of the Northern Ireland state itself.

The Civil Service

The Northern Ireland Civil Service (NICS) has most frequently been cited by Unionist apologists as a bastion of bureaucratic practices, corresponding to liberal parliamentary democracy.[1] In fact, the NICS and its composition were the centre of a struggle over the attenuation of such

* See Biographical Note on p. 249.
† See Biographical Note on p. 263.
‡ See Biographical Note on p. 261.

criteria. At first sight this may not appear convincing. It is well known that a number of Catholics were appointed to senior posts, for example Bonaparte Wyse and Samuel Sloan.[2] Moreover, in 1925-26 Sir Russell Scott of the Treasury gave the NICS machine a fairly clean bill of health in terms of efficiency, though he did feel it necessary to warn against 'the influence of politics'.[3] Further confirmation of the optimistic view of the NICS would be found by some in the fact that 5 per cent of the original staff were British, and that this proportion was much higher in most senior grades.[4]

Yet clear instances of discrimination against well qualified Catholics occurred from the very beginning,[5] and over 60 appointments were made without normal selection procedures being observed at all.[6] Spender, who became head of the NICS in 1925, felt that these nominess were a long-term handicap to the service and on his appointment decided to institute examinations of equivalent standard to those in the British and Indian civil services.[7] The results of Spender's efforts were, however, modified by other pressures. At the Ministry of Home Affairs, Bates refused to allow Catholic appointments.[8] In 1926 the Minister of Labour, John Andrews, found two 'Free Staters' in his ministry when he returned from holiday. He immediately initiated a tightening of regulations to disqualify such candidates automatically.[9] In 1927 Edward Archdale, the Minister of Agriculture, boasted that there were only four Catholics in his ministry.[10] While Unionist politicians were included on civil service appointment boards, nationalist requests for this privilege were ignored.[11]

As the years passed, evidence emerged of Orange Order surveillance of Catholic civil servants and even civil servants married to Catholics. Prominent and respectable Unionists like Sir Robert Lynn (editor of the *Northern Whig*) and Sir Charles Blackmore (Cabinet secretary) were the messenger-boys for the Order in these matters.[12] Craig's attitude was at best ambiguous.[13] Predictably, the number of Catholics in the higher ranks of the NICS dropped consistently throughout the late 1920s and early 1930s.[14]

The group around Pollock, Milne Barbour and Spender fought against this trend. Milne Barbour was in favour of having a sizeable number of Catholics in the NICS, 'though it may be a risky thing politically to say'.[15] Pollock reminded the Cabinet in 1927, 'It is our policy to maintain our civil service as far as possible on [British] … lines.'[16] Populists derided him for his self-image as 'father of the civil service'.[17]

Under the premiership of John Andrews populist attenuation of bureaucratic procedures increased further. In 1943 Andrews informed Spender of his doubts about employing Catholics in the NICS, claiming that the church hierarchy's attitude made it impossible for them to be loyal. Spender thought Andrew's views unfair and alarmist, pointing out that in any case none of the Permanent or Assistant Secretaries was Catholic. Andrews refused to be reassured by this response and demanded the compilation of a register of Catholic civil servants.[18]

The strongest evidence of the modification of bureaucratic by populist practices comes from critical comments on the NICS by senior members of other civil services. In 1933 Sir Richard Hopkins of the Treasury threatened Spender with a general inquiry.[19] Spender fended this off, but in 1934 a retired senior member of the Indian Civil Service named Anderson unexpectedly called on Spender and gave him,

> a somewhat lurid picture of the province, stating that he could not understand the attitude of our officials, who seemed bent on encouraging increased expenditure rather than reducing expenditure … in this respect, as in many others, the officials of Northern Ireland acted quite contrary to the traditions he was accustomed to in the Indian Civil Service.[20]

For reassurance Spender wrote to his old friend Sir Ernest Clark. Clark had effectively founded the NICS during his days as Assistant Under-Secretary at the Irish Office and was now Governor of Tasmania. 'Your service,' Clark replied, 'both in its recruitment and management, is not strictly on Civil Service lines, because the political element has entered into your appointments. If you don't mind me saying so, you are yourself an instance of this.'[21]

The Ministry of Finance

Bureaucratic procedures were also markedly modified with respect to the position of the Ministry of Finance which, as has been indicated, was the main base of the anti-populists. Contrary to the conventional view, the position of the ministry in relation to other state apparatuses was in no way comparable to that of the Treasury. While its formal status was equivalent,[22] its real control of other departments fell far short of its British equivalent. As Spender himself wrote in 1932:

> It was much more difficult for a government which was so close to the people to resist demands made upon it, than it was for a government of a larger country ... we [i.e. Spender and Pollock] endeavoured as far as possible to follow the high British standards but I had to admit that owing to our own peculiar local circumstances pressure was sometimes brought to bear on the Ministry of Finance by the Prime Minister and others in a way that would not happen in ... the Treasury, and on this account we did not have the same Treasury control that obtained in Britain.[23]

Far from exercising control, 'over-zealous' Ministry of Finance officials, when transferred to other departments, were hounded out of the civil service.[24] When the ministry opposed Craig's populist policy of 'distributing bones' to Unionism's supporters it was frequently ignored.[25] In one remarkable instance, that of the Ulster Transport Board, it found that the Ministry of Home Affairs had greater weight in what was essentially a matter of economic policy.[26]

Social Service Expenditure

The Spender-Pollock-Milne Barbour group disliked heavy expenditure on social services. Pollock expostulated, 'I am not sorry to see that strong pressure is coming from important blocks in Parliament to force the government to undertake reductions in social services.'[27] An exaggerated fear of idlers exploiting the dole led the inappropriately named Spender to suggest the drawing up of a black list.[28] Craig specifically condemned this kind of attitude.[29] However, the anti-populists received praise and support on this score at least from Sir John Anderson, a key figure in the British civil service. Anderson was delighted, for example, when he found Northern Ireland failing to implement costly British social reforms, particularly in the field of education.[30] The issue is of critical importance and lies near the heart of the populist/anti-populist divide. For in a curious way, on this issue at any rate, it was the populists who took a 'greater

British' and the anti-populists a 'little Ulster' stand. It must be understood, of course, that these terms bear no relation to their later connotations in the Unionist crises of the 1970s.

The Status of the Northern Ireland State

The disagreements between the populists and anti-populists are encapsulated in the maiden speeches of Craig and Pollock in the Northern Ireland House of Commons. Craig dwelt not so much on the legislative powers given to the new parliament as on the administrative powers which local government now possessed. He opened up the prospect of a new type of regime for Ireland – one deeply responsive to local pressure. Pollock, however, was more interested in the constitutional aspects of devolution. He claimed that Northern Ireland was 'an autonomous state with a federal relationship to the United Kingdom'.[31] His stress on autonomy went hand-in-hand with an emphasis on strict financial housekeeping.

While Pollock opposed the automatic extension of British social reforms to the Six Counties, the populists regarded the doctrine of parity or 'step by step', that is, the maintenance of an equivalent level of social services, as an article of faith. From this point of view the essential advantage of the ('Colwyn') financial arrangements agreed with Britain in 1925 was that Northern Ireland services could be ranked as a first charge on the area's revenues. The main question of devolution was whether Britain could be persuaded to replace the imperial contribution (whereby Northern Ireland was expected to pay its share of UK defence expenditure) by a payment making parity possible. Even after this position had in effect been reached, owing to the implementation in 1926 of a separate agreement subventing Ulster's employment fund, the populists continued to argue for a general British payment.

The debate reached its climax in the early 1930s. Pollock's view of the situation was supported by the Attorney General, Sir Arthur Quekett, who argued that the Colwyn Committee's purpose was not to revise the Government of Ireland Act but to find workable arrangements within the outline of its provisions.[32] The main populist spokesman was Andrews, who wrote:

I think there is a very general confusion in the mind of many people with regard to the constitutional position of Northern Ireland. Statements are often made which assume that Northern Ireland is autonomous or in the position of a Dominion ... in fact ... it is no more than a subordinate authority ... to which the sovereign legislature for its own convenience has devolved certain limited functions in respect of local services ... This being so, it seems to me unanswerable in equity that these measures of limited devolution are accompanied by those standards which are regarded as necessary and proper for the whole of the United Kingdom.[33]

Craig supported this view against Pollock's.[34] Divisions on this issue were severe enough to lead the anti-populists to weigh in on the side of the Treasury when the latter challenged populist arguments about equal standards, or tried to insist upon Northern Ireland bearing the burden of the cost of equalisation.

For example, the Treasury felt that the over-generous mode of derating[35] in 1929 and (for a considerably longer period) underrating in Northern Ireland were irregularities that ought to be rectified. As early as 1925 G.C. Upcott was noting:

In Great Britain 44 per cent of education expenditure and 50 per cent of police expenditure are borne by local rates, in Northern Ireland the local charge for these services is negligible ... If Northern Ireland claims that she is entitled to maintain her services on the standard prevailing in this country we are, I submit, justified in replying that they should raise the burden of local rates to the same level.[36]

The anti-populist accepted the logic of the Treasury position, and the scene was set for a conflict with those populists, in particular Craig, who did not. Craig at first dealt with the problem by denying its importance – despite clear warning over at least three years, it was not until December 1933 that he admitted the depth of the crisis in Stormont-Treasury relations.[37] Even then he was to claim repeatedly that through personal contact with Whitehall he had won dramatic concessions. These concessions were invariably products of his for once enlarged imagination.[38] As Hopkins explained to the Chancellor of the Exchequer,

'Lord Craigavon [i.e. Craig] in discussions of this kind is very inclined to assume that decisions are in his favour, unless it is made unusually clear to him what the decisions are.'[39]

Spender and Pollock, on the other hand, fought hard to gain acceptance of the Treasury line in Northern Ireland. Spender even went so far as to alert the Treasury on his own initiative if Craig showed signs of 'forgetting' his commitments.[40] The rating proposals of 1934 signalled Craig's defeat in this area.[41] He was effectively excluded from London-Belfast financial affairs until the negotiations between Whitehall and Dublin in 1938 permitted a rather less than glorious return to the stage. In his absence financial matters were dealt with mainly by the permanent officials in an atmosphere of increasing confidence.[42]

While they had lost one battle, the populists were to win the war, in this as in other fields, over both the anti-populists and the Treasury. The latter had re-opened discussions in 1931 with the intention of reversing the Colwyn Committee award's advantages for the Northern Irish. 'We started these discussions,' the Treasury official Brittain recalled, 'on the general principle, first, that it is not right that the Imperial contribution should in effect rank after all local expenditure in Northern Ireland.'[43] The discussions came to an inconclusive end, he added, when the Treasury's whole attention became concentrated on the economic measures of September 1931. As Ulster's economic position continued to weaken markedly in the 1930s, it became impossible to raise the matter again in the same terms.

As Hopkins, who replaced Niemeyer as Controller in 1927, was to put it near the end of the decade:

> When the Northern Irish government was set up it was expected that their revenues would be sufficient both to meet their expenses and to provide a substantial contribution to Imperial services (defence, debt, &c.) This expectation was realised at first fully and later in a diminishing degree. Since 1931 Northern Ireland has been in effect a depressed area. So far from receiving any large Imperial Contribution we have invented a series of *dodges* and *devices* to give them *gifts* and *subventions* within the ambit of the Government of Ireland Act so as to save Northern Ireland from coming openly on the dole as Newfoundland did.[44]

Hopkins's note implies that the general position of Britain and Northern Ireland within the world economy was not subject to control by the northern government. Other documents make it clear that this was in fact his view and explain his willingness to resort to what he later described as 'wangles' and 'fudges' to help the regime.[45] 'The fact is that they copy all our legislation and that therefore we set their general standard, for better or for worse. In times like these, that standard means bankruptcy for a small community which is suffering terribly from unemployment.'[46]

Political Forces and Social Classes

A Purely Political Explanation?

The content of the 'Protestantism' of Craig's 'Protestant state' is now somewhat clearer: in essence it amounted to a combination of clientilism, 'responsiveness' and a practical 'Keynesianism'. It was modified by liberal democratic practices, rather than the other way round. The extent to which this happened was a result of the presence of anti-populists within the state apparatus. The question is then as to the basis – if any – of the conflict, and how populism apparently prevailed. A purely political explanation is possible. Such an analysis would stress the differing political motivation of the two principal figures involved in it, Sir James Craig and Sir Wilfrid Spender.

In the case of Craig there can be little doubt that British indifference to the chaos in Ulster in the period of state formation affected him profoundly. He frequently stated that it was his intention to make the British government pay the 'debt' it owed Ulster on this account. On one occasion Spender charged him with pressing for advantages over and above those given to other British regions. Craig, Spender reported, merely smiled to himself in an amused fashion.

Spender's comments in his diary on Craig's death saw the Prime Minister as having become the epitome of 'little Ulsterism', over-responsive to almost any non-Catholic pressure-group in the province, whilst remaining more or less indifferent not simply to the Treasury but to wider Greater British and Imperial concerns.[47] Other Irishmen have wasted their talents through profligacy. Craig's great talent *was* profligacy. During the negotiations between

Whitehall and Dublin in 1938, for example, he literally asked only to be 'bribed' with armaments contracts to give his acquiescence to a London-Dublin deal.[48] He displayed little interest in the broader strategic considerations (for example the return of the so-called 'Treaty ports' in the South, now surrendered by Britain) which so concerned Spender.

On the other hand, Spender adhered to very different political traditions. He was an English army officer who had adopted the Ulster Unionist cause primarily on the grounds of imperial security. He saw Pollock, his minister, as the soundest imperialist in the Cabinet. In retrospect he even presented Pollock's championing of the Loans Guarantee Act (which did so much to make Belfast shipbuilding viable) not so much as an aid to regional employment but as the necessary condition for building some of the ships so badly needed for the coming world war.[49] Nor was this a matter of Spender projecting his own obsessions onto Pollock. The latter's first budget speech made the point that, 'We are the children of the Empire, we Ulster people.'[50]

It is tempting therefore to regard a purely political stress on differing 'world views' as a complete explanation. This is certainly the position of conventional political scientists and their advocates.[51] Richard Rose, for example, has committed himself to the view that the divisions in the Unionist bloc from 1921 onward can be explained simply by reference to the division between those who owed full allegiance to the British state and those who did not.[52] Is it not a simple matter to suggest that the fully allegiant group is that which has been described as anti-populist, and the ultra-loyalists or non-allegiant (in Rose's terminology) are those we have called populists? The idea assumes further credibility when it is considered how Rose deepens his account of this central division. The fully allegiant group accepted the ultimate sovereignty of the British government. The 'ultras', however, rejected it when it conflicted with the principle of maintaining Protestant dominance. On this basis it is a relatively easy matter to accept 'fully allegiant' as a characterisation of the Ministry of Finance group and 'ultra' as an adequate assessment of the Craig-Bates-Andrews circle.

Yet it is at this point that Rose's account runs into a paradox. The supposedly fully allegiant or anti-populist group had a more exalted conception of the Northern Irish parliament and state than the 'ultras'. It is the anti-populist group that talks of Stormont's autonomy in all fields, of its 'federal' relation with the UK. On the other hand, it is the 'ultras' who use phrases like 'subordinate regional authority'. In other words, great care is necessary to ensure that the analysis of inter-war Unionist divisions is not derived by projecting back in time an ideological reading of the dissensions of 1968-72.

While it is beyond doubt that differing political attitudes did play a critical role in determining the nature of intra-Unionist conflicts in the 1920s and 30s, they are not wholly explicable at this level. Recourse has to be made to an examination of the relationship between these attitudes and differing class forces.

Economic Explanations

In analysing the various forms of government which came to power in different European countries between the two world wars, a number of writers have focused their attention on the divisions between competitive and monopolistic businesses.[53] Is this approach helpful in the case of Northern Ireland?

In Ulster both monopolistic and competitive businesses, in the form of shipbuilding and the linen industry respectively,[54] were well represented at the political level, the former above all because of the state's heavy financial and political interest in its fortunes. Linen, too, had its representatives in the corridors of power in the shape of men like Andrews and Milne Barbour, who were not even required to give up their directorships when they became ministers. There was some grumbling on the part of linen interests that the Loans Guarantee Act ought to have been extended to their sector, but this was of marginal significance. The Cabinet as a whole tended to reflect the consensus of the linen trade that protection rather than a reorganisation and amalgamation of the many rather inefficient units was the answer to secular decline. Andrews, while accepting that some consolidation was inevitable, wrote to Craig, 'It is not competition among ourselves that is the trouble, so much as competition under quite unfair conditions overseas.'[55] Sir Gilbert Garnsey, a London accountant called in by the Ministry of Commerce, merely confirmed the view that the linen manufacturers would resist any move towards combines. It was probably with relief that Craig replied to Andrews, 'I am quite prepared to set on one side any possible reorganisation of the trade.'[56]

To approach the problem from a different angle: it is difficult to present the anti-populist grouping's policies as a reflection of the specific interests of one particular business interest against another. While continuing to receive support for certain basic objectives from competitive as opposed to monopolistic bodies such as the Belfast Chamber of Commerce,[57] the anti-populists were also the architects of the Loans Guarantee Act, which was clearly in the interests of monopolistic businesses. It should be observed that the implementation of Pollock's views on 'sound finance was in fact necessary for the smooth functioning of the Act.

If there was a politically significant economic division in Ulster's business community it was not between competitive and monopolistic interests but instead arose from the resentments of that group commonly called Ulster's 'minor' or 'miscellaneous' businesses at the domination of the state by shipbuilding and linen interests.[58] This group, which the Ulster Industries Development Association (UIDA) attempted – with no great success – to represent, was engaged mainly in producing for the home market. 'Buy Ulster Goods' was its slogan. Craig offered the Association some support, particularly in the early 1930s, but it was markedly unpopular with the Ministry of Finance. In his last Stormont speech in 1935 Pollock gave vent to years of private misgivings: 'I have no sympathy with the theory which seems to be shouted on all occasions "Use only Ulster goods".'[59] It is also important to note that this group – particularly through its links with Unionist critics of the government – was involved in the successful agitation of 1937 for a greater state role in the economy. The anti-populist Minister of Commerce, Milne Barbour, had reluctantly broken with the *laissez-faire* tradition of the Ministry in November 1931 to propose a scheme for attracting industry to the province by offering free sites and other inducements.[60] The scheme succeeded in creating very few jobs, and Milne Barbour was anxious in November 1936 to let it lapse.[61] Within a period of just over a year, however, the government was forced not only to keep the legislation alive but to expand its provisions substantially.[62]

Apart from this the UIDA was effectively marginal to political decisions and divisions. Its main grievance, after all, was that it did not get enough consistent support at the heart of the state apparatus.

Differences Between Britain and Ulster

Robert Skidelsky's approach to political and economic history in Britain between the wars is fruitful and repays detailed study.[63] His central concern is economic stagnation and the explanation he offers is illuminating. The conflicts and changes necessary to generate economic development could never occur, he argued, since the dominant political trend was the minimisation of conflict:

> The Baldwin-MacDonald politics of decency and consensus were designed to dissipate [the threat of class war] and they succeeded remarkably well. Unfortunately, the consensus created was based on mass unemployment and the dole, rather than full employment and growth.[64]

He quotes A.J.P. Taylor: 'The very forces which made Great Britain peaceful and stable prevented her from becoming the country of the New Deal.'[65]

Minimisation of conflict on a national scale was made possible by the survival of economic internationalism and minimal government as the twin political watchwords. These policies, promoted by Baldwin, together with the mass unemployment they caused, effectively split the working class into a 'constitutionally educated' wing following the Labour Party on the one hand, and a tiny and isolated Marxist wing following the Communist Party on the other.[66] The alternative was the more belligerent strategy adopted by Churchill in 1926, a vigorous mobilisation of frightened provincial employers, which would have turned society into a battleground.

The Baldwin-MacDonald 'politics of decency and consensus' implied a continued domination of banking over industry. The MacDonald government of 1929-31, for example, rejected the alternative of exploiting the differences between industry and the City as these had been outlined[67] in what Tom Nairn called 'the major document of the era',[68] the

Macmillan *Report on Finance and Industry* of 1931. The idea of promoting economic recovery through deficit budgeting (as, for example, in the United States, Germany, France and Sweden) was turned down. So too was the positive use of public works and other Keynesian suggestions. By and large, those who sought to make unemployment and domestic industrial development the central concerns of British policy – Lloyd George in 1929, Keynes and Mosley – were pushed to one side.

It is worth considering again the problem of the social identification of competing political forces in Northern Ireland in this light. In Britain the alternative political lines gained their coherence from the particular form taken by the conflicts engendered by the economic crisis. The two options open to the political elite were to try to give this challenge a voice amenable to its control (the Labour Party) while minimising its militancy through unemployment, and Churchill's line of bludgeoning it into the ground. In Northern Ireland the situation was completely different. There was no comparable challenge from the left, and in this sense the weakening and 'education' of a united working class were unnecessary. On the contrary, given the historical make-up of Unionism, a secular 'constitutionally educated' working class was undesirable. The clue to the nature of Ulster politics is the historically exaggerated dependence of the Unionist elite on the Protestant working class. Its object was the continued split between the Protestant and Catholic working class. Disunity between the different religious camps within the working class was Unionism's *sine qua non*. Populism was a strategy which made sense only in this context and its 'solution' to the danger of a unity between Protestants and Catholics was to weld ever more tightly the links between the Unionist elite and the Protestant working class.

But what of anti-populism? Anti-populism was not a strategy at all but a rhetorical device located at the heart of another, real, strategy. Its aim was to save the populist position from its own excesses. In short, its coherence was entirely dependent on the populist position and it was therefore doomed to remain forever a minority position within the government.

In scope the populist strategy departed considerably from

'consensus and decency' and its forms of implementation. The tying of the Protestant working class to the political leadership above all required a different approach to the problem of unemployment from that in Britain. It required an approach that was in essence 'productivist', protectionist and, in a purely practical way, Keynesian. As it happened, the regional economy's profound handicaps meant that this sort of policy would have had to have been pursued to a degree incompatible with membership of the United Kingdom if a complete solution was to have been found. Nevertheless, it was followed as far as possible and was expressed most clearly in the Loans Guarantee Acts and expenditure on public works. The latter was seen specifically as the proper lesson of the 1932 Outdoor Relief riots,[69] that unique occasion when Catholic and Protestant workers rioted not against each other but against a particularly niggardly system of outdoor relief payment for the unemployed; and was pressed on with long after Ministry of Finance entreaties demanded it should stop.

Why, it may be asked, was it necessary to go this far? Why could not Orangeism alone suffice? Its practice might even have been consistent with acceptance of the dominant British political watchwords, and the consequent avoidance of interstate conflict. The problem of Orangeism, however, was that its support amongst Protestant trade unionists was considered to be weak. The Orange Order was obviously a historical asset. Nevertheless Craig made perfectly clear his view that the Order was not up to the task. He stressed instead the role of the Ulster Unionist Labour Association (UULA). It – and not the Order – he insisted was the 'most wonderful organisation in Ulster'.[70] When the Orange Grand Master, Sir Joseph Davidson, protested at his institution's unwonted demotion, Craig was unrepentant. The UULA won the 'cream' of the working class and 'so many influential trade union leaders' to Unionism. Without irony, he observed there was nothing like it anywhere in the world.[71]

The effect of these policies was to maintain the dominance of industry. Craig was quite prepared to make explicit his preference for industrial as opposed to banking interests.

He had been spending the bulk of his time recently in consultation with the heads of the great business concerns in Ulster, whose advice he always liked to take in preference to that of banks or stockholders, and although it might seem to be impertinent of him to say so, if Britain had obtained advice from the manufacturers, a great deal of misfortune might have been avoided.[72]

In both a local and national context the maintaining of populist supremacy and the ascendancy of industrial interests that was its consequence had certain implications.

Generally speaking, and particularly with respect to home affairs, an unflinchingly populist line was pursued in the 1930s. In 1932, after widespread attacks by Protestant mobs on pilgrims travelling south for the Eucharistic Congress, Bates arranged with the Attorney General and Chief Crown Solicitor that the Protestant offenders should be treated leniently.[73] Events like this induced delusions of grandeur in Orange quarters. In 1935 Bates, at Orange insistence but without notifying Pollock, who was acting Prime Minister, lifted a government ban on Orange parades.[74] The result was massive inter-communal violence.[75]

As has been indicated, the pursuit of policies that effectively approximated to a crude Keynesianism generated considerable conflict with the Treasury, until the latter itself turned Keynesian. Andrews's demands on public works for example, were claimed by the Treasury to be typical only of left-wing socialists in Britain (with all that this implied).

To say that a policy was unpopular with the Treasury is to imply equal disfavour on the part of the City of London. It is certain that many of the officials involved in the critical dialogue with the Northern Irish government had the closest links with the City. Sir Richard Hopkins is a good example[76] and Sir John Anderson an even better one.[77] The opposition of Hopkins, the Treasury controller, and Anderson, the government's unemployment 'expert' in the 1930s, to the populist group is clear.

This was in the last resort as dangerous as mass inter-communal violence, since, as Spender was fond of saying, the chairman of the Midland Bank stood in the same relation to the Ministry of Finance as the Governor of the Bank of England to the Treasury. The Midland was the Northern Ireland state's exchequer bank and an important force in the boardroom of Harland & Wolff, on whose inner directorate of five it had two members. Of the remaining three, one represented the other banks, one the Ministry of Finance and one the Treasury – reflecting more or less accurately the extent of these bodies' investment. Sir Ernest Clark, the Ulster government's representative, later recalled having 'to face the Midland Bank every month to beg for enough to carry on in the bad times'.[78] At one point in 1936 the Midland even threatened to let Sir James Lithgow, the Scottish shipbuilding magnate, gain a controlling interest in the firm. Lithgow was well known as a fierce critic of the Belfast yard, holding that it was operated at over-capacity. He had indeed already used his influence at the Board of Trade against the 'unfair' advantages given to Belfast shipbuilding by the Loans Guarantee Act.[79]

In these respects the populist line had to be checked. It is here that the positive function and the true meaning of the anti-populist position may be appreciated. The anti-populists were extremely sensitive to the need to employ financial methods approved by the banks. Spender wrote to S.D. Waley at the Treasury that Andrews might well benefit from a trip to London if he learned thereby 'of the co-operation that he is likely to get from the financial magnates in London if our government adopts *sound methods of finance*'.[80] The Midland Bank, to take the obvious case, had an important interest in certain shipping lines, for example Union Castle, as well as in the Belfast yard. The greatest care was needed in Loans Guarantee operations – which became even more substantial in the 1930s – and clearly such projects had to be copper-bottomed by the creditworthiness of the Northern Ireland state.[81] The Midland was naturally a strong force in support of orthodox financial methods. The anti-populists' sensitivity to the bank never went as far as servility, but they did use it to make the government face up to what they saw as 'the basic facts of life'.

Spender sometimes appears a rather obsessive figure. In the later 1930s and early 1940s he was to grow more and more afraid of 'creeping socialism' – often working through such unlikely protagonists as Lord Reith.[82] Simultaneously he became less in touch with the changing paradigms of British economic policy. Sir Richard Hopkins, a firm anti-Keynesian in 1930[83] and such an important figure for Spender, was an ardent Keynesian by 1940.[84] It was too much for Sir Wilfrid. 'I think the world quite mad ...

my views on economics are quite too old-fashioned for
modern conditions,' he wrote to the Treasury on 12 January
1939, adding, in an attempted sting, 'and I am even fool
enough to believe that one ought to live on one's own
income.'[85]

Nevertheless the contribution of the anti-populists to the
stability of the government was to become more and more
crucial as the years passed. This was because Craig's
populism (and that of his successor, Andrews) was to
become increasingly frivolous and unrestrained as time
passed. He frequently perambulated the province on the
most extraordinary tours and in the process visited almost
every Unionist local authority. These waited upon him with
a list of projects and complaints for his attention. At
Portstewart, for example, a case was made out for classifying
the road to the golf links as first-class.[86] Almost invariably his
response to such trivia was favourable. In 1937 he demanded
that money be poured into the renovation of Musgrave
Street police barracks, Belfast, because a raw ex-public
school RUC officer cadet complained of conditions there.[87]
Had such expenditure been implemented *carte blanche*, it
would have exasperated the Treasury beyond self-control.
There was only one thing as dangerous for the local elite as
a unified working class – a unified opposition of Catholics
and the British state.

Conclusion

The most systematic Irish nationalist attempt to grasp the
nature of the state was produced by 'Ultach' in 1940. This was
a rigorous attempt to demonstrate in a precise analogical way
that the Northern Irish statelet was totalitarian. 'I should like
it to be understood here that I am not indulging in the
emotional exaggerations of political propaganda.'[88]

In this endeavour he drew on certain features of an already
burgeoning theory of totalitarianism which insisted on the
essential similarity of the Soviet and fascist regimes. In this
perspective the Soviet, Nazi and Orange systems required a
state of political high tension to keep the masses in
movement.[89] All three presented measures of coercion as, in
fact, measures of self-defence against dangerous enemies.[90]
The Unionists, it is true, had permitted elections, but only

those they were sure to win. 'Ultach' argued that the abolition in 1929 of proportional representation for parliamentary elections had been designed to enforce a false unanimity of opinion among Unionists. The abolition of proportional representation and gerrymandering in local government served to remove any possible focus of opposition from nationalist local authorities. He even claimed – less convincingly, perhaps – an analogy between the Unionist practice of allowing criticism of the government by extreme Orangemen with the Soviet practice of 'self-criticism'.[91] Above all, however, 'Ultach' explicitly insisted that in the totalitarian regimes, as in Ulster, the state had to be conceived as the 'instrument' of the party.[92]

In general terms it may be observed that 'Ultach's' borrowed methodology tended to give a falsely monolithic impression of the state apparatuses under consideration. Baldly instrumental conceptions – whether the subject wielding the instrument is said to be a class or a party – make it difficult to perceive the state as a set of relationships shot through by conflicts of the sort analysed in this chapter. Hardly surprisingly, 'Ultach' was at a loss to explain the 'liberal' features of the regime – why, for instance, if it was in the fullest sense totalitarian, it allowed a strong nationalist press to function with considerable (if not total) freedom.[93]

Unlike 'Ultach', we have found not unanimity but fissures and divisions. The stress on the populist/anti-populist division has been intended to break down the view of the Unionist state as an undifferentiated entity. It has been argued that this division contributed to the resilience of the state: in particular, the anti-populists acted as a curb on certain populist practices which invited conflict with the British government. 'Ultach' was correct in diagnosing the regime's vulnerability: 'Its weakness lies in the fact that it can be removed when England wishes.'[94] However, he was unable to explain why 'democratic' England should continue to support 'totalitarian' Unionism.

Towards the end of the inter-war period clear proof of our thesis is provided by the outcome of British government enquiries into allegations by the Eire government of maltreatment of the Catholic minority in Ulster. The Dominions Office and the Home Office both prepared minutes on the subject.[95] In general, the tone of the

Dominions Office comment is rather critical of the Ulster regime, while that of the Home Office is predominantly defensive.

Sir Harry Batterbee of the Dominions Office would, in particular, have liked to have seen more information on, for example, 'the charge that the government service is practically closed to Catholics. Could not the figures be given ... The Head of the Education is an exception, but is he the exception which proves the rule?'[96] The Home Office countered by claiming that Catholicism was in general the religion of the masses in Northern Ireland, while Protestantism was that of the upper classes.[97] It was hardly surprising that Protestants predominated in jobs requiring a certain educational level.

However, the decisive factor in warding off the Dominions Office concern was the attitude of Sir Wilfrid Spender. Spender expressed himself pleased by the way in which in the late 1930s an increasing number of Catholic applicants were coming forward to join the NICS. He tried to show that entry was not decided on sectarian criteria – in so far as he could control it.[98] There is little doubt that Spender's obvious sensitivity on the question greatly reassured the British civil servants.

It was felt that it was enough simply to register a certain concern about the situation. Batterbee wrote:

> To sum up, except as regards gerrymandering, the Home Office [in defence of Ulster] put up a fairly good case. There is no reason to suppose that there is a deliberate injustice to Catholics on the part of government. But, as Mr Stephenson (of the Home Office) points out in his minute, the bias of the Northern Irish authorities is bound to be in favour of those who are supporters of the present regime; it is everywhere inimical to good and impartial administration where government and party are as closely united as a Northern Ireland. In the South, Mr de Valera was at one time largely dependent on the IRA for support, but he has been able to throw off his dependence on that body in a way that the government of Northern Ireland have not been able to throw off their dependence on the Orange Lodges.[99]

This passage is a fairly accurate representation of Dominions Office views. It was certainly felt that the original Catholic boycott of the Leech Commission to enquire into local government boundaries was no excuse for sustained gerrymandering in this area. On the other hand, Spender had reassured his British colleagues about the conditions in government service. In general, it was sufficient to hope that the Home Office had now been alerted to the fact that there were real problems and that it would not continue to allow the situation to drift. This relatively mild and hopeful conclusion demonstrated the fundamental importance of anti-populism for the survival of the Stormont regime. As long as the crucial people in the British state apparatus felt that strategic figures in the Northern Irish administration were attempting to implement British methods, they were unlikely to respond to 'Ultach's' demand for strong British intervention to secure 'normal conditions' in Ulster.[100]

Notes

1. cf. R.J. Lawrence, *The Government of Northern Ireland*, Oxford 1965.

2. Sloan was Establishment Officer of the NICS. Whilst born a Catholic, he did in fact lapse. Shortly before his death in February 1940 he reverted to his religion. This fact leaked out and intensified Orange pressure on the NICS (Spender to Gramsden, 28 August 1940, PRONI D715).

3. cf. Scott to Spender, 24 October 1925, PRONI Cab. 7Q/7.

4. 53 of the 1,012 appointments of the first eighteen months were British – 38 of them in Labour and twelve in Finance (*Belfast Newsletter*, 24 December 1922).

5. cf. paper by J. McColgan read at the Institute for Irish Studies, 1977. Also P.J. Gannon, 'In the Catacombs of Belfast', *Studies*, Vol. II (1922), App. V, p. 295, is significant for the background. H.P. Boland, for example, brought to his interview with Sir James Craig in late June a strong recommendation from his Treasury superiors: 'There is every probability that you will find a man of this type indispensable,' it was said. However, Sir Ernest Clark replied that, 'The answer of the Northern government is "Thank you very much, but no." I believe you know why.' Boland was southern Irish and Catholic, John McColgan's fascinating research is now to be found in 'Irish Government Administration: British Administrative Policies in Ireland, 1920-22', unpublished PhD thesis, University College, Dublin, 1977. Gannon appears to establish a pattern of discrimination in Belfast Corporation appointments.

6. *Belfast Newsletter*, 24 December 1922.

7. Spender, *Financial Diary*, 30 May 1938, PRONI D715. At first this had the effect of making a majority of administrative grade appointees British.

8. *Irish Times*, 4 May 1967, and Spender, *Financial Diary*, 5 June 1941. In a rare moment of candour Dr John Oliver, who enjoyed a wide-ranging career within the NICS, gives a glimpse of Bates's general style of work: 'For example, I was told that in the very earliest days of the Ministry of

Home Affairs the Minister decided to meet a request from the Inspector General of the Royal Ulster Constabulary for motor tyres for the police fleet by telephoning the managing director of a business firm in Belfast and placing an order. Why not? ... Why bother to go through a long rigmarole of tiresome civil service procedure, advertise, receive sealed tenders, open them, pick the lowest tender, only to find the tenderer turns out to be an unreliable, inexperienced supplier who lets you down?' (J.A. Oliver, *Working at Stormont*, Dublin 1978, p. 46.)

9. PRONI Cab. 4/182/25; cf. Cab. 4/182/24. The 'Free Staters' had good British army backgrounds. It should be added that Andrews justified his position by referring to the Irish language qualifications for jobs in the Irish civil service. Indeed it is true that, while the Irish government even under de Valera 'in general' saw no need for a nationality clause in the civil service, the language requirements were a good substitute (SPO GC2/36, 20 December 1938). However, de Valera was prepared to allow a probationary period in which a civil servant could acquire this proficiency (SPO GC1/6, 28 January 1938).

10. M. Farrell, *Northern Ireland: The Orange State*, London 1975, p. 90.

11. *NIHC*, Vol. VIII, c. 667.

12. Spender, *Financial Diary*, 7-22 December 1935. There was even a case of a Catholic gardener at Stormont who was dismissed – despite a good army record and a reference from the Prince of Wales (!) – following Orange Order pressure on Craig (ibid., 15 January 1934).

13. In 1927 he resisted the extension of Whitley Councils to the NICS by claiming that it was necessary to prevent any further outbreak of that public hostility' to the service which had marked the early days of the regime. Craig had then been prepared to resist this pressure (PRONI Cab. 4/200/6). 'Then again they were charged that they employed Englishmen in their civil service ... it made him blush to hear such statements' (SPO S4743). Five years later he seemed prepared to use such sentiments as a means of controlling the service.

14. Spender, *Financial Diary*, 7-22 December 1935. This was Spender's personal impression. To be fair, by the late 1930s Spender believed that Catholics were presenting themselves for civil service examinations in relatively high numbers – though not quite in proportion to their share of the population (PRO D.O. 35/893, Spender comments included in Sir E.J. Harding's report, 18 November 1938). They dropped in the RUC too, from 541 in 1924 (*Belfast Newsletter*, 4 January 1924) to 489 in 1935 (PRONI Cab. B236) and 454 in 1944 (quoted in G.L. Dobbie 'Partisans and Protectors: the Police in Northern Ireland, c. 1920-70', unpublished paper).

15. *NIHC*, Vol. VIII, c. 667-8.

16. PRONI Cab. 4/200/18.

17. J.W. Nixon, *NIHC*, Vol. XVIII, c. 2464-5.

18. Spender, *Financial Diary*, 29 March 1943. The register was compiled, but Brooke did not use it.

19. Ibid., 5 May 1933.

20. Ibid., 4 January 1934.

21. Clark to Spender, ibid., 6 December 1935.

22. It controlled the NICS establishment and regulations, was the

largest ministry, had accounting officers attached to other ministries and the parliamentary draughtsman as one of its officials, etc. As late as June 1941 Bates even used the excuse of the wartime emergency temporarily to break the Ministry of Finance's formal control in this area (Spender, *Financial Diary*, 5 June 1941).

23. Ibid., 5 March 1932.

24. Ibid., notes of a discussion, 9 January 1934; diary, 30 June 1934.

25. Quoted in P.J. Buckland, 'The Unity of Ulster Unionism', *History*, 60 (1975).

26. PRONI Cab. 4/333/16, Cabinet memorandum, 5 January 1936.

27. Pollock to Craig, 15 June 1932, PRONI Cab. 7F/57/1.

28. Spender to Blackmore, 25 March 1930, PRONI Cab. 7A/3/1.

29. Craig's speech to the UULA, 2 January 1937, PRONI Cab. 8PF/22.

30. Record of an interview at the Treasury, 24 July 1930, PRONI Cab. 7A/3/1.

31. G.C. Duggan, *Northern Ireland: Success or Failure?*, Dublin 1950, p. 4. The maiden speeches are in *NIHC*, Vol. I, c. 33-7, 45-62 (Craig), and c. 119-34 (Pollock).

32. Quekett memorandum, 2 April 1930, PRONI Cab. 7A/3/1. Also A. Quekett, *The Constitution of Northern Ireland*, Belfast 1928, Vol. I, pp. 48-50.

33. Andrews memorandum, 18 November 1930, in Cab. papers, 1 May 1933, PRONI Cab. 7A/3/1.

34. Secret and confidential Cabinet conclusions, 19 November 1933, ibid.

35. Especially in agriculture.

36. Upcott to Craig, 3 August 1925, PRO T. 160/269/111999.

37. Spender, *Financial Diary*, Conference on the General Financial Position of the Province, 12 December 1933.

38. *Financial Diary*, 2 November, 4 December 1933, 20 January 1934.

39. Hopkins to the Chancellor, 16 May 1933, PRO T. 160/550/F6563/021/1.

40. PRO T. 160/550/F6563/021/1. cf. the correspondence of Hopkins to Spender, 12 October 1933, and of Spender to Hopkins, 20 October 1933, which is clearly the result of a warning by Spender. See also *Financial Diary*, 25 April 1932. Support for the Ministry of Finance line was expressed consistently by the Belfast correspondent of the *Economist* from 1927 to 1929.

41. Lawrence, *Government*, p. 58.

42. Spender, *Financial Diary*, 12 August 1935, May 1936.

43. Formulae for the Northern Ireland contribution, 16 March 1933, PRO T. 160/550/F6562/021/1.

44. Hopkins's document for Sir F. Phillips, 8 February 1939, in PRO T. 160/1138/15586. As early as 24 November 1930 Bewley wrote to Waley, 'Any honest statement of the position cannot help pointing out the fact that we now subsidise Northern Ireland to the tune of £1 million a year or more,' PRO T. 160/430/12302.

45. Hopkins to the Chancellor, 16 May 1933, PRO T. 160/550/F6562/021/1.

46. Hopkins to the Chancellor, 10 May 1933, ibid.

47. Spender, *Financial Diary*, 28-30 November 1940. See also the retrospective undated addendum for May-October 1943.

48. As D.W. Harkness (in *History and the Irish*, Belfast 1976, p. 13) has pointed out, the language is indeed explicit. On 22 March 1938 Hopkins wrote to the Chancellor of the Exchequer, 'the position at the moment ... is that Lord Craigavon said he would be forthcoming if he were bribed' (PRO T. 160/747/14026/04/2). Spender noted, 'I should perhaps make it clear that although my general views coincided with those of Lord Craigavon, they were coloured by a different background. Where he was determined to make the interests of Northern Ireland the great purpose of his life, I was still obsessed with questions of the defence of the UK' (*Financial Diary*, loc. cit.).

49. Ibid., August-September 1936. See also May-October 1943, pp. 208ff.

50. *NIHC*, Vol. II, c. 626.

51. See the defence of the empiricist view of politics by B. Hindess, 'The Concept of Class in Marxist Theory and Marxist Politics' in J. Bloomfield (ed.), *Class, Hegemony and Party*, London 1977.

52. e.g. in R. Rose, *Northern Ireland: A Time of Choice*, London 1976, p. 16.

53. cf. N. Poulantzas, *Fascism and Dictatorship*, London 1974.

54. In 1922 the Ministry of Commerce estimated that 340,000 of a population of 1.24 million were 'nominally engaged' in the linen trade ('Memorandum on the Linen Trade', PRO T. 172/1287).

55. Andrews to Craig, 23 July 1928, PRONI 7F/67/1.

56. Craig to Andrews, 25 July 1928, ibid.

57. Belfast Chamber of Commerce *Journal*, 19 May 1932.

58. Delegation of UIDA to meet Craig, 31 May 1937. Also Cleland to Milne Barbour, 26 November 1937, PRONI Cab. 7F/108/2 and 7F/126/3.

59. *NIHC*, Vol. XIX, 18 March 1937, c. 643. For some nationalist comments on Craig's views, see ibid., Vol. X, c. 109. It was the view of the Ministries of Finance and Commerce that the intended beneficiaries of this campaign did not seem to benefit by it. These were firms producing biscuits, meal, furniture, hosiery, ink, matches, pickles and sauces, preserves, footwear, soaps, etc. ('UIDA, note of its establishment and functions', PRONI Cab. 7F/108/1).

60. Memorandum dated 6 November 1931, PRONI Cab. 7F/126/3. In 1923 Craig had argued that industrial undertakings 'should be left to the initiative of the great commercial magnates' (PRONI Cab. 4/70/7).

61. Milne Barbour to Craig, 13 November 1936, PRONI Cab. 7F/126/3.

62. *Belfast Newsletter*, 5 and 26 November 1937.

63. R. Skidelsky, 'The Reception of the Keynesian Revolution' in M. Keynes (ed.), *Essays on John Maynard Keynes*, Cambridge 1975.

64. Ibid., p. 101.

65. Ibid.

66. M. Cowling, *The Impact of Labour, 1920-24*, Cambridge 1971, pp. 407-8.

67. Skidelsky argues that this was an objective possibility in *Politicians and the Slump: The Labour Government, 1929-31*, London 1967, pp. 387-8.

68. T. Nairn, *The Break-up of Britain: Crisis and Neo-nationalism*, London 1977, p. 50.

69. Spender, *Financial Diary*, 9 January 1934. The outdoor relief riots of 1932, though short-lived in their impact on working-class politics, had seen the most significant moment of proletarian unity in Belfast since the state had been created. Craig claimed that, 'The agitation had got so serious that he believed that they might have found themselves confronted with wilful damage which would be out of all proportion to the £300,000 paid away on Relief schemes.'

70. Craig to Davidson, 12 January 1933, PRONI Cab. 8PF/32.

71. Ibid.

72. *Belfast Newsletter*, 19 November 1931.

73. Bates to Craig, 26 July 1932; Craig to Bates, 28 July 1932, PRONI Cab. 7B/200. British Home Office interest in such matters – as both publicly and privately expressed – was slight; see D. Harkness, 'England's Irish Question' in G. Peele and C. Cook (eds), *The Politics of Reappraisal*, London 1975, p. 61, and P. Bew, 'The Problem of Irish Unionism', *Economy and Society*, 6 (1977), p. 107, n. 16.

74. Farrell, *Orange State*, p. 138.

75. PRONI Cab. B236; 'Disturbances in Belfast', *Financial Diary*, first week in June 1936.

76. M. Beloff, 'The Role of the Higher Civil Service' in Peele and Cooke (eds), *Reappraisal*, p. 213.

77. Skidelsky, *Politics*, p. 217. Anderson rejected the advice of Keynes and others and declared, 'everything must wait upon the forces of nature'. He had studied the problem for seven weeks.

78. Clark to Spender, 12 November 1943, *Financial Diary*.

79. Note on visit by Sir J. Lithgow, 17 October 1933, PRO M.T. 9/2560/8426.

80. Spender to Waley, 6 December 1938, PRO T. 160/1138/15586.

81. Spender to Blackmore, 11 October 1930, PRONI Cab. 7A/3/1.

82. Spender, *Financial Diary*, 20-25 July 1942.

83. S. Howson, *Domestic Monetary Management in Britain, 1919-38*, Cambridge 1975, p. 143.

84. S. Howson and D. Winch, *The Economic Advisory Council, 1930-39*, Cambridge 1977, p. 152. cf. the Keynes-Hopkins conflict on public works described in D. Winch, *Economics and Policy*, London 1972, pp. 120-1.

85. PROT. 160/1138/15586.

86. cf. an itinerary, PRONI Cab. 7B/136.

87. Spender, *Financial Diary*, 26 September 1936.

88. 'Ultach', 'The Persecution of Catholics in Northern Ireland', *Capuchin Annual*, 1940, p. 162.

89. Ibid., p. 165.

90. Ibid., p. 164.

91. Ibid., p. 163.

92. Ibid., p. 162.

93. Ibid., p. 163.

94. Ibid., p. 174.

95. See PRO D.O. 35/893/XII/123, 'Treatment of the Catholic

minority in Northern Ireland'. Cf. also D.O. 35/893/XII/251, UK/Eire, political and constitutional relations: allegations made by the Eire government as to the maltreatment of the Catholic minority in Northern Ireland arising out of partition.

96. PRO D.O. 35/893/XII/123, Sir H. Batterbee minute dated 7 November 1938.

97. Loc.cit., minute by Stephenson, 13 March 1938.

98. PRO D.O. 35/893/XII/251, notes by Sir E.J. Harding, c. 7 November 1938. Harding was Permanent Under-Secretary of State for Dominion Affairs.

99. PRO D.O. 35/892/XII/251, Dominions Office comment on Home Office views, Sir Harry Batterbee, 18 November 1938.

100. 'Ultach', 'The Persecution of Catholics', p. 175.

3   War and Welfarism, 1943–1951

The Second World War was a major watershed in British social and political history and, try as its rulers might, Northern Ireland could not remain untouched by the effects of the conflict. The war led to a substantial increase in state planning and economic management. As one of the leading historians of the period has pointed out, these developments were associated with a significant move towards acceptance of a 'managed' economy and the welfare state.[1] They also owed much to the political pressure of the working class, which, as Eric Hobsbawm has observed, 'injected a deliberate element of social equity into public policy, such as had been notably absent in the First World War'.[2] The effects of these developments on the political elite in Ulster were to be of particular significance because of the clear divergence between its main political strategy after 1921 and that pursued by its British counterpart. The latter was Baldwin's aim of 'educating the Labour Party', of integrating it into responsible, constitutional politics. This was necessitated by the massive increase in trade union membership and militancy after the First World War.[3]

The Unionist Party in Ulster was spared the problem of developing a fresh strategy by the intensification of the national struggle in 1920. This enabled it to disarm the working class by branding its leadership as 'Bolshevist Sinn Feiners'. The local labour movement suffered severely in the expulsions of 1920 and the subsequent 'cleansing' of Belfast workplaces of 'alien elements'. The consequent disorientation, pogroms and repression, followed by two decades of severe unemployment, provided local employers with sufficient leeway to continue with business as usual. Foster has pointed out that it was bankers who favoured the strategy of 'educating labour' in Britain. Industrialists, particularly in the provinces, were equivocal or hostile, tending instead towards the Churchillian alternative of mobilisation 'to defeat labour, discredit its leaders, attack its trade union base and decisively reassert the ... values of the existing order'.[4] Bankers were, of course, also present in Ulster, but they did not act as a decisive force in Unionist affairs. The dominance of the representatives of manufacturing industry, together with the weakness of the local labour movement, meant that the war acted on a political elite whose traditions were not such as to produce a 'British' type of flexibility.

This chapter examines the steady 'de-insularisation' of the economy, politics and ideology in Northern Ireland during and immediately after the Second World War. Four aspects of this process, each with different effects, will be examined. Each exemplifies the limits on the manoeuvrability of the political elite implied by its traditional political inflexibility. Together they illustrate the solution to 'de-insularisation' adopted by the political elite and the restrictions on future options which it embodied.

Industrial Mobilisation, Post-war Reconstruction and the Fall of Andrews

The issue of post-war reconstruction first emerged in 1941 when the British government committed itself to a far-reaching programme and the discussions began which led in 1942 to the Beveridge Report. In a letter to the Chancellor of the Exchequer in August 1942, John Andrews, who had succeeded Craig as Prime Minister in 1940, outlined the political problems such plans created for the Unionists:

> In numerous public utterances of responsible people the minds of our people have been directed more than ever before towards what is called a 'new order' or a 'fair deal', the 'scandal that poverty should exist' and the 'horrors associated with the slums'.[5]

He feared the emergence of political difficulties if the Unionists appeared to be prepared to do less than the British government:

Our people frequently chafe at their feeling of inability to exercise any sort of initiative in their desire for reform. For a very considerable time a very definite and sustained demand has been pressed upon me that I should give a real lead as regards the government's intentions on social problems in future years. We cannot maintain the necessary interest in our parliamentary institutions if we are not allowed to exercise some initiative.[6]

The background to Andrews's concern was rising public dissatisfaction with the government's performance in industrial mobilisation. Long after Dunkirk, when there was an acute labour shortage in Britain, unemployment remained high in Northern Ireland.[7] It appears that the change-over to war production was considerably hindered by the hostility of government ministers and the middle class generally to the integration of the province into the UK structure of area boards, set up by the Ministry of Supply.[8] Such falls as there had been in local unemployment were largely accounted for by the export of labour.[9]

Dissatisfaction with the government had manifested itself in two Stormont by-election defeats. An independent Unionist had won North Down, while Harry Midgley of the Northern Ireland Labour Party (NILP) had taken Belfast Willowfield.*

Shortly before his correspondence with the Treasury, Andrews had raised the issue of post-war reconstruction at a Cabinet meeting, pointing out the extent to which many social services in Ulster were inferior to those in Britain. Sir Basil Brooke,† who had been widely expected to succeed Craig and was now Minister of Commerce, made it clear that a public commitment to make up such 'leeway' would require Treasury clearance.[10] As a result it was agreed to set up a Post-war Planning Committee chaired by Brooke and composed of the Minister of Finance and the Permanent Secretaries for Home Affairs, Agriculture, Labour and Commerce. Spender, who was a member, thought the committee would be a check on Andrews's populism: 'I think that both the chairman and the secretary will act upon sound principles and prevent as far as possible any stampeding of

---

* See Biographical Note on p. 260.
† See Biographical Note on p. 250.

our government into premature action.'[11]

Despite this, and apparently without Treasury approval, Andrews proceeded to commit the government to its own programme of reconstruction in a Stormont speech at the end of July. He promised slum clearance, a housing programme, educational expansion and large-scale extension of mains water, sewage and electricity provision to rural areas. He emphasised that the programme was his own government's concern, though it would be related to British plans.

The speech provoked an extremely hostile reaction at the Treasury. In an internal communication, an official noted:

Mr Andrews has chosen to disregard not merely the financial responsibility of his government towards ours, but even the element of inter-government courtesy [a reference to the fact that the speech had been made before the Treasury received a copy of it]. Mr Andrews appears to be trying to establish the principle that whatever tune Northern Ireland calls, the Imperial Government will pay the piper.[12]

In a message to Spender, Compton of the Treasury spelt out his department's main objections:

It seems to commit your government to specific services on a very generous scale and without any prior consideration as to whether they can be met out of the available resources in the post-war years. Further, it pays no regard to the maintenance of parity of services between your government and ours. In this connection surely the sentence in para. 6 [Andrews's reference to the programme as a domestic concern] is misleading ... We *are* concerned, just because you may be proclaiming standards which conflict with our policy, secondly because there is evident danger of your being committed to a programme which would imperil the financial structure of your government.[13]

The British Chancellor of the Exchequer, Kingsley Wood, himself wrote to Andrews on 6 August. He emphasised the dangers of capitulation to contemporary tendencies to consider social reforms independently of their financial consequences, and the implications of this for Belfast-London relations. In particular, no programme which threatened parity could be endorsed.[14] The same message was conveyed in still stronger terms by Wood to Maynard Sinclair, Parliamentary Secretary to the Ministry of Finance, when they met at the Treasury:

> The Chancellor admitted that there was a similar demand in Britain but this came mostly from the Socialists ... in Northern Ireland it comes principally from our own supporters; he [Wood] feels that a reconstruction programme of any kind, and particularly one showing substantial advances in our social services, will be difficult to achieve and will not be possible in the immediate post-war period.

In recording this in his diary, Spender echoed the Treasury position and criticised Andrews's behaviour:

> I am quite convinced in my own mind that the best interests of Ulster will be ensured by the closest co-operation with the British government and that any attempt to make political capital by forestalling the British post-war measures will not be to the advantage of our province. In the end I believe that it would also prove disastrous to our present government if such a policy was pursued for purely political reasons.[15]

Sinclair revealed the Treasury position to the second meeting of the post-war planning group, adding that he had assured Wood that the government's only intention was to make up 'leeway'.[16] This same line was taken by Andrews in his reply to Wood. By now, however, it was too late. The Treasury viewed Andrews as a dangerous demagogue.

The difficulties were accentuated by general doubts, both locally and in Britain, about Andrews's competence. These sealed an alliance in Ulster between Brooke, the civil servants on the planning committee and Spender. For the latter, disquiet was mainly financial in character. An existing anti-populism had been reinforced once more by the Treasury. Wood and his department were the proponents of a traditional policy on government expenditure and were to be the major opponents of the Beveridge Report.[17] Brooke did not entirely share their views. For him, the articulation of this position was strictly subordinate to political considerations. He did not oppose populism as such, but rather its degeneration into a rhetoric detached from practical possibilities. As the degree of Treasury opposition became known, Andrews stood condemned not as a populist but as an inept – and in this sense a dangerous – one.

In fact Andrews continued to enrage the Treasury. In a speech at Stormont at the end of the war he claimed that in September 1942 he had secured agreement from the Chancellor that Ulster could incur extra expenditure to make up 'leeway', her backwardness in basic infrastructure and social services.[18] While he did in fact claim as much at the time, the Treasury view was that this was a 'dangerous doctrine' on which he needed to be corrected.[19] In a letter to Andrews, Wood assured him that the case for making up leeway was being sympathetically received, but added, 'The times are now such and will be after the war that both of us must have regard to the financial situation as a whole.'[20] Yet Andrews in his reply interpreted this too as an acceptance of his position. Compton, one of the main Treasury officials concerned, commented, 'Andrews naïvely notes the points on which obligations rest on the Imperial Treasury and ignores the points on which obligations rest on Northern Ireland'.[21]

Other problems too continued to be encountered. Alongside Brooke's planning committee, the government had appointed a planning consultant, W.R. Davidge, to report on the preparation of a town plan for Belfast.[22] In his preliminary report in September 1942, Davidge recommended a reconstruction plan for the city and a large part of the surrounding area, a plan for the city and county of Derry, and plans for the improvement and development of Armagh, Tyrone and Fermanagh. On his recommendation, and with the support of Andrews and Bates, a Planning Advisory Board was created. Brooke's group reacted with hostility and refused to meet until there was a clear division of powers. This was apparently not forthcoming and in December the Brooke committee was disbanded.[23]

The issue of industrial mobilisation meanwhile continued to attract public criticism. Owing to the intervention of another independent Unionist, the government lost the Westminster seat of West Belfast to a Labour candidate in February 1943. This was the first time it had passed from Unionist hands since 1922.

The Andrews initiative was in ruins. Brooke had emerged as the champion of 'responsible' government. It was only a matter of time before he became Prime Minister. This would not represent the eclipse of the dominant populist practices of the 1930s, but rather a tactical adjustment in the aftermath of an unsuccessful attempt to extend them. Andrews had allowed his fears of the criticisms of the Unionist war effort to stampede him into a piece of demagogy which had endangered relations with that section of the British state whose goodwill was essential to the financing of increased government expenditure. Internal political pressures had moved him too far ahead of the existing balance between reformism and orthodoxy in Britain. Brooke's line, on the other hand, acknowledged that in the context of the political and ideological transformations brought about by the war, traditional tactics were insufficient. Promises of 'bones' in the future, especially when made so patently under the pressure of political criticism, were no substitute for the obvious inadequacies in the government's handling of industrial mobilisation. Andrews, clinging to his geriatric Cabinet, was stumbling from expedient to expedient. Just as they failed to win the Treasury's approval, they failed to win approval at home. Ironically, by the end of the war British orthodoxy had accommodated a degree of interventionism and welfarism sufficient to create the conditions for just the sort of developments that Andrews had wanted in 1942.

For the present, events conspired to ensure that he was incapable of producing the style of active leadership required to offset the national unpopularity of the discredited Conservative appeasers of the 1930s. In 1943 the threat from the NILP had not yet assumed the dimensions it was to acquire in the last two years of the war. Brooke was able to take advantage of the internal divisions between partitionists and anti-partitionists in the Labour Party (which had culminated in Midgley's resignation to form the Commonwealth Labour Party in December 1942) to give his incoming government a coalitionist, 'national' flavour like that in Britain. Midgley was brought into the Cabinet.

Economic Policy

Apart from Midgley and his party, the forces Brooke gathered behind him to implement the realignment of the populist position indicated in the clearest possible way that it would provide only a little more flexibility than its predecessor. Particularly in his struggle against the Andrews line, Brooke had depended heavily upon a revival of residual anti-populism. Although the discrediting of Andrews should not be seen as a victory for this tendency within the Northern Irish state, certain critical changes had occurred in its position which now made it a more substantial, if less coherent, entity.

The first and most important of these was that its views on public expenditure had come to be increasingly articulated by a section of the local manufacturers who had previously been largely populist. Linen interests, which had been identified with this group at least in their protectionism, appear to have become alarmed at the tendency of industrialists generally to emphasise productivist and Keynesian views. While retaining their close links with the members of the Cabinet and the parliamentary party, the linen manufacturers now provided the backbone of opposition to proposals involving 'extravagance'. A second and more deep-seated change in anti-populism was that it became divested of its broader non-partisan implications and ceased to be associated with general attempts to institutionalise the *via Britannica* locally. While the basis of this transition is unclear, it was obviously tied in some respect to the change in allegiance of the linen manufacturers.

Newly circumscribed anti-populist proposals, and the linen industry's views more generally, increasingly found a voice through the previously ineffective Ministry of Commerce. As minister from 1941 to 1943, Brooke generally followed them on industrial matters. As a result of his own developing influence, they became part of the state's industrial policy. While acknowledging the problem of industrial mobilisation, pro-Brooke Unionists departed from independent Unionists and the NILP in attributing this failure solely to Andrews and not to the linen industry's failure to adjust to the wartime situation.

In January 1943 Brooke appointed a committee to consider post-war problems for the industry and such measures as might be necessary for it to overcome them.[24] Of its eleven members, ten were directors of linen firms.[25] Its proposals were basically conservative,[26] and were welcomed by the industry.[27] But to the industry's critics they simply served to make more unlikely the reforms in its structure which were regarded as a necessary condition of its survival in the predictably unfavourable post-war situation.

One such critic, writing in 1944, pointed out that although the inter-war period had seen an increase in the degree of vertical and horizontal integration in the industry, it was still dominated by a large number of small or medium-sized firms. Large-scale 'rationalisation' was necessary if the generally low level of efficiency and associated high costs of production were to be eliminated. 'Rationalisation' would greatly improve the quality of management. Many small, uneconomic firms were able to stay in business only by paying low wages or accepting very low returns on capital.[28] The industry had failed in the 1930s to adopt any measures of rationalisation comparable to those in shipbuilding and cotton. The consistently *laissez-faire* line of both Andrews and Brooke had clear effects on the war effort.[29]

Thus it was that the implementation of the linen manufacturers' line within the state ensured a policy towards the industry that was bound to increase the government's political difficulties as Labour and independent Unionists criticised its handling of the war effort.

Populism and the 'Fifth Column'

In considering the events discussed so far, their most important characteristic should not be overlooked. While together with their effects they represented modifications of the traditional populist strategy, these were essentially marginal. Neither of the modifications discussed effaced the core element of populism – the relationship between the Protestant middle class (through the state) and the Protestant working class. Brooke's new administration, while in part the result of an anti-populist reaction to the policies of the Andrews regime, in no way diverged in its principal strategy. This is clearly illustrated in the continuity of concern demonstrated by both administrations at the issue of the importation of southern workers.

Here the decisive aspect was the reimposition of a form of sectarianism on a potential class issue: unemployment. Throughout 1942 the independents and later Midgley had consistently raised the issue of the persistence of serious unemployment. The issue was, however, raised within a predominantly populist framework that made it relatively easy to deal with. In February 1942 at Stormont Midgley accused the Unionists of 'solving' the problem by encouraging workers to move to British industrial centres.[30] The notion that the Andrews administration was 'exporting' Ulstermen was taken up by Independent Unionists like T. Henderson and J.W. Nixon, the MPs for Belfast Shankill and Belfast Woodvale. The latter linked this claim to the accusation that the government was allowing workers from Eire to get jobs in the North. Henderson claimed that, 'There are more Fifth Columnists in Northern Ireland than in any other country in Europe and they are still being brought in here.'[31]

Because of the conditions under which the state had been born the issue was of great significance. The question of the employers' attitude to the 'peaceful penetration' of the First World War had been a major source of conflict within the Protestant bloc from 1918 to 1920. It had been resolved by employers' acquiescence in expulsions and the Vigilance Committees, and by the institutionalisation of this position in the B Specials and, to a lesser extent, the state more generally. The government became acutely sensitive to grievances of this kind. In the 1930s the anti-populist group had attempted to put into perspective the usually fanciful and lurid accounts of 'Eirean' infiltration which Craig sometimes received from local Unionists. After the collapse of the Pollock-Milne Barbour-Spender circle there was no attempt made to curb this aspect of populism. Rather, it was indulged by both Andrews and Brooke in a successful attempt to hegemonise opposition over unemployment.

Owing to the enlistment of skilled workers and an increased demand for certain types of skilled labour, the Ministry of Labour had brought in some skilled southerners. In response to criticisms it was pointed out that no unskilled workers were imported under ministry auspices, although some private employers had done so independently.[32] Efforts were initially made to control this, but by the beginning of 1942 Andrews was pressing for more action. The possibility of an order under Defence of the Realm Act regulations to make it compulsory for all employers to engage workers through employment exchanges was rejected, and it was agreed to set up a joint ministerial committee (Home Affairs, Labour and the new Ministry of Public Security) to investigate alternative methods of restriction.[33]

The progress of the committee was slow and Andrews became increasingly agitated. By April he claimed to have evidence of 'increasing public criticism of the ease with which workers from Eire could obtain employment in Northern Ireland'.[34] At his suggestion it was agreed that the Minister of Home Affairs should arrange to see the British Home Secretary to secure his approval for some sort of restrictive measure.

In September 1942 the British Cabinet, in keeping with the vigour of its war effort, agreed to Belfast's proposals for a 'Residence in Northern Ireland Restriction Order' by which the period of an immigrant's residence would be controlled by permit.[35] Andrews and his Minister of Labour, J.F. Gordon, were still dissatisfied. Their anxiety to deflect their supporters' disquiet, no matter how trivial its basis, was demonstrated in subsequent events. In January 1943 Andrews reported receiving a complaint from the Downpatrick district that local building trade workers were being dismissed from a contract while men from Eire were being retained.[36] Gordon promised to make immediate enquiries, stating that in his own view the existing measures were still insufficient. The Cabinet agreed that he should draw up proposals to strengthen the order.

The fall of Andrews and his supporters – including Gordon – had nothing to do with this issue and it continued to be a matter of the greatest importance for the Brooke Cabinet. The only criticism of Andrews on this score was of the degree to which his Cabinet's fixation on it had led to other wartime problems being ignored.

Its significance for Brooke may be illustrated simply. In July 1944 a Protestant clergyman made a speech in which he alleged that the Belfast government had complete discretion in issuing residence permits, with the implication that the order would be used to exclude southern Catholics. Brooke became concerned that if the government was to be attacked in the future for being soft on southerners it should be made clear that it was not its own master in this area. He discussed the speech with his Minister of Home Affairs, William Lowry: it was agreed that a statement should be issued

denying that the administration of the Act was solely a
Northern Irish matter and pointing out that the Home
Office had to be consulted. The statement referred to the
fact that permits could not be issued on a confessional basis.
The rest of the Cabinet reacted strongly:

> There was considerable discussion as to the wisdom of
> emphasising too strongly that the Order could not be
> administered on the basis of the religious persuasion of the
> applicants. It was recognised that the Minister of Home
> Affairs was responsible to the Home Secretary for the
> manner in which the Order was administered and that there
> could not be any process of selection on a sectarian basis.
> On the other hand, the repetition of this principle ... was
> like trailing one's coat and seemed in the view of the Cabinet
> to be unnecessary and particularly undesirable at the period
> of the 12th celebrations.[37]

Lowry's defence of the statement was in the same liberal
spirit:

> He thought it essential as a matter of policy to indicate quite
> clearly that discrimination according to religion was beyond
> the powers of the government, although he was fully in
> sympathy with the view that unless some steps were taken to
> ensure the Protestant Ascendancy, the future of Northern
> Ireland was in jeopardy.[38]

In his Minister of Public Security (later to become Minister
of Labour), Harry Midgley, Brooke had as staunch a populist
as Gordon, but a more perceptive one. From mid-1944,
when the government began to anticipate the problems
associated with demobilisation and reconstruction, Midgley
emphasised that the real issue in this area would be that of
ex-servicemen from the South obtaining work in post-war
Northern Ireland. A veteran of the First World War and an
organiser of an ex-servicemen's group in the 1920s, he seems
to have feared a repeat of the mass Protestant working-class
disaffection with Unionism in 1919 and 1920, which in its
sectarian mode attacked local employers for taking on
Catholics between 1914 and 1918. Midgley was particularly
worried that the implementation of the Beveridge proposals
in Northern Ireland would lead to a 'deluge' of southerners,
who, apart from increasing competition in the labour market

and arousing loyalist hostility, would 'gravitate to the disloyal element in our population and increase our political difficulties'.[39]

Brooke took note and at a Cabinet meeting in February 1945 announced that he planned to meet Churchill to discuss inter-state relations, as 'there might be several areas on [*sic*] which Northern Ireland's constitutional powers needed strengthening',[40] particularly, of course, control over southern immigration. Later in the month Maynard Sinclair, Minister of Finance, reported that at several recent political meetings he had found 'very strong dissatisfaction about the number of Eire workers employed in Northern Ireland, and still coming here while so many of our own people were unemployed'.[41]

In March, Midgley reported that a critical situation was developing, as some trade unions were claiming that when workers became redundant Northern Irish dilutees should be paid off before skilled southerners. There was Cabinet agreement that in such cases the residence permits should be withdrawn, even if this resulted in a strike.[42]

Brooke duly travelled to London to discuss the employment situation with British ministers, raising the topic of control of immigrants from Eire and 'the difficulties which were likely to arise in Northern Ireland in the absence of any statutory power to control entry after the war'.

No attempt was made to verify empirically the hypothetical deluge of workers from the south, nor to gain even an impressionistic estimate of the 'danger'. Rather, concern seems to have been directly related to the expression of alarm by groups and organisations considered influential with the Protestant working class. Early in 1946 Brooke reported that the British Legion had made representations to him about the large number of civilians employed in some establishments run by London-based departments like the Air Ministry. The Legion asked the government to have such people replaced by ex-servicemen. For once, a cursory investigation of the situation was made and Midgley found that of 5,500 employees only 2,000 were ex-servicemen. Worse still, a considerable proportion of the civilians came from Eire. British government regulations made no provision for preferential treatment of former members of the forces, but Brooke nevertheless insisted that the London departments remove the southerners.[43]

Despite the important changes in the political and ideological climate brought about by the war, the political elite's principal traditional strategy of dividing the working class was retained. The important questions concern the social basis for this continuity and the new tactics developed in relation to it.

Welfarism

A fourth issue involving the de-insularisation of Northern Ireland was that of the welfare state. While enthusiasm for welfarist legislation was evidently strong amongst the Protestant working class, and was expressed in the growth of the NILP, its major effect was to continue the process of redivision of the political elite which had begun during the 1942 dispute over post-war reconstruction.

The major aspect of this realignment was the final transformation of anti-populism from its original status as a non-partisan critical force whose most important allies were in Whitehall, especially the Treasury. By the late 1940s this element remained anti-populist only in its parsimony. Not only had it ceased to be non-partisan and non-sectarian, but it had become associated with a section of the Orange Order. It developed an obsessive concern with 'socialistic' British legislation and, as Keynesian thinking on budgetary control became dominant, lost its allies in the Treasury. Populism, on the other hand, was reproduced with only minor modifications. It was able to absorb welfarism in its stride, as it had relief works in the 1930s.

While these were important changes, they should not divert attention from the most fundamental one of all in these years, implicit throughout this chapter. In the process of the political redivision of the Unionist elite differences between populists and their opponents descended from a strategic to a tactical level. While anti-populism had never been a comprehensive strategy for establishing leadership over the Protestant working class in the way populism had, it nevertheless contested the basic aim of dividing the working class along religious lines, and not simply the tactics for doing so. Promoting such a division had not previously been part of anti-populism.

By 1950, however, this was no longer so. Both populists and their opponents took for granted the overall objective of tightening the bond between different sections of the Protestant community. They differed not on this but on the degree to which the Northern Ireland state could secure welfarism whilst resisting the erosion of its autonomy by other aspects of Westminster legislation.

Another significant change was that, unlike earlier divisions, the new ones were not reproduced within the central state apparatuses themselves. These appear to have been united in their defence of the government's populist policies against critics both at Stormont and in the constituencies.

Many of the government's critics were middle-class, and many of the arguments the government used against them were justified by reference to working-class demands. This was evidence not that the state was becoming neutral in class terms but that the populists' relative independence was made necessary by the implementation of a line which would perpetuate the status quo.

At least partly as a result of its alliance with traditional anti-populists against Andrews's post-war reconstruction speech, the Brooke circle's original reaction to the Beveridge proposals had been cautious. Brooke argued:

> I do not see how any government could possibly commit itself until it knows what the financial position is going to be after the war ... If you deprive industry, whether socially owned or privately owned, of its means of producing work and wealth, then those magnificent schemes put forward by Sir William Beveridge must fall to the ground for lack of funds.[44]

At the same time it was clearly recognised that the maintenance of the Unionist class alliance required not merely a sectarian position on an issue like workers from Eire but action of some sort on social and economic issues.

In 1943 the NILP concentrated on the backwardness of local health services – Ulster had the highest infant mortality rate in the UK, and the position was similar for deaths from tuberculosis, facilities for the treatment of which were, like the maternity services, pathetically inadequate.[45] On the industrial front, the winter of 1942 saw strikes at Short's and other engineering works and the development of a militant

Belfast shop stewards' committee.[46] Further strikes and
prosecutions under Defence of the Realm Act regulations
followed in 1943, and in 1944 the NILP began for the first
time to form industrial groups, the first of them in the
shipyard. The number of trade unionists affiliated to the
party increased sharply.[47] In March and April 1944 a strike of
engineering workers at the yard, the aircraft factory and
some of the largest engineering plants led to a conflict with
the government when five shop stewards were arrested. The
shop stewards' committee ordered a mass walk-out from
Belfast factories, which forced the release of the men and a
favourable settlement of the original wage claim.[48]

While the degree to which the Beveridge proposals could
be implemented depended on the results of the
forthcoming Westminster election, the government in
Northern Ireland could only adopt a strategy of piecemeal
accommodation to popular pressure. In March 1944 a new
Ministry of Health and Local Government was created.
Brooke had also reformed a post-war reconstruction
committee under Sir Ronald Nugent,[49] but it was recognised
that in lieu of a national scheme its activities would be
cosmetic.[50]

The Unionists fought the 1945 general election on a
strongly anti-socialist platform, emphasising the dangers to
local industry of Labour's commitment to nationalisation
and planning.[51] In the same campaign, however, they also
committed themselves to introduce whatever social reforms
were passed in Britain.[52]

At the Stormont election the same year the NILP
nominated eight candidates in Belfast and although it
captured only two seats, in constituencies where there was a
substantial Catholic working class (Oldpark and Dock), all
its candidates won substantial votes. If it is remembered that
the Protestant oppositional vote was shared with six
candidates for Midgley's Commonwealth Labour Party and
three for the then pro-Union Communist Party of Northern
Ireland, whose candidates received an impressive 12,456
votes, it becomes clear that the government's post-election
strategy had to acknowledge this labourist upsurge.[53]

What, then, would be the relationship of the government
in Ulster to Labour's implementation of Beveridge? In his
analysis of Protestant politics A.C. Hepburn argued that:

Perhaps the main reason for the Unionists' effortless maintenance of power lies in the ultimate insignificance of the local parliament. Once a working agreement was reached between Westminster and Stormont on the financial aspects of devolution ... social progress could be maintained, with no additional effort or expense, simply by reproducing Westminster legislation.[54]

Needless to say, the introduction of welfarism to Ulster was not such a frictionless process as this implies. The implementation of 'socialistic' laws threatened not only to produce disunity within the ruling elite but possibly to encourage the Protestant cynicism about Stormont. In December 1945 the Cabinet discussed a memorandum drawn up by Brooke on a proposal by BBC Northern Ireland to broadcast a series of talks called 'The Week in Stormont', to be given by back-bench MPs in proportion to party strength. Although Britain already had a similar programme about Westminster, Brooke argued that in the Six Counties 'there are special circumstances which make such a programme of talks highly undesirable'. These naturally included the fact that 'the Nationalist members are aiming at the destruction of our Constitution', but also, and more interestingly, that,

Our parliament meets on only one day in some weeks, and the business may be of a relatively unimportant character. In such a week there would be very little material ... the radio talk would create the impression that our parliament (as some of our opponents are constantly saying) is of little importance and talks of the character proposed should impress the public with the value and prestige of our parliament.[55]

The problem for the Unionist government arose from the fact that a government which Unionism had identified as a major enemy of Protestant interests was introducing a series of significant improvements in everyday life. The problem was solved by the outbreak of intra-Unionist division, which enabled the Brooke Cabinet to present itself as the champion of popular interests.

Once the Cabinet began to consider the Attlee government's legislative programme, concern with both its 'socialistic' nature and its implications for the existing division of powers between the two governments became evident. In September the Supplies and Services (Transitional Powers) Bill was discussed. Under it, orders made by Northern Irish departments using delegated powers would have to be laid before the British parliament. Brooke argued that although it might be administratively convenient for control to be exercised from London, it would be a mistake to 'allow them to take over our legislation'. Nugent, the Minister of Commerce, commented on the 'deterioration' of the situation since the British election, 'Whereas it was the desire of the last government to have controls removed as soon as possible, the present government was showing a tendency in the other direction.'[56]

Eventually it was decided that the Bill did not threaten Stormont's powers and it was accepted. The issue was raised again in October over another piece of Westminster legislation, the Investment (Control and Guarantees) Act. Maynard Sinclair pointed out that certain clauses dealing with investment control related to a transferred service.[57] Although the close links between local and national banks and insurance companies were obvious grounds for central control of capital issues, a major policy issue was at stake:

> My own feeling is that we should take no step which would in any way weaken the constitutional position of the parliament and government of Northern Ireland ... [Although the present issue was not vital] I can forsee a circumstance in which any precedent which might indicate our readiness to allow the Imperial Parliament to legislate in respect of a transferred service might prove embarrassing.[58]

As a result, separate legislation was introduced in Stormont.[59]

In November Brooke referred to the investment Bill as an index of what was now seen as a potentially serious threat to existing relations between Stormont and Westminster:

> The adoption of some of the measures which were being passed by the present government at Westminster could be justified on the grounds that they were an unavoidable part of the aftermath of war, but as time went on more extreme socialistic measures may be introduced which on account of the financial relationship between Northern Ireland and Great Britain, would have to be followed here. At any time the government might have to face a situation in which the

measures they considered they had no alternative but to introduce would be unacceptable to members of the Unionist Party, and if the government could not rely upon their support chaotic conditions would result ... he was extremely uneasy on this score and had been considering whether any changes could be made to avert such a situation. The possibilities were dominion status or a return to Westminster.[60]

In Cabinet discussions in January and February 1946 Nugent and Brian Maginess, Minister of Labour, submitted memoranda favouring dominion status, whereby Northern Ireland's constitutional position within the United Kingdom would have been changed to allow it the same status as other effectively independent states in the Commonwealth like Australia and Canada. It appears they were considered seriously by the rest of the Cabinet. Both ministers took as their starting point the following characterisation of the UK:

Britain seemed to have shifted significantly leftwards, and governments, Labour or Conservative, would hereafter assume much tighter planning and control, irksome to Ulstermen used to 'independence'.[61]

They both stressed that the new status should not militate against the introduction of welfare legislation and Maginess believed that, 'Our industrial, though not our social legislation can no longer run on parallel lines.' He also felt it was necessary to request 'a greater degree of responsibility and at the same time ask for continued financial assistance'. Dominion status was rejected if it meant Ulster having to live within its own resources. Maginess argued that,

It might mean that our present standards might have to be lowered, [which] would tend to lessen the difference to the worker between Northern Ireland and Eire and therefore by so much would weaken one of our most telling arguments against Union with the country ... on the political side it would present the Labour Party here with the best election platform they could ever hope to have

Brooke and Sinclair made speeches throughout the winter of 1945-46 emphasising that the relative autonomy of Stormont remained intact even when it implemented measures for which Westminster was financially responsible. On one occasion Sinclair managed to combine this with a typically populist blast:

> Family allowances would cost more per head of population in Ulster than in the rest of the UK. He did not think this was due to the Unionist population. He rather thought there was another reason ...
>
> Ulster would always be able to make her budget balance and make an Imperial contribution because she was going to be in a more prosperous condition than after the 1914-18 war.[62]

In his budget speech Sinclair denied that 'parity' and 'step by step' meant that Ulster should 'slavishly follow' the whole pattern of life in Britain. 'We should preserve in the administration of our services the greatest possible degree of flexibility.'[63] Speaking at an Orange meeting in December 1945, Brooke read out a letter from an English Tory attacking the Labour government and thanking heaven for a bastion of conservatism at Stormont. Brooke went on to forecast difficult times ahead in relations with Westminster.[64]

It was soon to become clear, though, that feeling within the Cabinet was for playing this down. As early as November the Minister of Home Affairs, Edmond Warnock, made a speech arguing that Labour represented no threat to Ulster's constitutional position and that, although it differed in some principles, the party's social programme was 'not unlike our own'.[65] In fact the Cabinet was coming under attack from the right for importing too much 'socialist' legislation. Brooke's speech had been partly motivated by the need to defend Unionism's conservative credentials.

In December William Grant, Minister of Health and Local Government, introduced a Bill to create a publicly owned house-building authority, the Northern Ireland Housing Trust (NIHT). It was bitterly attacked by local builders' organisations. Grant pointed out that it departed from the British pattern by providing subsidies for private builders.[66] Nevertheless at the UUC in February 1946 he was attacked as an opponent of private enterprise, and a resolution demanding more concessions to private builders was adopted.[67]

The criticisms of the government by back-benchers and the constituency organisations were to increase in 1946, culminating in a campaign for dominion status to save Ulster from 'creeping socialism'. There was a certain reflection of this campaign in the Cabinet where some ministers feared a potential constitutional clash with London over possible nationalisation measures.[68] Brooke's support for the status quo was, however, underwritten by the favourable financial relations negotiated with the Treasury.

In a series of agreements with the Treasury from 1946 onwards the Unionist government was able to obtain the financial guarantees that would underwrite the reforms Andrews had promised in 1942.[69] Apart from the fact that they fully integrated the province into the welfare state, they enabled the domestic exchequer to put money into local services rather than it going to Whitehall. This had become particularly important in the area of capital expenditure, where Northern Ireland could have found it difficult to make up 'leeway' without getting into debt. From 1947 the Treasury permitted the Ministry of Finance to divert revenue from the imperial contribution to a Capital Purposes Fund for industrial development and other projects. At the same time Westminster made it clear that these concessions were incompatible with an increase in devolution.

Equally significantly for the Cabinet's change in attitude was the fact that by the summer of 1946 Brooke and his colleagues had become convinced of Attlee's goodwill towards them on partition, and had acquired a more balanced view of the actual extent of his proposals for nationalisation.[70] As Rumpf and Hepburn put it, 'It became clear at quite an early stage that no one in the Attlee Cabinet was inclined to upset the Unionist applecart.'[71] The Home Secretary, Chuter Ede, rebuffed attempts by both the NILP and the Friends of Ireland group of back-bench Labour MPs to raise issues such as electoral law and practices, discrimination and the Special Powers Act in Ulster.

Nevertheless, an important section of the Ulster business class remained more concerned with the province's integration into an enveloping system of 'socialist control' than with the problem of perpetuating the political and ideological conditions for maintaining their political dominance. Their discontent was clearly influenced by the increases in taxation during and after the war, which were regularly denounced by Unionist back-benchers as 'death-blows' to local enterprise.[72] Their increasingly bitter reaction to the main lines of Unionist government policy threatened to provoke major conflict within the Unionist Party. The issue that crystallised the opposition was the government's attempt in 1946-47 to introduce a Statistics of Trade Bill.

In November 1946 the Attlee Cabinet announced its intention of introducing legislation to empower the Board of Trade to collect figures from employers on numbers employed, wage rates, value and ownership of fixed capital, stocks and subsidies from central and local authorities. The Northern Ireland Ministers concerned – Sinclair and Nugent – observed that similar legislation would have to be introduced at Stormont, since the statistics were an element in the formation of national policies from which they hoped the province would benefit. At the same time Sinclair raised an important objection: 'There is a natural reaction of the business community against disclosing all these particulars … I feel we may wish to operate something far less drastic.'[73]

Nugent replied that it was imperative the legislation be similar, citing the general benefit of existing economic and financial relations:

> The main object in collecting these statistics is to provide the Imperial government with a sound foundation of facts and figures on which to base their policies of full employment. We are committed to a similar policy in Northern Ireland and stand to gain considerably by the prosecution of that policy on the part of the Imperial government. It would be difficult to substantiate our claim to be treated as a development area in the government's policy with regard to the distribution of industry if we are unable to provide up-to-date information on trade and business [here].[74]

The government agreed with Nugent.

When this became known in September 1947, opposition was substantial. Unionist back-benchers were already attacking the Health Services Bill, the NIHT, and the creation of a Northern Ireland Transport Board (which involved the nationalisation – on generous terms – of the almost bankrupt local railway system). In the furore over these measures the demand for dominion status to save

Ulster from socialism was for the first time given public prominence.[75]

Unionist ministers were now forced to defend the Attlee government, emphasising its defence of Ulster's constitutional position.[76] Brooke praised Chuter Ede, and argued that, as a subordinate assembly, the Ulster government had no alternative but to introduce some of the legislation being adopted.[77]

The Belfast Chamber of Commerce and various other industrial and commercial bodies passed resolutions against the Statistics of Trade Bill.[78] In Unionist constituency parties, pressure from business interests resulted in similar resolutions being accepted. As opposition mounted (supported by the *Belfast Newsletter*), Nugent told a specially convened UUC Executive Committee meeting that he had decided to invite 'representative businessmen' to form a committee to examine the Bill. He gave an assurance that a second reading would not take place until it had reported.[79] The eventual result was complete government capitulation and the introduction of a much weakened Bill in March 1949. While this represented a defeat for Brooke, he was able to profit by it. The Ulster middle class's hysterical outcry against 'socialism' provided him with a means of completing the incorporation of welfare measures into the Unionist alliance.

In a series of speeches in late 1947 he represented the government as the champion of a humane, progressive middle way between two extremes:

> In a modern democratic state, the government must assume responsibility for a wide range of activities in the interests of the community, but the indiscriminate charge of 'socialism' is unjustified and absurd ... there is a need for a middle course between the extreme philosophy of *laissez-faire* and the fetish of socialisation.[80]

The demand for dominion status was singled out for attack in a speech to a Unionist rally in Larne, where he combined an appeal to fear of nationalism with an open avowal of the significance of welfarism for the Unionist alliance:

> To attempt a fundamental change in our constitutional position is to reopen the whole Irish question. The government is strongly supported by the votes of the

working class who cherish their heritage in the Union and to whom any tendency towards separation from Britain is anathema The backbone of Unionism is the Unionist Labour party. Are those men going to be satisfied *if* we reject the social services and other benefits we have had by going step by step with Britain?[81]

By now it was evident that although most of those who advocated dominion status were critics of 'socialisation', not all anti-socialists were proponents of dominion status. Thus J.M. Andrews, who was unsympathetic to the government, made an extended attack on the idea which was welcomed by the *Newsletter*.[82] The *coup de grâce* was probably a speech in favour of the idea by an anti-partitionist Labour MP, Jack Beattie.[83] By the end of 1948 it found support only on the wilder fringes of the party.[84]

Although it proved possible to use a division within the elite to present the state as the progressive guarantor of parity with the new standards of British welfare, there was no fundamental change in relations between populist and anti-populist practices. The relatively full employment of the post-war period, together with the Brooke circle's defence of the welfare state, seemed to the correspondent of the *Round Table* to offer the prospect of evolution towards a more normal type of regime:

> One result of the last three years has been a certain realignment of the Unionists themselves. The lessening of the threat of constitutional change which so long strengthened the right wing has enabled the party to regain more of the liberal tradition. The Prime Minister has not deferred to the older and more diehard element in going ahead with social reforms. It is too soon, perhaps, to see the effects of this broadened outlook on relations with the minority, but notably in the new educational system inspired by the Butler Act, Unionist dissidence was safely risked in order to make concessions to the Roman Catholics.[85]

Yet within two years the Minister of Education who proposed these concessions had been forced to resign in the face of another sordid capitulation to pressure from the Protestant churches, the Orange Order and many MPs when he proposed to increase state grants to voluntary (mainly Catholic) schools from 50 to 65 per cent.[86] Later, in 1951, a

Public Order Act was passed to enable the RUC to suppress 'inflammatory' nationalist marches more effectively.[87]

Populist Orange pressure was evident in the government's subsequent decision to augment the Public Order Act with the Flags and Emblems Act in February 1954. This obliged the RUC to protect the display of the Union Jack anywhere in Northern Ireland. Although the Minister of Home Affairs reported to the Cabinet that the Inspector General of the RUC was unhappy with what he referred to as 'an impossible task' and two other ministers warned that the legislation showed the government to be 'yielding to the agitation of the extremists', Brooke insisted that he had already given a public assurance that people displaying Union Jacks would not be forced to remove them, it was essential that the legislation be introduced.[88]

If these manifestations of the 'Protestant' nature of the state confounded the hopes of optimistic liberals, there was a tendency to see them as a natural reaction to the victory of a new coalition in the southern elections of 1948. The Fine Gael-Labour government included a social-republican party, Clann na Poblachta, and within a year it had taken Ireland out of the Commonwealth, changed the state's name from Eire to the Republic of Ireland and launched an all-party Anti-Partition Campaign which financed candidates in the General Election Brooke called in January 1949.[89]

The argument that liberalising tendencies fell victim to events in the south betrays a fundamental misconception of the nature of the Unionist class alliance. Middle-class dominance of this alliance was achieved by the strenuous efforts to reconcile practices that were often at odds with one another and sometimes conflicted directly. There was disagreement within the elite about welfarism only because part of it saw that Protestant working-class disaffection was bound to arise if British legislation was not put into effect. In no way did this imply any liberalisation of the state's attitude towards Catholics. A commitment to some form of welfare state was to become an integral part of post-war British Conservatism and was compatible with many elements of traditional Conservative ideology.[90] In Ulster, Brooke and his circle made it clear that welfarism involved no threat to the local middle class whose industrial policy they continued to implement. It was a politically and ideologically neutral development both in Britain and in Ulster. Such significance as it had was determined by *existing* political and ideological practices: in Britain, those of a social democratic party; in Ulster those of an exclusivist Unionism. The Unionist leadership clearly saw welfarism as a necessary element in maintaining the support of the Protestant working class. This is not to say that other practices which had secured domination in the past were redundant. The Cabinet's reaction to the proposed BBC programme mentioned above makes it clear that even before anti-partitionism intensified in 1948 the primary attitude of the state towards Catholics was still exclusivist. Farrell also cites a speech of Brooke's in February 1947 to the City of Derry and Foyle Unionist Associations in which he applauded a fund they had set up to prevent Catholics buying Protestant-owned property, and further restrictions on the local government franchise the previous year.[91] The anti-partition campaign simply provided an opportunity for the elite to merge welfarism into populism with greater ease. Welfare benefits were presented as the fruit of the British connection and Catholics stigmatised as two-faced intransigents for accepting the benefits while continuing to reject the legitimacy of the state.

The effects of the political, ideological and economic deinsularisation of the province from 1940-45 had been weathered successfully by Brooke and his circle, certainly in a fashion apparently beyond Andrews's limited resources, cerebral or otherwise. The 'solution' was a series of tactical modifications to populism, during which anti-populism briefly revived and then collapsed beyond recognition as a political force.

For all the formal changes in the state (new ministries, policies and general administrative expansion), its nature and its inflexibility remained much as they had been. Indeed, it could be argued that the recent changes had diminished its flexibility. By committing itself to welfarism and 'step-by-step' the Unionist elite was redefining its dependence on the Protestant working class and the British state in potentially dangerous ways.

This would not become apparent for some time, however. Unionism would enter the new decade buoyed up by the unintended effects of the Dublin government's September 1948 decision to repeal the External Relations Act and thus sever the last constitutional link between the southern state and the Commonwealth. When Brooke and his colleagues set about exploiting the decision they found the Attlee administration, mindful of the South's neutrality in the war and the North's consequent strategic importance, sympathetic.[92] In fact the Labour Cabinet had received civil service advice that,

> It has become a matter of strategic importance to this country that the North [of Ireland] should continue to form part of his Majesty's Dominions. So far as it can be foreseen, it will never be to Great Britain's advantage that Northern Ireland should form a territory outside his Majesty's jurisdiction. Indeed, it would seem unlikely that Great Britain would ever be able to agree to this even if the people of Northern Ireland desired it.[93]

In fact the government recoiled from such an absolutist position although the 1949 Ireland Act did reflect the strengthened Unionist position by, for the first time, giving statutory assurance that Northern Ireland would not cease to be part of the United Kingdom without the consent of the northern parliament.

The upsurge of anti-partitionism associated with the repeal of the External Relations Act provided Brooke with favourable conditions in which to call a Stormont election for February 1949. The NILP, which had experienced increasing tensions between its Unionist, labourist and anti-partitionist strands, made a public declaration in favour of the existing constitutional position in January 1949. Nevertheless, the NILP and the various anti-partitionist labour forces did disastrously in the inflamed conditions in which the election was fought.[94] Brooke noted in his diary, 'A magnificent victory ... all socialists knocked out.'[95] When the NILP threat returned it would do so in very different circumstances.

Notes

1. P. Addison, *The Road to 1945*, London 1975.
2. E.J. Hobsbawm, *Industry and Empire*, London 1972, p. 245.
3. J. Foster, 'The State and the Ruling Class During the General Strike', *Marxism Today*, May 1976.
4. Ibid., p. 140.
5. PRO T. 160/F 14464/043/04/1327.

6. Ibid.

7. In 1939 the unemployment rate was 22 per cent; in 1941 it was still 12.3 percent (*Ulster Year Book*, 1947).

8. J.W. Blake, *Northern Ireland in the Second World War*, Belfast 1956.

9. L. O'Nuallain, *Ireland: The Finances of Partition*, Dublin 1952, pp. 131-2.

10. PRONI Cab. 4/513/7.

11. Spender to Brooks, 8 July 1942, PRO T. 160.

12. PRO T. 160.

13. Ibid.

14. Wood to Andrews, 6 August 1942, ibid.

15. Spender, *Financial Diary*, PRONI D715, 15 August 1942.

16. PRONI Com.7/6.

17. Addison, *Road*, pp. 229, 237.

18. R.J. Lawrence, *The Government of Northern Ireland*, Oxford 1965, p. 70. Harbinson refers to this illusory agreement as Andrews's 'most abiding memorial', *The Ulster Unionist Party, 1882-1973*, Belfast 1973, p. 140.

19. Comments on Andrews's letter, 30 August 1942, PRO T. 160.

20. 14 September 1942, ibid.

21. Ibid.

22. PRONI Com. 7/6.

23. PRONI Com. 7/4.

24. Summarised in A. Maltby, *The Government of Northern Ireland, 1922-72: A Catalogue and Breviate of Parliamentary Papers*, Dublin 1974, pp. 64-5.

25. *NIHC*, Vol. XXVI, c. 607.

26. The report suggested a refund of 20 per cent of excess profits tax and the provision of low-interest government loans for modernisation of plant and machinery. Flax and linen research should be under unified control and the industry should have the determining voice on proposals for investment. On internal structure, reference was made to the recommendations in 1928 of four representatives of the principal branches of the industry that as an ultimate object the whole industry be amalgamated into one unit. This was felt 'impractical', and instead a policy of vertical integration was advocated.

27. Brooke to Dalton (Board of Trade), PRONI Com. 7/36 PW55.

28. A. Beacham, 'The Ulster Linen Industry', *Economica*, November 1944. Almost identical views had been expressed by a local linen manufacturer, W.J. Larmour, in a lecture in Belfast in 1929 ('Northern Government Accused of Masterly Inactivity', *Belfast Newsletter*, 23 February 1929).

29. 'The resources of the textile industry were not utilised to the fullest possible extent – the logic of total war demanded maximum production from the working part of the industry, the closure of the remainder and the transfer to other work of the labour released ... but no attempt was made' (Blake, *Second War*, p. 394).

30. *NIHC*, Vol. XXV, c. 21.

31. Ibid., c. 161.

32. Ibid., c. 198.

33. PRONI Cab. 4/496/5.
34. PRONI Cab. 4/507/7.
35. PRONI Cab. 4/525/8.
36. PRONI Cab. 4/533/12.
37. PRONI Cab. conclusions, 4/592/2.
38. Ibid.
39. PRONI Cab. 4/597/7.
40. PRONI Cab. 4/614/9.
41. PRONI Cab. 4/615/5.
42. PRONI Cab. 4/618/6.
43. PRONI Cab. 669/12.
44. *NIHC*, Vol. XXVI, c. 65.
45. Lawrence, *Government*, p. 136; J.F. Harbinson, 'A History of the NILP, 1881-1949', unpublished MSc thesis, Queen's University, Belfast, 1966, p. 149.
46. M. Farrell, *Northern Ireland: The Orange State*, London 1975, p. 173.
47. Harbinson, *NILP*, p. 159.
48. Ibid., p. 169; Farrell, *Orange State*, p. 174.
49. Spender, *Financial Diary*, 13 April 1944.
50. Ibid., 20 April 1944.
51. In one speech in Oldpark, Brooke proclaimed, 'Once they started nibbling the biscuit of socialism, before they knew where they were their children would be tied hand and foot.' Grant, the Minister of Labour, attacked the Labour Party commitment to full employment more floridly still: 'There never had been a time when there was full employment in this country, full employment was a fallacy.' *Belfast Newsletter*, 6 June 1945.
52. Speech by Sinclair, *Belfast Newsletter*, 30 May 1945.
53. Harbinson, *NILP*; Farrell, *Orange State*, p. 190. Terry Cradden points out that in the voting for the Belfast constituencies in the Stormont election in 1945 the 'non-nationalist left', i.e. the NILP, Commonwealth Labour Party and Communist Party, received 66,506 votes to a total Unionist vote of 96,273, i.e. almost 70 per cent. See his *Trade Unionism, Socialism and Partition*, Belfast 1993, p. 46.
54. E. Rumpf and A.C. Hepburn, *Nationalism and Socialism in Twentieth-Century Ireland*, Liverpool 1977, pp. 179-80.
55. PRONI Cab. 4/646/5.
56. PRONI Cab. 4/635/14.
57. PRONI Cab. 4/636/9.
58. Ibid.
59. PRONI Cab. 4/678/7.
60. PRONI Cab. 4/642/9.
61. This and other quotations from memoranda are from an account of the discussion by D.W. Harkness, *Irish Times*, 16 November 1977.
62. *Belfast Newsletter*, 12 November 1945.
63. Ibid., 22 November 1945.
64. Ibid., 13 December 1945.
65. Ibid., 30 November 1945.
66. Ibid., 22 December 1945.
67. Ibid., 9 February 1946.

68. Thus Nugent, the Minister of Commerce, expressed hostility to Westminster policies and supported dominion status in memoranda to the Cabinet in 1947 and 1948: PRONI Cab. 4/730/17, 10 November 1947, and Cab. 4/772/5, 11 November 1948. We owe these references to Denis Norman. These issues are also considered in Brian Barton, 'Relations Between Westminster and Stormont During the Attlee Premiership', *Irish Political Studies*, Vol. 7, 1992.

69. Lawrence, *Government*, pp. 78-81.

70. cf. Harkness, *Irish Times*, 16 November 1977.

71. Rumpf and Hepburn, *Socialism*, p. 202.

72. O'Nuallain, *Finances*, pp. 109-10.

73. PRONI Cab. 4/690/5.

74. PRONI Cab. 4/694/3.

75. By W.F. McCoy, Unionist MP for South Tyrone (cf. *Round Table*, XXXVII, 1947).

76. cf. W. Topping's speech, *Belfast Newsletter*, 29 September 1947.

77. *Belfast Newsletter*, 21 September 1947.

78. Ibid., 29 October 1947.

79. Ibid., 5 November 1947.

80. Ibid., 14 November 1947.

81. Ibid., 27 November 1947.

82. Ibid., 22 November 1947.

83. *NIHC*, Vol. XXXI, c. 2894.

84. e.g. T. Lyons and the Revd G. McManaway, Unionist MPs for North Tyrone and Derry City.

85. *Round Table*, XXXVIII (1948).

86. Farrell, *Orange State*, p. 196.

87. Ibid., p. 200.

88. PRONI Cab. 4/924, 7 January 1954.

89. Farrell, *Orange State*, pp. 183ff.

90. Addison, *Road*.

91. Farrell, *Orange State*, p. 181.

92. Barton, Relations Between Westminster and Stormont', p. 11.

93. PRO CP (49)4, quoted in Troops Out Movement, *Close to Home*, London n.d., p. 38.

94. Cradden, *Trade Unionism, Socialism and Partition*, pp. 174-82.

95. Barton, 'Relations Between Westminster and Stormont', p. 11.

4 The Origins of O'Neillism, 1952–1964

This chapter is concerned with the problems of analysing the relationship between economic changes in Northern Ireland from about 1950 to 1963 and the political crisis that manifested itself at the close of the period as Terence O'Neill became Prime Minister.* Like the conflict within the Unionist Party some years later over civil rights, the crisis has been widely interpreted as an outcome of tension between 'traditionalists' and 'modernisers'. The modernisers were successful in installing O'Neill but not in maintaining him in power.

This type of analysis has dominated the left and has been forcefully restated by Michael Farrell, who posits a direct relationship between the difficulties of the economy, which became acute in the late 1950s, and the emergence of this division at the political level. The government's response to the growing difficulties of the traditional staple industries was 'complacent and lethargic'. In response to the defection of Protestant workers to the NILP in the 1958 election it made a conventional appeal to sectarianism. In evidence Farrell quotes a prominent Unionist, A.B. Babington, who advocated that the party should keep registers of unemployed Protestants from which employers could recruit.[1] Since the idea was repudiated in Stormont by the Minister of Labour, it cannot bear the significance Farrell attaches to it.[2] His other main source for the characterisation of 'traditional' Unionism – O'Neill's autobiography – is also suspect if it is

* See Biographical Note on p. 262.

103

not seen for what it was, a contribution to political debate and controversy.

Such analyses, having set out the traditionalist-modernist division, attribute it to economic tension between local businesses, said to maintain their power by according sectarian privileges to Protestants, and external businesses, said not to do so. As this argument was originally applied to the events of 1968 and has subsequently been projected back a decade, fuller discussion of it will be postponed until the next chapter. Nevertheless, a few words on its strictly theoretical implications and its characterisation of 'traditional' industry are in order here.

The main problem with this approach is its reduction of a political crisis to a conflict between businesses of different origins. It reduces questions which can be posed only at the level of the state and its relationship to the Protestant working class to the needs of different sectors of industry. Despite its close links with local industrialists, the government's policies reflected a more complex set of measures and, in particular, its at times uneasy relationship with the Protestant working class. The Northern Ireland state was thus subject to a wider range of pressures than those outlined by Farrell.[3]

As a result of ignoring the significance of the state in the crisis, Farrell is reduced to a form of psychologism. Certain 'real' pressures are outlined-the changing economic structure in the North, British business's need for good political relations with the South as the latter becomes an increasingly important market and sphere of investment, and so on.[4] These pressures push O'Neill into a series of reforms which enrage the Unionist bloc's traditional base. O'Neill is seen as a mouthpiece of the multinationals, while local industry is regarded as a spent force ('the Ulster-based industries had all but disappeared'[5]). The Unionist backlash is explained in terms of the disruptive effect of 'modernisation' on the collective psyche of the Protestant masses:

> The Orange ideology was too deep-rooted to be dispensed with overnight, especially at a time of change and confusion when new industries were replacing old ones, threatening small businessmen and established skilled workers, when new blocks of flats were replacing old slums, new towns replacing old villages. Orangeism provided stability and status in a changing world and defended jobs and position.[6]

While it is possible that Orangeism did function like this for *some* Protestant workers, this approach greatly exaggerates its influence and underplays more secular labourist responses.

The previous chapters have argued that the key role in perpetuating the Protestant alliance was played by the state. This, however, should not be taken to imply that the state could, at will, impose particular political attitudes onto the population at large. Rather, its function was to give a specific form to the contradictions within society in such a way as to ensure harmony between the classes in the Protestant community. The ideology of triumphant sectarian exclusivism associated with the expulsions of 1920, for example, was not a tactical device on the part of the Unionist leadership but the result of the endorsement and taking over by that Unionist elite of relatively independent sectarian traditions.[7] Throughout its subsequent history the state's endorsement of sectarian activities remained an important element in the renewal of the Unionist alliance. The backtracking on education in 1950, the passing of the Public Order Act and the Flags and Emblems legislation were all post-war examples of this phenomenon.[8]

Yet if this was an important element in the maintenance of Unionist hegemony, it was not the only or even the dominant one. The essential basis of the reproduction of the alliance was the state's sensitivity to the political impact on the Protestant working class of changes in their material conditions.

Once this is recognised, the real problem of the 1950s is seen to be Northern Ireland's autonomy within the United Kingdom at a time when the main parties in Britain were committed to full employment and were recognising the 'regional problem' for the first time. The political crisis of the early 1960s can be understood only if it is recognised that many members of the Protestant working class were not the dupes of Orangeism in their reaction to local economic decline but were influenced by a secular ideology of opposition to regional deprivation articulated by the NILP.

By effectively ignoring the state, or treating it as an epiphenomenal expression of the economic interests of different types of business, writers like Farrell and Boserup fundamentally misinterpret the history of the 1950s and early 1960s.[9] The ironic consequence is that both end up crediting O'Neill with the intention of reforming sectarian structures, although his attempts are then dismissd as feeble. In fact he had no such reforming zeal. The belief that he had is the other side of the coin to the view that the middle class 'created' sectarianism, and so sees sectarianism as a tactic to be adopted or dropped depending on political circumstances.

Historical analysis has shown that, far from being a product of the needs of business, support by a large section of local industry for exclusivism in the workplace was mixed, and dependent upon specific political and ideological conditions.[10] Another study of the structure of the Protestant alliance in its classic period has demonstrated that its organisation involved the assimilation of the practices of exclusivist Orangeism to a much wider coalition of social forces which included skilled workers and the explicitly anti-Orange (if anti-nationalist) ideology of liberal Unionism.[11] An elite wedded simply to exclusivist practices would have been incapable of winning the struggle against Home Rule, and the preceding chapters have shown that once the state was created dominance was maintained only by a combination of different strategies.

Sectarianism was neither a 'tactic' nor unequivocally tied to the needs of local industrialists. It was a set of institutions and practices which acquired significance in the context of the state's relations with the Protestant working class. The failure of existing analyses to understand sectarianism is symptomatic of their failure to comprehend this general relationship. In this connection Farrell's analysis of the interaction between economic problems and the political crisis of the 1960s is mistaken. The 'modernisation' associated with the change-over from Brooke to O'Neill was a product not of the economic decline of traditional industry but rather – as Farrell partly recognises, without attributing it its full significance – of a specific political problem.[12] This was the potential loss of control over key sectors of the working class as persistent high unemployment assumed the dimensions of a political issue by contrast with full employment and a bipartisan commitment to the elimination of regional disparities in Britain.

In its attempts to deal with the problem the O'Neill

administration became formally associated with a national move to more vigorous forms of regional economic planning. This had specific effects. Notably it posed a threat to certain local apparatuses of Protestant domination, and meant a shift in the central state machine towards more power for the bureaucracy and a 'presidential' style of politics. There was certainly a backlash, but it was a localised one, the most significant effects of which were within the parliamentary and constituency Unionist parties. Not until after the development of the civil rights movement did it involve significant sections of the Protestant working class. It is also important to note that initially it had nothing to do with opposition to civil rights-type reforms, since O'Neill made no attempt to introduce any.

The Economy in the 1950s

In 1950 the dominant aspects of the North's economic structure were the continued pre-eminence of the two traditional staple industries and the high proportion of the workforce (by UK standards) engaged in agriculture. Of the total number of workers in manufacturing, 30 per cent were in textiles and linen and 20 percent in shipbuilding, engineering and vehicle repair.[13] Agriculture accounted for one-sixth of the gainfully employed and almost a quarter of gainfully employed males.[14]

1951 was the last year of the post-war boom in demand for manufactured products which had allowed the linen industry, for example, to enjoy conditions unknown before the war.[15] By the summer of 1952 production had declined in a number of industries.[16] In the three years prior to June 1954 linen employment fell by 15 per cent.[17]

Although general economic conditions improved in 1954 and 1955, the linen trade now entered a long period of rationalisation and contraction. As the textile industries of the advanced industrial nations faced increasing competition from low-cost ex-colonial producers, linen was confronted with the additional problem of the expansion of the synthetic fibre industry. With government assistance (see below), a programme of re-equipment and modernisation was initiated to increase productivity. As a direct result there was a large-scale reduction in employment. Between 1954 and

1964 the number of jobs in plants employing 25 or more (the great majority) fell from 56,414 to 33,957. The number of plants fell from 298 to 200.[18]

Rationalisation was accompanied by concentration. The importance of vertical and horizontal integration increased. So too did the proportion of total capacity controlled by 'combines' – firms owning plants engaged in all processes from spinning to making-up and disposing of their intermediate products solely to other departments of the same organisation. Even in 1954 combines had controlled over 30 per cent of spinning and weaving capacity. By 1964 there was a much greater degree of integration and the bulk of employment was in the control of a few large organisations.[19]

Government assistance was crucial in this process. Little direction seems to have been exercised over the disbursement of funds to specific firms, and as a result a number of modernised plants went bankrupt in the 1958 slump. These were acquired by combines which proceeded to strip their assets.[20]

By concentrating solely on the gross decline of employment in the linen industry Farrell is led to accept a distorted view of this process. It was not simply a case of the decline of the linen manufacturers within the middle class as a whole. Although significant numbers of small and medium-sized firms closed in the period, a linen complex still existed at the end of it. Moreover the industry was now dominated by a small number of firms which had clearly benefited from the decade of rationalisation. The decline of employment in a classic staple should not be seen as an index of the virtual disappearance of the traditional linen manufacturers. As the Hall Committee was to point out, the 1950s saw a strengthening of the industry in some respects. Productivity had increased, research into the use of new fibres and fabrics had intensified and new materials were being used on a limited scale.[21] A process of concentration had occurred and, although reduced in numbers, the linen manufacturers were far from being an insignificant force.

The important feature of the history of shipbuilding in the same period was not so much decline itself as its timing. In 1950 more than one-tenth of Ulster's manufacturing jobs and about a one-fifth of those in Belfast were to be found at

Harland & Wolff. Employing 21,000 in four yards and eighteen berths on the Queen's Island, it was the largest single localised shipbuilding complex in the world.[22] Until about 1955 its main problem was a shortage of steel due to the rearmament programme. By that date, however, the building programme had caught up with the post-war backlog of demand. From then on, the international market because increasingly competitive. British firms came under increasing pressure from Continental and Japanese yards, which as a result of the war had been obliged to undergo more substantial re-equipment. By 1958 the number of ships afloat exceeded requirements. UK shipbuilding output fell back to its 1954 level in 1959, and by 1960 it was 22 per cent below its post-war peak.[23]

In Belfast, although there had been some lay-offs in the late 1950s, the major decline occurred over a very short period. Between 1961 and 1964 employment in shipbuilding and repairing and marine engineering dropped by 40 per cent (11,500).[24] The compression of such a substantial decline into such a short period, and its concentration in Belfast, had critical political repercussions.

Agriculture in the post-war period also experienced an intensification of the process of amalgamation, the elimination of marginal holdings and an advance in mechanisation.[25] An increase in output of 80 per cent was achieved between 1938 and 1960, despite a declining workforce. Between 1950 and 1960 total agricultural employment fell by nearly one-third (28,000).[26]

The contraction of the staples was reflected in a high level of unemployment throughout the decade. In the manufacturing sector, a small decrease occurred in total numbers employed between 1950 and 1960. Although new industry was attracted by various government inducements, the employment it created did not cancel out the effect of the decline in the staples. There was an increase in service employment of 18,500 due mainly to government investment in education and personal and public health. But the contraction of agriculture and a relatively high birth rate meant that throughout the decade unemployment never fell below 5 per cent and averaged 7.4 per cent. This was four times the national average.[27] If it was nothing like the figures of the 1930s, the fact remained that it was now taking place in the context not merely of full employment in the UK but of a relatively better performance by Britain's other regional black spots (see Table 2).

Table 2 *Unemployment in the Development Areas, 1956-64*

	1956	1958	1959	1960	1961	1962	1963	1964
Scottish	2.2	3.7	4.1	3.4	2.9	3.5	4.6	3.5
Welsh	2.2	4.1	3.8	2.5	2.4	3.0	3.4	2.4
Northern	1.4	2.2	3.0	2.5	2.0	3.2	4.3	2.9
Merseyside	2.0	3.6	4.2	3.1	2.7	3.9	4.9	3.4
South-West	1.8	2.8	2.5	2.8	1.8	2.2	3.1	2.4
Northern Ireland	6.8*	9.3	na	6.7	na	7.5	7.9	6.6

* Figure for 1955
na Not available
Source: G.McCrone, *Regional Policy in Britain*, London 1969, p. 154.

Before considering the effects of these results, it is necessary to bring up to date the history of the government's post-war industrial policy.

The State and the Economy to 1954

In 1944 the Northern Ireland Cabinet had decided that existing legislation aimed at diversifying the economy from its staple base was inadequate. Under the New Industries (Development) Acts of 1937 and 1942, which had offered grants towards the cost of rent and income tax, plus loans, 35 firms employing a total of 2,500 had been attracted.[28] It was feared that the end of the war would precipitate unemployment in the staple industries and it was decided to introduce an Industries Development Act (IDA) aimed at attracting larger enterprises by providing factory premises and equipment, with the necessary infrastructure.[29] The Act gave the government power to lease, purchase or erect premises and to let or sell them to incoming industrial undertakings. It allowed the Ministers of Finance and Commerce discretion in the type of assistance granted. Under the Act grants of up to one-third of capital costs were normal, and could be exceeded in 'desirable' projects.[30] Most of the expenditure went on building factories. The rents charged were below the cost required to service the capital outlay.[31] In terms of inducements, the measures appear to have given Northern Ireland an advantage over the British regions. Because Stormont was empowered to enact this type of legislation the main foundation of British regional policy, the Distribution of Industry Act, 1945, did not apply to the province. In some ways its provisions were more stringent. A Treasury committee had to be satisfied both that each project was commercially sound and that finance could not be raised from another source. Regional policy was in any case being given a low priority in Britain at the time. The building of advance factories on the mainland was stopped altogether in 1947 and did not recommence until 1959.[32]

Northern Ireland's own industrialists were not particularly sympathetic to a vigorous policy of industrial attraction. In January 1946 Nugent had announced that, under the new legislation, ten new plants had been established and were expected to create 4,710 jobs. They included Courtauld's and Metal Box.[33] But he had already reported local industry's disquiet over these developments to the Cabinet: 'There seemed to be a feeling that the government, in their efforts to attract new industries, were overlooking the necessity for encouraging and helping existing manufactures.'[34]

During the conflict over the Statistics of Trade Bill local industry's representatives in parliament attacked this aspect of government policy. In a debate on the Ministry of Commerce estimates in 1947 both Milne Barbour and Andrews criticised the effects of the Industries Act, which, they claimed, led to labour being drawn away from the linen industry to new firms. Andrews defended the local industries: 'They have stood the test of time, and no matter how many of these new industries are established, it will be on the old ones that we will have to depend chiefly in the days that lie ahead.'[35]

In defending the policy, Nugent and his successor, Brian Maginess, made it clear that they were relying upon the traditional industries to provide the mainstay of the North's economy for the forseeable future. In 1949 Maginess announced that, since 1945, 136 firms with an expected employment capacity of 23,000 had set up in the North. He added, however, that it was the traditional industries which 'in the testing time ahead would allow Northern Ireland to avoid large-scale unemployment by their ability to adapt and sell in competitive world markets'.[36]

Such reassurances to business interests were given concrete form in November 1950, when a Re-equipment of Industry Bill was introduced at Stormont. It provided 'for the payment of grants towards expenditure incurred in the re-equipment or modernisation of industrial undertakings'.[37] The rationale for the Bill was set out in a speech by the Minister of Finance:

> While I am sure the [Ways and Means] committee are in full sympathy with the government's policy of attracting new industries, thereby diversifying our industrial set-up and mitigating, as far as possible, the effects of any setback in world trading conditions upon our principal export trade, there is undoubtedly a feeling that these new industries may have had an adverse effect on existing industries, notably in the attraction of labour to modern, well laid-out factories erected in many cases with generous governmental financial assistance.[38]

It was pointed out that the aim of the IDA was to expand manufacturing capacity and that existing firms could obtain grants only if they could show that there would be a consequent increase in their workforce. Yet what existing industries needed were grants for re-equipment which would probably tend to restrict employment opportunities by increasing the productivity of the present labour force.[39] Under the new Act, therefore, grants of 33 per cent of capital cost were to be made available.

The legislation was introduced at a time when the linen industry was still experiencing boom conditions due to the effect of the 1949 devaluation on exports to North America.[40] By mid-1951 the industry was being hit by an international slump in textiles which, coinciding with a shortage of steel, led to a serious recession in local industry. Unemployment rose to 10 per cent by January 1952.[41] As the economic outlook deteriorated, the government was again criticised for 'submissiveness' to London. The issue this time was the allegedly 'crippling' levels of death duties, estate duties and excess profits tax, which were 'threatening the annihilation of the family firm'.[42] This was a popular complaint, since the province had a much higher proportion of family firms than the UK as a whole. The budget of 1951 conceded exemption for gifts *inter vivos* made three, rather than five, years before death.[43] But this was of little economic significance, and a section of local industry once again revived the cry for dominion status to ensure lower taxes and the payment of the imperial contribution.[44]

The political context in which these questions were debated appears to be transformed by the return of the Conservatives in the General Election of 1951. The nine Ulster Unionist MPs at Westminster constituted half the government majority. The *Round Table*'s commentator gave what was probably an orthodox Unionist opinion on the new situation:

On no previous occasion have [the Unionists' seats] been such a material factor at a general election. Never before has the association between the Conservatives and Unionists proved so timely and advantageous.[45]

Any hopes of advantage were to be confounded. To cope with the inflationary pressure of rearmament in the national economy, the new administration introduced measures to restrict credit and control public expenditure. The effect was to push local unemployment higher. In response, some Unionist MPs began to claim that the Cabinet was failing to assert Ulster's interests with sufficient vigour. At first Brooke argued that Ulster had no choice but to suffer for the sins of national financial profligacy: 'As a nation we have for a considerable time been living beyond our means ... we are now faced with the stern necessity of making our books balance.'[46] This remark was made in December 1951, when unemployment was 7.5 per cent. By February 1952 it had reached 11 per cent. Middle-class disquiet about government 'inactivity' increased, still coupled with a conviction that the solution to the problem lay in measures to subsidise local industry and to increase its non-taxable surplus. Faulkner* continued to bemoan the 'confiscatory' level of taxation.[47] Further reductions in death duties would be made, but their economic effect was limited.

* See Biographical Note on p. 256.

If the Faulkner line was to be put into effect a substantial revision of Belfast-London relations would have been involved. The consequent threat to welfarism acted as a basic limit of the policy options debated within Unionist politics. Throughout the decade there was to be a largely rhetorical note in demands for a revision of the Government of Ireland Act, which tended to collapse pathetically into demands that the government 'at least extract more' from the Treasury.

In 1952, however, Brooke was forced to forego his earlier fatalism and there took place what the *Round Table*'s correspondent hailed as 'a ministerial conference without precedent in relations between these two parts of the United Kingdom'.[48] Brooke and four of his ministers[49] met Churchill and other British ministers in London to discuss the North's economy.[50] In his report to Stormont Brooke told MPs he had emphasised the critically high level of unemployment. It had been agreed that the British would try to increase the allocation of steel and other raw materials 'consistent with the rearmament and export programmes'.[51] Apart from this nebulous commitment, it had been agreed that the Admiralty would order three ships from Harland & Wolff, that Short's would produce the Comet airliner under sub-contract and that 'it was hoped' the placing of textile orders for the defence programme would be accelerated. The *Round Table* nevertheless considered that the most important outcome was an agreement that the Chancellor and the Minister of Finance would collaborate in an investigation of those factors (including transport costs) which militated against full employment locally.[52]

In April 1952 Duncan Sandys, Minister of Supply in Churchill's government, visited Ulster for further discussion with Cabinet ministers and industrialists. In his subsequent comments, while agreeing that his government would do what it could to help, he concluded, 'In the long run this is an Ulster problem which only Ulster can solve.'[53]

Undoubtedly this statement ignored the effects of national economic policies on Northern Ireland. It was characteristic of what one authority has called the 'freewheeling' policy of the Conservatives towards the regions in the 1950s.[54] The post-war boom in most traditional industries continued until 1955, and unemployment in many of the regions remained low. As McCrone comments,

Governments may, perhaps, be excused for supposing during this period that the regional problem was virtually solved. In fact, however, though policy measures immediately after the war had achieved considerable success, the economies of the Scottish, Welsh and Northern regions were still heavily dependent on their traditional industries. Immense tasks remained if their infrastructure and environments were to be recreated to stimulate new economic growth. The continued boom in the traditional industries had ... only masked [the problem].[55]

The harmful effects of shelving regional problems were compounded by those of national policies to deal with the inflationary pressures and the threat of the balance of payments that developed during the investment boom of 1954-55. As a result the regions bore the brunt of the credit squeeze and autumn budget of 1955, the post-Suez measures and Thorneycroft's increase in Bank rate in 1957.[56] Northern Ireland was particularly hard hit. The close political links between the government and the Conservatives were now to contribute to major political divisions in the Unionist ranks.

Before considering this development it is necessary to examine a further turn in Stormont's industrial policies. In March 1954 Lord Glentoran, Minister of Commerce, announced the government's decision to replace the Re-equipment of Industry Act with a Capital Grants to Industry Act (CGIA).[57] Under the former grants of £3.25 million had been allocated to 150 schemes. Glentoran considered this stimulus insufficient, arguing that it had not prevented an overall decline in investment in buildings and machinery. Incentives on a much broader front were now to be offered. No longer would re-equipment schemes have to be substantial to qualify. It was proposed to give grants of up to a quarter of the cost for any investment in plant, machinery or buildings, whether it involved re-equipment or expansion in the labour force. £5 million was made available for this purpose over the next three years.

Glentoran had concluded his announcement with a plea to local industrialists to come forward with schemes. But the linen industry, despite the fact that conditions had improved, was still complaining of over-taxation. In response the Minister of Finance announced a further

reduction in estate duties.[58] Again it was not enough for
Faulkner, who predicted that the concession would not
reverse the 'deplorable' tendency for investment to
decrease.[59] A reaction to these views was also evident,
however. The *Round Table*'s correspondent reported
criticism of government policy on the grounds of its over-
dependence on the local middle class. 'Economists doubt
whether this preservation of privately owned businesses
can deal with the basic problems.'[60] The budget and the
new Industry Bill were a challenge to local industrialists: if
they could not make the economy viable the government
would face a severe crisis. This opinion seems to have been
based upon a highly critical survey of Ulster's economic
structure and of government industrial policy which had
been commissioned by Brooke's Cabinet, but which it was
now reluctant to publish. It is with this report that an
account of the political significance of economic
questions must begin.

The Politics of Unemployment

The report, an 'Economic Survey of Northern Ireland', by
two economists at Queen's University, K.S. Isles and N.
Cuthbert, had been commissioned by Nugent in 1947. Its
authors presented it to Glentoran in June 1955 at the latest,
but it was not until over two years later that it was made
public. The reasons for the delay become clear when the
report's substance is considered. Although Glentoran was to
claim that it broadly supported government economic policy
since 1945, it in fact supported the NILP's critique of this
policy.[61] It pointed out that under the IDA and the CGIA,
schemes with a total employment potential of 26,000 had
been introduced. This represented a yearly average of 2,500,
which compared unfavourably with 'shake-out' by the staple
industries. 'The degree of resilience and expansionism in
the economy has not been great.'[62]

Although reference was made to the province's 'natural
disadvantages' (remoteness, etc.), the authors' analysis
centred on a critical view of local industry and the
government's pliability to its needs and desires. Their views
amplified those of earlier critics, mentioned in the previous
chapter. The linen complex was dominated by small-scale

family-owned units, fiercely traditional and unamenable to planned rationalisation. The preponderance of private companies (60 per cent in Ulster, compared with 35 per cent in the UK as a whole) prevented the investment of domestic savings in local industry.[63] It was the dominance of these enterprises which, they argued, was responsible for the failure of Ulster's industries – particularly textiles – to adjust to changed conditions in the world market. Principal shareholders were reluctant to seek an increase of capital for fear of losing control over decision-making. The majority of private firms had forsaken any ideas of expansion and preferred to invest their undistributed profits in government securities or to divest them by paying high dividends and directors' salaries.[64] Lacking any breadth of experience in production, management or marketing, they were as a rule ill-equipped to modernise or diversify. Indeed, Isles and Cuthbert were so critical that they probably exaggerated the inertia of local industry and its inability to rationalise.

The report also highlighted an important restrictionist and monopolist tendency which had built up in the inter-war period, when trade associations had been formed to maintain prices. There was a widespread habit of concentrating on profit margins rather than volume of sales, accentuated by a general ignorance of 'modern business methods'.[65] These tendencies had particularly bad effects in cross-channel shipping, where transport prices were needlessly high, and in the coal trade, where restrictive practices were entrenched.[66] The report recommended the creation of a nationalised cross-channel shipping service and the referral of the existing situation to the Monopolies Commission.

The most important political implication of the report was that it rebutted the Northern Ireland government's defence of local industry. Lack of investment was due not to 'confiscatory' levels of taxation but to an archaic industrial structure and the myopic self-interest of local business. The government, particularly the Ministry of Commerce, had failed to take a broader view in its industrial policy. In suggesting the formation of a Development Corporation to encourage the establishment of new industries, if necessary by public enterprise,[67] the report took the Ministry of Commerce to task for its failure to attract new industry, its lack of enterprise and flexibility and its wasteful concentration of resources on existing firms. The authors' criticisms were made more explicit still in their contribution to a contemporary reader on Northern Ireland:

> In such a small business community as that of Northern Ireland there is inevitably a good deal of scope for the exercise of special privilege, and under self-government therefore it is difficult for the administration to always be thoroughly impartial.[68]

In its efforts to force concessions on the Statistics of Trade Bill and death duties, local industry had been relatively successful. In Lord Glentoran it had a rigid defender of its record against the critics. Traditional industry was also well represented in the Unionist parliamentary party. Of the fourteen Belfast MPs at this time, twelve had direct links with traditional industry as either proprietors or managing directors.[69] The two Ministers of Commerce in the 1950s exemplified the close links. H.V. McCleery, who held the post from 1949-53, was a managing director of a flax-spinning firm; Lord Glentoran was a member of the Dixon family who, as well as being closely involved in Conservative politics from the 1890s, were shipowners and timber merchants.

The argument is not that such close personal interlocking of local industry and the state apparatus determined the latter's character. The significance of the heavy representation of local industry within the state was mediated by another significant relationship – that of the state towards the Protestant working class. If, in contrast to the immediate post-war period, the dominant policies appear to have reflected the wishes of local industry this was because of a drop in the level of actual and potential class conflict since the earlier period. The shipyard and engineering workers who had been the prime recruiting ground for the NILP during the war years were relatively quiescent from 1950 to 1957 as the yard and the major plants maintained production. If relations within the Unionist bloc were tranquil this allowed a certain attenuation of the state's relative autonomy to develop, and the tendency appears to have been most marked in the Ministry of Commerce.

When Isles and Cuthbert's survey was published the

principal reaction in the Unionist parliamentary party was to ignore it. When its criticisms were raised by Unionists they were confined to the question of the coal trade.[70] Two of the three MPs concerned (Henry Holmes of Belfast Shankill[71] and William Fitzsimmons of Belfast Duncairn) were local businessmen. Not only were their criticisms of the coal importers not take up by other MPs, but when the third MP involved (Edmund Warnock of Belfast St Anne's) became persistent, the possibility was raised of expelling him from the party.[72] Although productive industry had no interest in the preservation of restrictive practices, the survey induced a collective desire to close ranks and to ensure that as little open discussion as possible took place.

This recourse was hampered by a further significant rise in unemployment at the end of 1957, following a rise in Bank rate. A minority of critics now linked the question of the effects of national deflationary policy with the accusation that the government was resisting parliamentary discussion of the survey.[73] Eventually, in November, a debate took place. Glentoran attacked many aspects of the report; in particular its suggestion of a Development Corporation 'showed a sorry lack of faith in the vitality of Ulster industry'. He also rejected the authors' contentions about monopolistic practices in shipping.[74] The best Stormont MPs could do was rally to the somewhat weary cry that whatever the defects of Ulster industry they were the result of the 'unfairness' of existing fiscal arrangements. According to Herbert Kirk (Belfast Windsor), British levels of taxation were inappropriate locally. Together with the consequences of unsuitable national economic policies, they justified a demand for a subsidy from the British Exchequer to offset present 'discriminatory' arrangements.

1958 saw unemployment rise to 10 per cent in the province. In Belfast it rose by almost half. The city's textile industry, which had a heavy concentration of the most viable plants, now felt the force of the depression that had eliminated firms elsewhere in the province earlier in the decade.[75] Prior to the February Stormont General Election Brooke went to London for discussions on unemployment. On his return he gave a press conference at which the major announcement was a bland endorsement of UK monetary policy. 'If the value of the pound fell, nothing else mattered.'[76] The election results indicated a weakening of working-class support for Unionism in Belfast, where four seats were lost to the NILP. Three of these were marginals and there was no question of large-scale defections, but the government's inability to reduce unemployment was clearly reducing its authority.[77]

A major crisis for Belfast's economy set in at the close of 1960, when the building programme at Harland & Wolff came to an end at a time of worldwide recession in the industry. Early in 1961 the yard announced that 8,000 of its 21,000 workers would have to be made redundant by the summer. The future of 8,000 workers at Short's was also in doubt, as orders for its main aircraft were insufficient. In response, the Confederation of Shipbuilding and Engineering Unions organised a mass walk-out and a demonstration of over 20,000 workers to demand government action.[78] Further marches were held during the spring as the situation deteriorated. In April the largest spinning firm in the city, which employed 1,700 and had received a substantial amount of government aid, announced it was going into voluntary liquidation.[79] In July the 8,000 shipyard workers were indeed made redundant,[80] and the regional unemployment rate stood at 7 per cent compared with 1.2 per cent nationally. Over the next twelve months 2,000 more were laid off at Harland & Wolff,[81] and Short's management announced that unless orders were received soon the plant would close. In 1961 there were 20 per cent fewer aircraft workers than three years earlier. In the UK the contraction had been only 5 per cent.[82] By the end of the year a Northern Ireland Joint Unemployment Committee was formed by local trade union branches and the NILP, with the aim of modifying government policy.[83] A Save Short's campaign of demonstrations and meetings was launched. The 1962 May Day march was reckoned to have been one of the largest since the strike of 1919. While the NILP did not gain any extra seats in the Stormont election of 1962, its average share of the vote increased by 15 per cent.[84]

Between 1958 and 1962 discontent with government economic policies grew within the Unionist Party. Two factors were at work. One was acute fear, especially among the Belfast MPs, that unless the government took a new initiative the drift to the NILP would intensify. At the UUC annual conference in 1961 there were complaints about government 'lack of energy' on unemployment, and the leader of the UULA delegation suggested the nationalisation of Harland & Wolff.[85] In Stormont Desmond Boal, the new Shankill MP, and Edmund Warnock led the critics. In March Boal supported a critical motion by David Bleakley of the NILP. He blamed the situation on the structure of financial relations with Westminster and the failure of the government to put enough pressure on the Conservatives. In a statement loudly cheered by NILP MPs, he said, 'The government must make up its mind whether it owes loyalty to the Conservative Party or to the working people of Belfast.'[86] He went on to argue that, as a 'progressive' government, the Unionists should provide full employment.

Yet if at the level of rhetoric Boal appropriated some elements of labourist ideology, the dominant critical response still centred on the long-standing dissatisfaction with existing financial relations. It was most clearly formulated by Warnock.[87] The substance of his position was that Ulster could not support the current burden of taxation. 'Why had Ulster to rely upon outsiders to provide employment? One answer was that the country had been denuded of capital to an extent which crippled development.'[88]

The second source of criticism was pressure from local industry for a 'solution' which would mean either a decrease in tax levels or a direct subsidy from Britain. Increasingly the Brooke government's problems arose not from too close a reliance on this class, as Farrell suggests, but from the critical stance it began to adopt.

The effects can clearly be seen by considering briefly the course of inter-government negotiations on the North's economy from 1958 to 1962. When in the 1958 debate on the Isles and Cuthbert survey the demand for a revision of financial relationships had been raised, the Minister of Finance, Terence O'Neill, had replied that Northern Ireland was already favourably treated by the Treasury under the terms of the various post-war agreements on 'leeway'. In particular, he added, she had been allowed a set of industrial inducements more favourable than anywhere else in the UK.[89] Under party and back-bench pressure this attitude changed drastically. In March 1961 Brooke took his principal ministers to London for the first 'summit' (as the *Newsletter* disarmingly described it) since 1954. All he managed to extract from the Conservatives was a pledge to continue support for existing measures of industrial promotion, together with agreement to initiate a joint study of the unemployment problem and how it might be dealt with. (This was later to emerge as the Hall report.[90])

Any positive effects he might have achieved were erased by the introduction of a UK payroll tax and a mini-budget which increased Bank rate and imposed credit restrictions. The payroll tax enraged the linen manufacturers, who claimed it would make their export competitiveness hopeless.[91] O'Neill managed to win the concession that the local government would have a free hand with revenue from the tax. This did not satisfy employers or the *Newsletter*, which became more and more critical of the government.[92] Presently Brooke had yet another meeting with London, and extracted what were announced as further concessions. There would be no slow-down in the industrial programme, local authorities would not be told to curtail any of their work programmes and building subsidies were to be increased. In addition an Economic Advisory Office was to be created within the Cabinet secretariat under Sir Douglas Harkness (then Permanent Secretary at the Ministry of Finance).[93]

The critics were not placated. In a debate at Stormont in 1961 Warnock reiterated the traditional cycnicism.[94] O'Neill responded with the equally familiar reply: that solution endangered 'leeway'.[95] The government continued with its twin tactics of creating more jobs (8,000 during 1961) and making concessions to its critics (the rate of grant to firms applying under the CGIA had been increased from 25 to 33.3 per cent in 1959).[96]

The increase in the NILP vote in 1962 and continued economic difficulties further demonstrated the inadequacy of this strategy. In any case, the introduction in Britain of the Local Employment Act, 1960, had decreased the attractiveness of the inducements the Six Counties could offer.[97] The government redoubled its efforts on the joint working party to negotiate an employment subsidy from the Treasury.[98] The proposal was for a grant of 10s a week for all employees in firms qualifying for CGIA aid. It was estimated that an increase of 50 per cent in aid to industry would be involved. Ulster, the argument ran, needed to lower her costs to become competitive: labour was a prime cost, but as wage rates were tending towards parity with the UK a subsidy was the only solution. The second line of argument was that in the future a large proportion of employment would be provided by the staple industries and that it was therefore as essential to maintain employment in them as to promote new ones.

The publication of the Hall report, which was to reject this position, was crucial in Brooke's fall. Throughout the summer the unions and the NILP had campaigned to save Short's and for the recall of Stormont.[99] Brooke in response stressed that Hall would resolve all difficulties. 'We are very proud of our contribution to it. We think that the proposals it contains should go a long way to solving some of the problems.'[100] The fact that even at the time there was no definite date for publication indicated to critics (including the *Newsletter*) that the British government was unsympathetic to Brooke's proposals.[101] Meanwhile the problem became more pressing. In August 12,000 workers marched to the City Hall for a mass meeting addressed by NILP, Independent, Nationalist and southern Labour Party MPs. A resolution was passed calling on the Conservative Prime Minister, Harold Macmillan, to take immediate steps to provide contracts and financial assistance for Short's. It was supported by Belfast Chamber of Trade and Unionist city councillors.[102] A NILP petition to recall Stormont gathered 100,000 signatures in four weeks. October saw an announcement that 620 more shipyard workers would be made redundant by November, and that 'two or three thousand more' would be paid off before the end of the year.[103]

A foretaste of the Whitehall position was received the same month. The Home Secretary, Henry Brooke, paid a visit to Belfast. He warned the population not to get the unemployment problem out of focus – 'Businessmen would not plant roots where a spirit of desperation was prevalent.'[104] Shortly after, the Northern Ireland Prime Minister again visited London, drawing Macmillan's attention to the political difficulties that would accompany a worsening of the economic situation.[105] The report was published at the end of the month.

The reaction of the *Newsletter* was strongly understated: 'disappointment will be general'.[106] The report defined the problem as 'essentially to make [Ulster's] industry fully competitive with similar industry in Britain ... and to do so fast enough to bring about a decrease in present levels of unemployment'. The solution was to reduce costs, principally through greater efficiency and productivity. Contemporary policies were ineffective – on the assumption that the level of economic activity in the UK rose at the same rate as in the 1950s, it should be possible to promote an average of 3,500 to 4,000 new jobs a year, compared with 2,500 in the 1950s. Yet this would not bring about any reduction in unemployment. Labour migration would have to be encouraged.[107] Industrial policy had been biased toward propping up local industry. The 'ideal' policy would be to ensure that in future allocations of government funds preference was given to encouraging new industries. Existing ones were relatively high-cost producers with no future. A policy which aided them hindered the long-term development of the region. The proposals for subsidising Northern Ireland would have a conservative effect on the structure of industry. The more successful they were in reducing unemployment in declining industries, the less attractive Ulster would be to new firms seeking a pool of available labour. It is of interest to note that there is no evidence in the report that the British side's stress on 'modernisation' and concentration on efficient new industry found any echo among the Ulster delegation.

Brooke's leadership was fatally damaged. In Stormont all he could do was express disappointment and hope that 'in the long term' management and labour would reduce costs by increasing efficiency. The Ministry of Commerce would be redirected to concentrate on industrial development. The *Newsletter* expressed Unionist demoralisation. The reform 'would have been wiser still a year ago'. The report was a personal crisis for Brooke.[108] Within six months he had resigned and O'Neill was Prime Minister.

Social Classes and the Crisis of the Brooke Administration

An analysis of the political forces at work does not support the notion of a crisis of modernisation brought about by the decline of locally owned firms and the rise of multinationals.

First, the decline of traditional industry is exaggerated. By 1963 some 50,000 jobs had been created in government-assisted undertakings since 1945, representing 30 per cent of total employment.[109] Of these, one-quarter were in firms of local origin.[110] The established middle classes were still the predominant force in the early 1960s.[111] What then were their relations with the Brooke government? According to Farrell the state apparatus was the mouthpiece of this class and its sectarian strategy towards the Protestant working class. Yet if there was a close community of interest between local industry and the state, specifically the Ministry of Commerce and parliament, it was concerned with economic strategy rather than ideological and political relations with the Protestant working class. Even in industrial strategy the state was far from a mouthpiece. The crucial concern for dominance over the Protestant working class dictated an industrial strategy aimed at some degree of diversification. Even after the increase of grants under the CGIA it was recognised that the existing structure of incentives favoured incoming firms.[112] It is this which explains the fact that the overriding criticism of economic policy in the early 1 960s was the same quaint and archaic one which emerged during the controversy over dominion status. The crisis for the administration was a product not of the decline of local industry but of its continuing strength as a political force.

It is this strength which determined the curiously hybrid nature of local attempts at solving the unemployment problem. The NILP victories of 1958 and their consolidation in 1962, together with a massive rate of actual and threatened redundancies, seemed to presage large-scale working-class defection if drastic action was postponed. To accede to the demands of Warnock and Faulkner would have been to threaten not only welfarism but regional industrial incentives. The result would not just have been to increase the danger of working-class disaffection. It would have meant renouncing the substantial benefits of existing arrangements for an uncertain gamble on the expansionary capacity of local industry. The outcome was a compromise. The proposals to the Hall working party defended existing financial relations and asked for a further subsidy.

The decisive force in the crisis was the section of the Belfast Protestant working class which voted NILP. Here was the phenomenon that threw existing industrial strategy into disarray and determined that a 'solution' which involved dismantling existing financial relations would be rejected. It is in this context that Babington's statement to a UULA meeting should be considered. Farrell adduces it as evidence that 'under [Brooke] the Unionists relied on traditional methods to keep their supporters loyal'.[113] In fact Babington's speech was an attack, along populist lines, on government 'inactivity' over unemployment.[114] It was repudiated, and it is noticeable that the relationship of the state to the working class throughout the period had a predominantly secular tone. There appears to have been some recognition that the NILP attacks would have to be answered on their own terms.

'O'Neillism' emerged not as the mouthpiece of modernising business in opposition to Brooke's sectarianism, but rather as an effect of the *impasse* which existing economic policies had reached with the Hall report and the persistence of high unemployment. The *opposition*, not the support, for Brooke came from traditional industry and the champions of an old-time populism.

O'Neill and Planning

It is commonly argued that one of the main differences between the Brooke and O'Neill administrations was the importance O'Neill attached to 'planning'. While it is undeniable that in his early years as Prime Minister a rhetoric of regional economic planning was adopted, the significance usually attached to it is problematic. The introduction of planning is seen as heralding the novel policy of relying on multinationals, as opposed to traditional industry. Yet as incentives already favoured incoming firms (to the chargrin of local industry), this did not represent any basic change of policy. Where innovations occurred, they were due to the Hall report and its veto on subsidies for traditional industry. Just as his predecessor had resisted attacks upon 'socialistic' laws after the war, so O'Neill had in the post-Hall period to retain dominance over the Protestant working class even if this meant adopting measures that caused friction with local businesses.

His new policies were clearly influenced by changes in

regional policy at the national level. The depression in many of the heavy industries at the end of the 1950s had led to increased unemployment in the British regions and a greater priority for regional policy.[115] This new concern was associated too with the first moves towards national planning. The official position on planning moved from a social (unemployment) to a technocratic basis (economic growth). Attention was focused on promoting regional expansion as a contribution to securing a higher national growth rate. The new ideology took shape in steps to establish growth areas and economic planning for the regions. The latter was to be related to physical and transport planning with the aim of 'creating an environment conducive to growth'. The role which new towns and infrastructure investment could play in the creation of a suitable environment was emphasised.

In his first speech as premier to the annual meeting of the UUC O'Neill outlined a strategy that clearly mirrored the new national ideology. He referred to the Matthew report on physical planning in the province:

> Our task will be to transform the face of Ulster. To achieve it will demand bold and imaginative measures. The Matthew Plan suggests a way in which Northern Ireland could capture the imagination of the world.[116]

In October 1963 O'Neill informed Stormont that he had set up an inter-departmental inquiry into the potential scope of economic planning in Ulster, with a view to the production of a 'comprehensive' plan. In fact both Matthew and the consequent 'Wilson plan' were a sham. References to 'natural properties' in Matthew's report suggest its inspiration to have been classical rather than technocratic.[117] When Professor Thomas Wilson's report was published in the winter of 1964-65, it too appeared curiously devoid of serious economic calculations. It accepted the Matthew 'growth centre' strategy as given, even though it had little academic support, and argued that the main obstacles to growth were physical rather than financial.[118] Its main proposals were improvements in infrastructure and industrial training.[119] As Steed and Thomas put it,

Analyses in depth of the expected social and economic transformations were conspicuous by their absence – no studies providing an economic basis for the choice of regional centres, no attempt to analyse the growth potential of various industries located in these towns.[120]

Above all, the blatantly cosmetic character of O'Neillist planning was shown in the fact that no economists were taken on by the government to implement the consultants' recommendations.[121] Planning merely represented, in a phrase which evidently pleased O'Neill, 'stealing Labour's thunder'.[122]

Behind the ideology of 'transforming the face of Ulster', planning represented an intensification of post-war dependence on subsidies from London. It meant working hard on the leeway argument to extract subsidies for a large-scale public works programme of housing, motorways, a new airport and improved port facilities. If subsidies were to be refused for traditional industry, then the new ideology could at least be used to extract resources providing employment in construction and services.

While this strategy offered the possibility of recuperating Unionist losses amongst the Protestant working class, it was to create new conflicts within the party. The most serious of these before 1965 arose from the effects of the Matthew recommendations on the relationship between central and local government.

One of the main recommendations – a new Ministry of Planning and Development – was originally turned down by the Cabinet. In explaining its decision, W.J. Morgan, Minister of Health and Local Government, observed that the suggestion was the most difficult in the report, and that action on it depended on the outcome of negotiations with the local authorities.[123] The implications of planning for local government were to prove a thorn in O'Neill's flesh.[124]

Subsequent legislation – the New Towns Act (Northern Ireland) – transferred the planning powers of local authorities in development areas to central government. The ministry responsible – Development – had been created only as a result of O'Neill's adoption of what his critics inside the party referred to a dictatorial style of politics. In the summer of 1964 he attempted to overcome resistance of his proposals by a ministerial reshuffle, setting up the new department while most of his colleagues were on holiday.[125]

The *Newsletter* observed at the time that the July reshuffle was surprisingly limited in terms of changes in personnel. In fact the paper criticised him for his continuing reliance on ministers from the Brooke administration.[126] The most significant change was a realignment of Cabinet responsibility which concentrated powers over planning, transport, roads, local government and housing in the Ministry of Health and Local Government, restyled the Ministry of Development in January 1965. The new ministry, with its task of developing a 'master plan' for Ulster, was the centrepiece of O'Neill's strategy for dealing with the NILP.[127] Right from the beginning, however, it was clear that resistance from local Unionist power centres would have significant effects on the implementation of the strategy. Thus the existing Minister of Health and Local Government, who was believed to have antagonised the Unionist-controlled Belfast Corporation, was replaced by William Craig* in a cosmetic attempt at appeasement.

More significantly, actual and potential resistance appears to have had a measurable influence on both the decision to create the 'new city' at Lurgan-Portadown and the Lockwood Report's recommendation that a new university be sited at Coleraine. Both projects were vital symbols of 'modernisation' and both were the product of a specific kind of political calculation. It had obviously been decided to treat the inevitably hostile reaction of local Unionists in the west of Ulster as a necessary price for the political benefits to be gained from concentrating resources in the Protestant 'heartland' of the east. The existence within the Derry Unionist leadership of a significant group that saw 'modernisation' as disruptive of the local power structure may have encouraged the O'Neill entourage to hope that resistance to Lockwood would be seriously weakened.[128]

'Modernisation' under O'Neill combined an overriding concern with symbols of a new direction with a series of piecemeal attempts to placate and divide the Unionist opposition at the local level. The controversy over Craigavon and Lockwood was in fact relatively easily contained. It did become linked up with a province-wide resistance to the

* See Biographical Note on p. 253.

government's New Towns Bill and its encroachments on the powers of local councils.[129] O'Neill, however, was able to placate some of the opposition by emphasising his basic commitment to some of the most traditional aspects of Unionist rule. In a revealing interview with a *Newsletter* reporter he replied to a question about the youth of Ulster becoming tired of hearing about 'Derry, Aughrim and the Boyne':

> I do not think we could or should turn our backs on a very honourable tradition which still means a great deal to the majority of Ulster people. What we have to do is to build modern policies upon the foundations which these traditions have given us.[130]

The ideology of modernisation could function quite simply to defend sectarian activity by defining nationalist and NILP concern as 'reactionary' or 'living in the past'.

The degree to which modernisation was aimed not at dismantling sectarian structures but at denying the legitimacy of a reformist strategy in this area was soon apparent to some of O'Neill's erstwhile liberal supporters. In March 1964 the *Round Table* discussed this question:

> It is indicative of government reluctance to admit that grievances exist and to forestall political attack that the National Assistance Board, the Housing Trust and the newly appointed Lockwood committee on university expansion are without Catholic members.

It speculated that O'Neill's failure to act would consolidate the growth in the Catholic community of the Campaign for Social Justice and eventually make liberalisation 'from above' impossible. It continued:

> Captain O'Neill's series of speeches on the 'New Ulster', stimulating as these have been in terms of a more modern outlook on town and country planning ... have not further defined the meaning of what he earlier called a 'unity of purpose'. 'A change of heart', to quote another phrase, has not been applied beyond civic pride and a quickening of the economy. The impression is that he has decided that material well-being is enough, without running the risk of dissension in his party through a direct attempt to ease the problem of segregation.

O'Neill's economic policies bore no relation to intercommunal relations. Their *raison d'être* lay only in political conflicts within the Protestant bloc. In June 1964 his disinclination even to begin the process of breaking down discrimination was confirmed for the *Round Table*. Two prominent Catholic professional men had written a series of letters to him enquiring why he continued to follow the traditional policy of not appointing Catholics to public boards. The letters were published because he did not reply. On the day of publication he attacked the Catholic hierarchy for maintaining social divisions by insisting on segregated education. The feebleness of his conciliationism (not to mention its illogicality) was demonstrated when, within a few days, he made his famous visit to a Catholic school.[131]

The political concerns of 'O'Neillism' had been determined by the loss of dominance over a section of the Protestant working class. The new departure required the centralisation of initiative at Stormont within a relatively small group of ministers and civil servants. This led to charges of ministerial and bureaucratic dictatorship from local Unionists. Opposition was manifested within the parliamentary party itself, especially over the New City and Lockwood decisions. Nevertheless, it is noticeable that until the end of 1965 the critics within the party at all levels could still be treated as a small if vigorous minority. Desmond Boal and Edmond Warnock attempted to associate O'Neill's meeting with Sean Lemass,* the southern Prime Minister, with the general question of a secretive and anti-democratic style of operating which supposedly threatened Ulster's security.[132] But whilst there was undoubted dissatisfaction in the parliamentary party over particular decisions, it did not reach the level of a significant political division about the overall direction of government policy. The latter appeared to be successful in its object of reconstituting Unionist leadership over the Protestant working class. The O'Neillite manifesto for the 1965 election crystallised the ideology of modernisation – 'Forward Ulster to Target 1970'. The vote showed an average swing to the Unionist Party of 7 per cent and a reversal of the Labour inroads of 1962, with the NILP losing two of its four Belfast seats.[133]

* See Biographical Note on p. 258.

The political success of O'Neill's strategy made it difficult for his critics to consolidate what could be represented as merely selfish local concerns. More significant, however, were the clear signs he had given of having no positive strategy for reform in the areas of civil rights and discrimination. The main question for the future development of his administration was whether the disorganised and passive state of Catholic politics would continue to allow him the political space for intra-Unionist dispute to be localised and defused.

Notes

1. M. Farrell, *Northern Ireland: The Orange State*, London 1975, p. 227.
2. *Belfast Newsletter*, 8 March 1961.
3. Farrell, *Orange State*, pp. 229-30.
4. Ibid., p. 328.
5. Ibid., p. 329.
6. Ibid.
7. H. Patterson, *Class Conflict and Sectarianism*, Belfast 1984, pp. 115-42.
8. See above, p. 97.
9. A. Boserup, *Who is the Principal Enemy?*, London 1973.
10. cf. Patterson, *Class Conflict and Sectarianism*.
11. P. Gibbon, *The Origins of Ulster Unionism*, Manchester 1975, pp. 112-42.
12. Farrell, *Orange State*, p. 228.
13. K.S. Isles and N. Cuthbert, 'Ulster's Economic Structure', in T. Wilson (ed.), *Ulster under Home Rule*, Oxford 1955, p. 101.
14. Ibid., p. 97.
15. M.D. Thomas, 'Manufacturing Industry in Belfast', *Annals of the American Association of Geographers*, 46 (1956), p. 189.
16. Ibid.
17. K.S. Isles and N. Cuthbert, *An Economic Survey of Northern Ireland*, Belfast 1957, p. 382.
18. G.P. Steed, 'Internal Organisation, Firm Integration and Locational Change: The Northern Ireland Linen Complex, 1954-64', *Economic Geography*, 47(1971).
19. Ibid.
20. One example was the important Herdman company. In this period it acquired two mills, one of which had been recently re-equipped. The mills were dismantled and sold off, whilst the best equipment was transferred to the main Herdman plants in Belfast and Sion Mills (ibid.).
21. Government of Northern Ireland, *Report of the Joint Working Party on the Economy of Northern Ireland*, Cmnd 446, Belfast 1962 (hereafter referred to as 'Hall'), para. 19.
22. G.P. Steed, 'The Changing Milieu of a Firm: A Case Study of a Shipbuilding Concern', *Annals of the Association of American Geographers*, 58 (1968).

23. G. McCrone, *Regional Policy in Britain*, London 1969, p. 117.
24. Steed, 'Changing Milieu'.
25. This process began during the war: in 1939 there were 350 tractors in Ulster, by 1960 some 30,000 (Hall, para. 23).
26. Ibid.
27. Hall, paras. 25 and 26; Government of Northern Ireland, *Economic Development in Northern Ireland*, Cmnd 479, Belfast 1965 (hereafter referred to as 'Wilson').
28. PRONI Cab. 4/604/8.
29. Ibid.
30. Hall, para. 48.
31. Ibid.
32. McCrone, *Regional Policy*, p. 115.
33. *Belfast Newsletter*, 7 January 1946.
34. PRONI Cab. 4/619/12.
35. *NIHC*, Vol. XXXI, c. 916.
36. Ibid., Vol. XXXII, c. 579.
37. Ibid., Vol. XXXIV, c. 1928.
38. Ibid., c. 1000.
39. Ibid., c. 1982.
40. *Round Table*, XL (1950).
41. Ibid., XLII (1952).
42. Brian Faulkner was one of the chief proponents of this quaint analysis; cf. *NIHC*, Vol. XXXV, c. 1105.
43. *Round Table*, XLI (1951).
44. See Sinclair's attack on them, *NIHC*, Vol. XXXV, c. 1023.
45. *Round Table*, XLII (1952). Glentoran provided his colleagues with an account of a visit to London in November 1951 to urge more action on Conservative ministers. At a meeting with Peter Thorneycroft, President of the Board of Trade, he told him that Northern Ireland's 26,000 unemployed was the equivalent of 1½ million in Great Britain: 'People in Northern Ireland had told the government that, now that their own party was in power in the United Kingdom, they would hope and expect that more would be done for Ulster.' Memorandum by Minister of Commerce on his visit to London 15/16 November 1951, PRONI Cab. 4/859/21, 26 November 1951.
46. *NIHC*, Vol. XXXV, c. 2572.
47. *Belfast Newsletter*, 20 February 1952.
48. *Round Table*, XLII (1952).
49. Those of Finance, Commerce, Labour and Agriculture.
50. *Belfast Newsletter*, 19 March 1952.
51. Ibid.
52. *Round Table*, XLII (1952).
53. *Belfast Newsletter*, 3 April 1952.
54. McCrone, *Regional Policy*, p. 116.
55. Ibid., p. 117.
56. Ibid.
57. *NIHC*, Vol. XXXVIII, c. 1499.
58. Ibid.,c. 1830.

59. Ibid.

60. *Round Table*, XLIV (1954).

61. *Belfast Newsletter*, 14 September 1947. In a memorandum to the Cabinet the previous year the Minister of Commerce, Lord Glentoran, had warned that he saw no alternative but to publish the report: 'I have thought it desirable, nevertheless, to draw the attention of the Cabinet to the controversial nature of a number of conclusions reached in the survey which, if acted upon by the government would involve important and, in the view of my Ministry, undesirable changes in existing policy.' 'The Economic Survey of Northern Ireland: Memorandum by the Minister of Commerce', PRONI Cab. 4/1004, 6 April 1956.

62. Isles and Cuthbert, *Economic Survey*, p. 382. (It is significant that the survey, unlike the later one by Wilson, was not published as a Command Paper.)

63. Ihid., p. 183.

64. Ibid., p. 187.

65. Ibid., p. 189.

66. Ibid., p. 350.

67. Ibid., p. 197.

68. Isles and Cuthbert, 'Ulster's Economic Structure', p. 101.

69. From the extremely useful appendix of biographical notes on Unionist MPs in Harbinson, *Ulster Unionist Party, 1882-1973*, Belfast 1973, pp. 188-203.

70. *Belfast Newsletter*, 23 October 1957.

71. An ex-chairman of the NILP.

72. *Belfast Newsletter*, 4 November 1957.

73. Ibid., 11 October 1957.

74. Ibid., 14 November 1957.

75. *Round Table*, XLIX (1959).

76. *Belfast Newsletter*, 28 February 1958.

77. The seats were Oldpark, Pottinger, Victoria and Woodvale. In the first two there was a significant Catholic working-class component of the Labour vote. See Sydney Elliott, *Northern Ireland Parliamentary Election Results 1921-72*, Chichester 1973.

78. *Belfast Newsletter*, 3 March 1961.

79. Ibid., 25 April 1961.

80. Ibid., 21 July 1961.

81. Ibid., 16 June 1962.

82. Ibid., 19 and 20 June 1962.

83. Ibid., 20 October 1961.

84. Ibid., 1 June 1962.

85. Ibid., 12 April 1961.

86. Ibid.

87. In an open letter to Brooke, ibid., 28 April 1961.

88. Ibid., 24 May, 22 June 1961.

89. Ibid., 15 November 1957.

90. Ibid., 12 April 1961.

91. Ibid., 18 April 1961.

92. *Round Table*, LI (1961).

93. Ibid.
94. *Belfast Newsletter,* 26 October 1961.
95. Ibid.
96. *Belfast Newsletter,* 23 June 1962.
97. Hall, p. 11.
98. Ibid.
99. *Belfast Newsletter,* 23, 26, 27 June 1962.
100. Ibid., 19 July 1962.
101. Ibid., 23 July 1962.
102. Ibid., 18 August 1962.
103. Ibid., 13 October 1962.
104. Ibid., 3 October 1962.
105. Ibid., 16 October 1962.
106. Ibid., 24 October 1962.
107. Hall, p. 11.
108. *Belfast Newsletter,* 31 October 1962.
109. Wilson.
110. Hall, p. 75.
111. It should be noted in passing that traditional industry should not be thought of as wholly local. Isles and Cuthbert estimated that about a third of total paid-up capital in all public and private companies registered in Northern Ireland was owned outside the province (*Economic Survey,* p. 161). In a sample of public companies it was as high as 76 per cent. The investment of mainly British external capital in both shipbuilding and engineering sectors became significant in the inter-war period (although John Brown's had bought a controlling interest in Harland & Wolff as early as 1906). This non-local section of traditional capital does not appear to have been interested in asserting an independent line in local politics or employment practices.
112. Hall, p. 50. The Belfast government had been pressing the Conservatives for a major concession to ease conflicting domestic pressures since the early 1950s. Thus in the run-up to the 1955 Northern Ireland election the Minister of Finance had pressed the Chancellor for a major concession: a transport subsidy to deal with Northern Ireland's peripheral position and a general production subsidy. These were refused and the Northern Ireland government had to make do with a subsidy for the creation of a Northern Ireland Development Council chaired by Lord Chandos with the aim of attracting more inward investment. See PRONI Cab. 4/970/9 and PRONI Cab. 4/970/8, 30 April 1955.
113. Farrell, *Orange State,* p. 227.
114. *Belfast Newsletter,* 8 March 1961.
115. McCrone, *Regional Policy,* p. 120.
116. *Belfast Newsletter,* 6 April 1963.
117. The three major reasons Matthew gave for siting the new city (Craigavon) in north Armagh were: '(1) [the] location ... beyond the head of the Lagan valley is in the *natural direction of development* ... (2) [Lurgan/Portadown] have good rail connections ... and can easily be linked to the proposed motorway ... *their proximity to Lough Neagh could take advantage of water transport should it develop* ... (3) *The configuration of*

the land is well suited to building ..' (emphasis added). Government of Northern Ireland, *Belfast Regional Plan*, Cmnd 451, Belfast 1963, p. 37.

118. M.D. Thomas, 'The Northern Ireland Case' in United Nations Research Institute for Social Development, *The Role of Growth Poles and Growth Centres in Regional Development*, Geneva 1968.

119. Wilson, pp. 188-90. It should be said in mitigation that some of Wilson's recommendations were not included in the accompanying White Paper, in particular that the government enter into negotiations with the Industrial and Commercial Finance Corporation about the possibility of establishing a new finance agency, and that it set up a full-scale enquiry into cross-channel shipping charges (*Belfast Newsletter*, 3 February 1965).

120. G.P. Steed and M.D. Thomas, 'Regional Industrial Change in Northern Ireland', *Annals of the Association of American Geographers*, 61 (1971).

121. The number of economists (other than agricultural economists) employed by the Northern Ireland government in 1963 was two. In 1968 it was still two. (*NIHC*, Vol. LXIX, c. 1404-5).

122. Terence O'Neill, *The Autobiography of Terence O'Neill*, London 1972, p. 47.

123. *Belfast Newsletter*, 9 May 1963.

124. It prompted a sharp reaction from local authorities (ibid., 4 July 1964).

125. *Round Table*, 216 (1964).

126. *Belfast Newsletter*, 23 and 24 July 1964.

127. Ibid., 30 December 1964.

128. The role of Derry Unionists in resisting the idea of expanding the local Magee College as an alternative to Coleraine was first underlined in an article by Ralph Bossence in the *Newsletter*, 19 February 1965.

129. In 1965 the Ulster Unionist Conference passed a resolution condemning 'the dictatorial outlook of recent government planning proposals' (*Belfast Newsletter*, 1 May 1965).

130. *Round Table*, 214 (1964).

131. Ibid., 215 (1964). O'Neill described it thus: 'I took my first step in the direction of improving community relations. I visited a Catholic school in Ballymoney.' Terence O'Neill, *Autobiography*, p. 59.

132. *Belfast Newsletter*, 4 January 1965.

133. J.A.V. Graham, 'The Consensus-Forming Strategy of the NILP', unpublished MSc thesis, Queen's University, Belfast, 1972, p. 183.

5   Collapse, 1965–1972

In 1972, after little more than fifty years of devolved power, the British government terminated the existence of an autonomous administration in Northern Ireland. Parliament at Stormont was prorogued and the civil service absorbed into a new Northern Ireland Office under a Secretary of State who was to take responsibility for most Stormont ministers' former functions. This process coincided with the administrative centralisation of almost all the hotly disputed functions of local government in Northern Ireland. Taken together, these events signified the end of the Northern Ireland state.

Formally speaking, the death of the state was occasioned by the refusal of its last Prime Minister, Brian Faulkner, to cede responsibility for security matters to Westminster. In fact, as one historian has pointed out, 'The move was evidently well prepared. It seems clear that the threat to take over Stormont's security powers was only a way to precipitate a crisis.'[1] The real collapse took place not on 24 March 1972 but during the preceding four years, as a result of an unprecedented combination of developments. This conjuncture, and its relation to some of the tendencies already described, are the subject of this chapter. For the collapse of the state was just as dependent on the regime's historically specific qualities as its survival had been.

There is an enormous range of interpretations of the failure of the state in Northern Ireland and little consensus even about its principal empirical dimensions. Nevertheless most commentators have generally agreed in emphasising three issues. Firstly, the changes in Catholic politics associated with the rise of the civil rights movement; these have generally been treated as the political expression of a novel social and economic force in the province, a Catholic middle class. Secondly, the policies of the British government; there is no agreement on what these policies were, though, let alone their precise effects. Thirdly, there is the issue of divisions within Unionism, the main subject of this study. Broadly speaking, Unionist differences in the period have been attributed to the same process which purportedly led to the rise of O'Neillist 'reformism' in the early 1960s – a polarisation between declining, reactionary traditional industry and progressive, modernising businesses. This polarisation is said to have intensified as a result of an increasing 'dissolution effect' of the latter upon the former. While their interpretation will be disputed, these three dimensions of the state's collapse may be taken as a starting point.

Changes in Catholic Politics

In 1968-72 the politics of the Catholic population underwent a major sea change. The process was characterised by two main trends. Firstly, almost the entire Catholic population became a united militant political force, at least for a short time in 1968-69. This unity was to swallow most nationalist-oriented organisations and assumed institutional form with the creation of the Social Democratic and Labour Party (SDLP) in August 1970. Secondly, and somewhat paradoxically, there was the reappearance after 1969 of a strong republican undertow – especially in the most deprived Catholic urban areas – which was to find expression in the Provisional IRA.

The first of these trends was unprecedented in Northern Ireland, at least since the formation of the state. Directly and indirectly, its effects were dramatic. Terence O'Neill was prevented from consolidating a moderate political centre and the stage was set for the events that were to lead to direct rule. The second, parallel impulse, which began to make itself felt more strongly after August 1969, amplified the overall effect of Catholic political mobilisation while simultaneously reducing the ability of its formal leadership to 'deliver' support for any particular compromise it was offered.

For a prolonged period this twin tendency, towards formal

unity on the one hand and the recreation of a familiar kind of disunity on the other, was to be buried beneath a general celebration of Catholic political mobilisation as such. So novel was the scale of this development that it intoxicated the great majority of the Catholic population and their political representatives alike. Bernadette Devlin observed that the atmosphere in Derry in January 1969, at the conclusion of the march from Belfast organised by the radical student militants of People's Democracy, was 'like that of V Day: the war was over and we had won'.[2] This sentiment was to surface frequently in the next three years. Shortly before Bloody Sunday, when British paratroopers killed thirteen demonstrators in Derry in January 1972, Austin Currie addressed an anti-internment rally in Falls Park in equally triumphalist terms:

> When Brian Faulkner turns on his TV set and sees the crowd here, by God, it will be the longest day of his life. Reginald Maudling came on TV and said we should be prepared to talk. I say to him, why the hell should we be prepared to talk to him? Because we are winning and he is not ... Even if Maudling got down on his bended knees and kissed all our backsides we would not be prepared to talk.[3]

Mobilisation itself was being accounted victory.

The novelty both of Catholic mass activity and the relative unity which became associated with it is best appreciated by a glance at post-war Ulster Catholic politics.[4] The major political division in the Catholic population between 1945 and 1965 was that between town and country. Rural areas were dominated by the Nationalist Party, a segmentary political organisation embracing all constitutionally minded Catholic activists. Supporters not only of the old Redmondite party, but of both major parties in the south, Cumann na nGaedheal/Fine Gael and Fianna Fail, had fallen in behind the Nationalists long before the war. Until the 1960s, however, the Nationalists had no party apparatus to speak of. Most parliamentary candidates were still selected by conventions dominated by the clergy and middle class of the small towns. Their only form of organisation was often the registration committee which doubled for the Republican candidates who by mutual agreement stood in place of Nationalists at Westminster elections. In 1965, as a result

both of Sean Lemass suggesting they become an official
parliamentary opposition and of the increasingly high profile
of Belfast MPs, the Nationalists endeavoured to create a
proper political machine.[5]

Catholic politics in Belfast and one or two larger towns, for
example Dungannon, were somewhat different. Until the
1940s most of the Catholic vote in these areas was accounted
for by the NILP, which until late in the decade took no
explicit line on partition. In some constituencies (e.g.
Oldpark) this continued to be the case during the 1960s. In
constituencies where Catholics formed a reasonable majority,
however, the NILP never recovered from its acceptance of
partition. In its place appeared various versions of Catholic
labourism. According to Rumpf and Hepburn,

> The confusing multiplicity of party labels in the Central,
> Dock, Pottinger and Falls constituencies between 1945 and
> 1969 was the result of an inability on the part of local politi-
> cians to agree on what sort of anti-partitionist party should
> fill the vacuum created by the expulsion of both the
> Nationalists and the NILP from Belfast Catholic politics. The
> main difficulty was simply that there were fewer seats than
> there were aspirants, while there were no compensating
> pressures to encourage political unity.[6]

Catholic politics in post-war Belfast were characterised by
competition between hustling politicians with a labourist
rhetoric and personal followings established by brokerage.
By 1966 Gerry Fitt, whose election to Westminster that year
as a 'Republican Labour' candidate was to prove significant,
had the largest following.

The Catholic masses meanwhile showed considerable
apathy towards these forces. Actual numbers involved in any
organisation, whether Nationalist, Catholic, labourist or
Republican, were minimal. The bread and butter of Catholic
politicians remained patronage and brokerage. Fitt, for
example, despite forays into 'Connolly socialism', was as
suspicious of the professionalism and secularism of the
Northern Ireland Housing Trust as back-bench Unionists
and Nationalists:

Mr Fitt: One of the points of criticism in which members of
   both sides have joined over a period of time is that as elected

representatives we should have some say ...
Miss Murnaghan: They should have none at all.
Mr Fitt: It is quite all right for the Hon. and learned member
for Queen's University to say that we should have no say at
all, but she has got no constituency interest in this...[7]

The vehicle for the unparalleled Catholic popular mobilisation which this situation gave way to was, of course, not the Nationalist Party, nor the political retinues of figures like Fitt, but the civil rights movement, an entirely new force.

The first and subsequently most influential interpretation of the movement's wide appeal was that its growth was due to the emergence in the 1960s of a 'much larger Catholic middle class ... which is less ready to acquiesce in the situation of assumed (or established) inferiority and discrimination than was the case in the past'.[8] This stratum was created by the extension of secondary and higher education to Catholics after the war, an innovation which had a dual effect. Integration into the British educational system, particularly in higher education, supposedly diminished the appeal of republicanism to the post-war generation, leading it to demand a role within the state. The civil rights movement was an expression of that demand.

While it has obvious attractions, the 'Cameron interpretation' is deficient in a number of ways. Firstly, its proponents offer little or no empirical evidence for the 'expansion' of the Catholic middle class nor even any precise definition of who comprised this class.[9] Secondly, as will be seen, Catholic middle-class political activity in the immediately preceding period evinced little evidence of any general trend towards secularisation and moderation as a consequence of educational changes. Thirdly, and most strikingly of all, this interpretation fails to show why such a narrow impulse should have generated such broad appeal and impact. Even if the 'expansion of the Catholic middle class' thesis is accurate in identifying the source of civil rights agitation, it hardly shows why the movement was to acquire an irreversible momentum among the Catholic population at large.

The problems underlying these difficulties may perhaps best be solved by an empirical investigation of the Cameron hypothesis. In 1975 E.A. Aunger published a review of the results of the 1961 and 1971 Northern Ireland censuses of religion and occupational class.[10] His figures indicate that during this period there was virtually no change in the social structure of the male Catholic population.[11] The finding that the male Catholic middle class was immobile rather than expanding might itself be thought sufficient ground for rejecting the Cameron argument, but it should rightly be placed in the context of a longer-term view of changes in social structure.[12] The 1926, 1937 and 1951 censuses lacked the necessary tabulation of occupation by religious affiliation, but that of 1911 did not. Its results are retabulated here as far as possible according to procedures identical to those employed by Aunger.[13] (The figures include all economically active males and females; because these figures were not available for 1961, comparison is made only with Aunger's figures for 1971.[14])

The twentieth century has, of course, been characterised by substantial general changes in the social structure in all industrial societies. The most notable have been a decline in the numbers employed in agriculture, a dilution of the craft skills of the manual working class and an expansion of non-manual strata.[15] The trends were reflected in Ulster as in the rest of the United Kingdom. Notable in Northern Ireland, however, is the way in which the last two of these trends worked out differently for Catholics and Protestants. Amongst the Catholic population the two most notable trends were a more than doubling of the professionally employed, partly accountable by a shift from lower grade non-manual employment, and a substantial rise in the proportion of unskilled manual employees, mainly account-able by a similar decline in the skilled manual group. Amongst Protestants the most notable trends have been a major decline in skilled manual labour and significant rises in the relative sizes of all other manual and non-manual categories – except the unskilled, who actually fell as a proportion of all Protestant employees.

While the figures to some extent confirm the Cameron hypothesis, they show that it describes only part of the overall picture. The proportion of Catholics in professional and managerial occupations has risen sharply – more sharply in fact than for the population of the province as a whole. But two other conclusions are equally significant. Firstly,

Table 3 *Religion and Occupational Class,*
Northern Ireland, 1911 and 1971, Percentages

Occupational Class	Catholic		Protestant		Total	
	1911	1971	1911	1971	1911	1971
Professional, managerial	5	12	8	15	7	14
Lower-grade non-manual	23	19	18	26	20	24
Skilled manual	24	17	34	19	31	18
Semi-skilled manual	28	27	22	25	24	26
Unskilled	20	25	18	15	18	18

N (1911) = 423,448; (1971) = 564,682
Source: See text and appendix p.265.

expansion at the top end of the Catholic social scale has been balanced by an equally important growth at the other end. Secondly, most of the changes seem to have taken place before 1961 and not to have been directly related to improved educational provision after 1944.[16] It should also be pointed out that the expansion of educational opportunities was implemented later in Northern Ireland than in Britain.

These qualifications illuminate the question of the origins and effects of the civil rights movement more than the original hypothesis. The movement's timing in relation to structural change suggests a specific political trigger to Catholic middle-class impulses for reform in the mid- and late 1960s rather than a purely economic one. On the other hand, the expansion at the base of the Catholic social structure throws light on why the movement should have had popular impact among the working class, whose enthusiasm was to prove more enduring than that of its leadership.

A possible trigger to Catholic middle-class political activity in the 1960s that has often been mentioned is a growing awareness of Protestant monopolisation of recent expansion in the state sector of the economy and public sector.[17] The

Plain Truth,[18] *Fermanagh Facts*[19] and other civil rights publications concentrated much of their attention upon the non-absorption of the Catholic professional classes into public service. Indeed, as has been noted, O'Neill was criticised by liberal Unionists as early as 1964 for failing to encourage appointments of this kind. No doubt there were real grievances amongst the middle class, but grievances alone do not generate political involvement. Two factors which had a bearing upon mobilisation as such appear to have been the return of a Labour government to Westminster in 1964 and the response of the Nationalist Party to O'Neillism.

There can be little doubt that the Labour victory of 1964 raised Catholic political expectations. Obviously it made the position of Unionism somewhat delicate and also evoked other political memories. The period of the previous Labour government in Britain (1945-51) had seen a large-scale mobilisation of Irish Catholics in the anti-partition campaign of 1949. Though in most respects a dismal failure, the campaign had succeeded in establishing a core of committed anti-Unionists within the parliamentary Labour Party. Thirty Labour MPs became associated with Geoffrey Bing's Friends of Ireland group and many more – including Harold Wilson – could be regarded as sympathetic. Some of this group were to provide the nucleus of Paul Rose's Campaign for Democracy in Ulster, founded in June 1965 at a meeting attended by 60 Labour MPs.[20] The CDU gained impetus with the return of Gerry Fitt to Westminster in 1966, and its membership soon rose to 90.[21] Evident numerical support and general sympathy in parliament for the campaign created a favourable atmosphere within Northern Ireland for a 'responsible' reform movement. Equally significantly, it was to have an important effect upon the forms of public protest the movement was to adopt. Another influential factor was developments within the Nationalist Party, and local Catholic politics generally, in the period 1965-66. The O'Neill-Lemass meeting of 1965 had been the occasion of the Nationalist Party's official reversion to constitutional opposition, but it had been edging in that direction for some time before. While retaining an essentially conservative outlook on social and economic questions, the party moved rapidly towards a conciliatory stance on community relations immediately after O'Neill's accession. It not only responded to O'Neill's gestures with what Farrell has called 'pathetic gratitude',[22] but reciprocated them disproportionately. In particular, traditional hostility to the security forces abated noticeably. In 1963 one of the party's Stormont senators described the RUC as 'a fine body of men who are doing a good job'.[23] By February 1968, when it was proposed at Stormont to grant a supplementary estimate of £29,000 for the B Specials, the party leader, Eddie McAteer, agreed to the proposal without qualification.[24] Reception of the administration's other policies was equally gentle, not to say deferential. When in April 1968 the government announced the appointment of Professors Wilson, Matthew and Parkinson as consultants for the 1970 economic plan, McAteer fatuously remarked, 'That would be a hell of a half-back line – those three.'[25] Indeed, as McAteer was himself to reveal inadvertently during the February 1968 debate on Brookeborough's retirement from Stormont, the party's assumption of official opposition had had the practical effect of opposition being renounced completely:

> In some way or another I am reminded of a very recent experience which I had discussing with a veteran Nationalist some of the difficulties surrounding the new soft-line approach. I talked for some time and I recall that he looked at me sorrowfully and said, 'Ah, sure, Eddie, there is hardly any such thing as politics now at all ...'[26]

The Nationalist Party had vacated its traditional role, possibly as much in response to the prevailing religious ecumenism as to local political realities, without finding a new one. This was most apparent on civil rights questions. Individual Nationalists continued to raise cases of discrimination against their constituents, but the party had a less coherent approach to the issue than either the Liberals or the NILP.[27] When a Unionist White Paper on local government was discussed early in 1968, McAteer was obliged to confess, 'I want to say frankly that our party's view has not yet fully crystallised on this subject.'[28]

Probable external receptiveness to a local 'civil rights' campaign, together with the Nationalist Party's loss of direction, ushered in a general period of fluidity and competition in Catholic politics, which created opportunities for marginal groups of Marxist revolutionaries briefly to capture the stage. The tendency was strongest in Derry, where after the riots of 5 October 1968 it impelled the local middle classes to head off what was perceived as growing popular support for Eamon McCann:

> ... word got round during the afternoon that 'all interested parties' were meeting to 'consider the situation' ... In the room upstairs there were about a hundred and twenty people. The Catholic business community, the professions, trade union officialdom and the Nationalist Party were well represented ... Various speakers congratulated us on the marvellous work we had done over the past few months. A few expressed their regrets, apologies, etc., that they had not 'been so active in the past as I would have liked'. All urged we now all worked together.[29]

The truth is not, as Cameron suggests, that a newly radicalised Catholic middle class dropped from the sky (or at least from post-Butler secondary and higher education). While growing in numbers, the middle class actually remained remarkable more for its conservative than for its radical qualities.[30] The situation was rather one in which the social basis, the political space and impetus and the opportunity of apparent success for a middle-class reform movement all coincided.

The movement's instantaneous popularity is another matter. Two factors, already mentioned in passing, may be considered here. Firstly it is evident from the statistical account of changes in social structure that the relative position of the least privileged members of the Catholic community deteriorated during the existence of the Northern Ireland state. Most significantly, while everywhere else (including the Protestant community) the unskilled section of the working class was diminishing as a proportion of the work-force, in the Catholic community it was actually increasing. No less than a quarter of the non-agricultural work-force was consigned to unskilled labour, excluded not only from political life but also from the rising standard of living enjoyed by other classes. This sector constituted an immense reservoir of opposition to Unionism and indifference to moderation.

The stimulus for the involvement of this and other strata

of the Catholic population in the civil rights movement was partly provided by the new-found activism of influential and respected, not to say patrimonial, community figures, as McCann has pointed out.[31] Perhaps more importantly, it was provided by the forms of public protest which this stratum had specifically devised as a means of capturing the outside world's attention and sympathy. While these forms of protest – the street march, the sit-down and so on – had their immediate pedigree in the moderate American civil rights movement and were intended to evoke its image, in practice their impact in Northern Ireland was at variance with this secular inspiration.

In Ulster demonstrations had distinctly non-secular implications. Marches in particular meant, and still mean, the assertion of territorial sectarian claims. To march in or through an area is to lay claim to it. When so many districts are invested with confessional significance by one bloc or the other, undertaking a 'secular' march creates the conditions for territorial transgressions and counter-transgressions. Most incidents of this nature occurred, as a matter of probability, in the inner urban areas inhabited by the unskilled as efforts at secular demonstrations spilled from town centres to adjacent zones. Quite apart from any independent sectarian attraction such demonstrations may have had for a portion of the population, they inevitably had a further tendency to involve the unskilled working class. This tendency gave rise to feelings of local solidarity and thus to the creation of 'militant areas' on behalf of civil rights.

Catholic unity reached its high point under the leadership of the Catholic middle class late in 1968 and early in 1969. Its volatile and somewhat contradictory character was exemplified in the remarkable selection (and subsequent election) of a young Trotskyist woman, Bernadette Devlin, as pan-Catholic candidate for Mid-Ulster in the spring of 1969. Thereafter, and without ever having been complete,[32] unity declined. The circumstances in which it did so were to reflect the disparity within the movement's social basis and to be critical for future developments.

As sections of both the Catholic and Protestant communities became more belligerent in the early summer of 1969, leading figures of the previous year lost influence to a greater or lesser degree, particularly in working-class districts. As early as May 1969 members of People's Democracy were ejected from Ardoyne.[33] As popular participation in public demonstrations increased, so did the unsought involvement of entire areas in violence, which became commonplace, even casual.[34] These events escalated into the quasi-civil war of August 1969, when the prevalence of intimidation and flight mobilised entire districts. The 'breakdown of public order' in July and August 1969 led to the evacuation of no fewer than 1,505 of Belfast's 28,616 Catholic households.[35] Such ills inevitably inspired local remedies – barricades, vigilantes, citizens' defence committees and so on. Where these prevailed, the leadership of the professional middle classes was broken.

Yet while conditions at one level were working towards a breakdown in the effective social unity of the Catholic community, other factors were promoting the formal institutionalisation of its political unity. Principal among these was British military intervention in August 1969 and the support it implied from British public opinion for amelioration of the Catholic position. As the formal civil rights organisations were now either in abeyance or had lost their authority, pressures which had begun after the collapse of the Nationalist Party in 1969 to favour a reorganised 'United Opposition' intensified. These were perhaps increased by the common desire of most Catholic politicians to isolate Bernadette Devlin, who they perceived as bringing their cause into disrepute.[36] Even so, competing personal ambitions seem to have delayed the setting up of the SDLP for a further year. Once formed, however, it rapidly came to monopolise Catholic political representation.[37]

Although Catholics now had a more effective political voice, the SDLP found that in some districts it had at least to co-exist with a new, localistically oriented current of Republicanism which had evolved from the 'local solutions' of August 1969. While Unionist policies became more extreme in 1971 and 1972, this undertow crystallising in the Provisional IRA, temporarily dictated the pace and content of the SDLP's moves. Unionism faced a more determined opposition than ever before. Yet despite its relative homogeneity, the authority and internal control of its constitutional leaders were weak. This discrepancy was to redouble the obstacles to Unionist dominance.

There remains the question of how this restructuring of Catholic politics, which proved so full of difficulties for Unionism, was influenced by the tendencies embodied in the apparatuses of the state prior to 1968. They appear to have affected it in two clear ways.

The more extensive effects were those due to the exclusivism intitutionalised by successive Unionist regimes. The most obvious consequences were the well known grievances over status among the Catholic middle class and the steady augmentation of a reservoir of potential support for extreme politics among unskilled Catholic workers. A corollary of these largely administrative and economic aspects was a political exclusivism towards the Catholic political parties which, with some Nationalist collusion, deprived Catholics of effective political representation. When a slightly more accommodating stance was eventually taken by Terence O'Neill, Unionist exclusivism ironically took a still heavier toll. Continued Unionist preoccupation with the border as the only permissible area of political controversy had enabled the Nationalist Party to survive as a credible political force despite its almost total lack of formal organisation, and hence of close communication with its constituency. The party's lack of contact with informed middle-class Catholic opinion was to rebound on it when in response to O'Neill's gestures it chose to adopt 'pathetic gratitude' as a political line.

A second aspect of the Unionist state apparatus directly affecting the restructuring of Catholic politics was the mutual insulation between it and the British state, tacitly and directly encouraged by both regimes. As will be seen, the consequences were most severe for British and above all Unionist politics. Its effects on Catholic politics were none the less real. The fact that civil rights leaders recognised its existence dictated the spectacular forms of public protest which they devised, and which had local repercussions well beyond their original intentions. Perhaps, however, this insulation had a further consequence with as much impact as any of those mentioned. It led to a common lack of cynicism about British politicians' intentions among both Catholics and Protestants. There seems little reason to doubt that both communities believed their grievances would ultimately be remedied, one way or another. For the leadership of the

Catholic community this seems to have acted as a restraining influence. Perhaps above all it prevented major political defections from that most conservative of communities. Had Catholic politicians taken a more militant stand in 1971-72, for example, they would surely have been overplaying their hand. As research has shown, even at the height of the rent and rate strike against internment of that year, less than a quarter of the province's Catholic households were taking part.[38] Traditional conservative nationalism never really showed its face between 1968 and 1972, but it is far from clear that it disappeared. By holding the movement back in the way it did, the SDLP was to keep this force submerged and so maintain a high degree of pressure on Unionism.[39]

The Policy of the British State

There is some dispute as to whether the British state had an Irish policy at all in the period between 1965 and 1972. Two well-placed individuals in Harold Wilson's court, Cecil King, chairman of IPC, publishers of the pro-Labour *Daily Mirror* and a director of the Bank of England, and Joe Haines, Wilson's press secretary, have categorically stated that it did not.[40] Most of the left-wing literature, on the other hand, has concluded that a coherent British strategy did exist but that its implementation was obstructed and modified by events.

Evidence can be produced to support both views. The apparently frank memoirs of both Haines and Richard Crossman show that discussion of the Irish question in the Cabinet was perfunctory, inconclusive and ill-informed – at one stage in his diary Crossman refers to 12 July as St Patrick's Day. On the other hand, leading British politicians with special Irish interests were in the habit of regularly making public statements embodying reformist zeal and seeming to disclose an intention of initiating long-term structural reforms.

Between the wars two economic trends in Anglo-Irish relations stand out. One is the completion of large-scale British landed disinvestment in southern Ireland. British landowners had been withdrawing since the Land War, but even in 1921 retained substantial interests. Against general imperial trends, these were now almost wholly terminated.[41] While commercial and financial investment was maintained, the value of property sold off before 1939 well exceeded new investment.[42] The other is the increasing marginality of Northern Ireland's middle class. At one stage in the nineteenth century it could almost have been regarded as an integral part of the metropolitan middle class, not simply sharing the latter's sources of finance but substantially engaged in the dominant industrial pursuits – shipbuilding and textiles. After 1925 an increasing disparity became evident. Ulster saw very little of the 'rationalisation' applied to these industries in Britain and none of the growth of monopolistically shaped consumer industries which in the Midlands and South-East came to dominate the industrial sector.

In the post-war period the currency of this trend not only in Northern Ireland but in Wales, Scotland and parts of England too became recognised as the 'regional problem'. Regional business leaders were considered backward, inflexible and incapable of delivering full employment. While not seeking to disengage themselves from them entirely, the metropolitan middle class's relation to its regional counterparts was no longer one of simple solidarity. As marginalisation continued, some enterprises were forced to site plants in the regions to avoid so-called 'overheating' in the metropolitan areas, while others went there voluntarily to take advantage of investment incentives and relatively cheap labour. To this extent the economic interests of the metropolitan elite were physically extended, yet the overall amount of investment was relatively small and in general the regions were an economic embarrassment. This was particularly the case with Northern Ireland, as the subvention began to rise sharply in the mid-1970s at the same time as new investment began to dwindle.[43]

Politically speaking, too, Ireland became marginal after 1925. By 1940 Ulster demonstrably had no part in the long-term political and strategic calculations of the British political elite. That summer Churchill effectively offered the province to de Valera on condition that he joined Britain in the war against Germany.[44] The empire was no longer considered an inviolable entity, and a strong current of opinion favoured intelligent adjustments to local opinion wherever it became organised, or even sacrificing large slices of territory where expedient. In the post-war period both the empire and Ireland became even less important political considerations. At any rate, no coherent force within the British political elite lobbied for the question to be reopened.

One political consideration not touched upon should be mentioned. This was Anglo-American relations. Because an Irish cultural identity persisted among a substantial sector of the American people, the US government periodically felt obliged to take up the mantle of guarantor of Irish national aspirations. After the Second World War, with the emergence of the 'special relationship' (in other words heavy British economic, political and military dependence on the USA), the potential significance of American government opinion increased.

A second general determinant of policy towards Northern Ireland was the institutional form of state-to-state relations between Britain and the province. These relations were largely conducted through Parliament, the Treasury and the Home Office. Constitutionally, Britain began insulating herself from the affairs of the Northern Ireland state even before partition took place. The process was completed by 1923 when the first definitive ruling was given that matters of administration for a minister in Northern Ireland could not be discussed.[45] In so far as this convention was modified, this was on the Unionists' own terms.

A process of insulation is also evident in the practices of the Treasury and the Home Office. The Treasury's control of financial matters has been discussed at length and only two remarks will be made here. Firstly, financial relations between the two areas, which had always been to Northern Ireland's benefit, became more and more so. Secondly, the Treasury's autonomy in handling these relations appears to have been very extensive indeed. It is doubtful whether ministerial decisions were involved in all the post-war period. Certainly Crossman did not recall them coming up before the Cabinet:

> Neither Jack Diamond [Chief Secretary to the Treasury, 1964-70] nor the Chancellor knew the formula by which Northern Ireland gets its money. In all these years it has never been revealed to the politicians and I am longing to see whether now we shall get to the bottom of this very large and expensive secret.[46]

Predictably, they did not.[47] The major quid pro quo of all this, from the Treasury's point of view, seems simply to have been that the Northern Ireland Ministry of Finance satisfy Whitehall that it was applying Treasury-style monetary management policy and techniques.

The Home Office was theoretically the main channel of inter-state relations, and Northern Ireland affairs were strictly speaking the responsibility of the Home Secretary. Yet just as in practice the various state departments in Britain serve as sponsors' of particular economic and political forces, rather than as executors of an independently conceived government policy, so the Home Office over the years acquired the role of sponsoring the Unionist interest in Whitehall. This was made stunningly clear by Sir Frank Newsam, Permanent Under-Secretary of State at the Home Office in 1954. Newsam listed the Northern Ireland functions of the Home Secretary as follows:

1. To act as the official channel of communication between the Governments of the United Kingdom and Northern Ireland.
2. To ensure that Northern Ireland's constitutional rights are not infringed and to watch Northern Ireland's interests generally.
3. To safeguard her interests with regard to schemes under the Agricultural Marketing Acts
4. To ensure that the views of the Government of Northern Ireland on matters affecting them are made known to the Government of the United Kingdom.
Questions of law and order are entirely for the Government of Northern Ireland.[48]

He added:

Personal contacts that have been established between Home Office officials and their Northern Ireland colleagues have led to mutual understanding and goodwill in the handling of thorny problems, despite occasional differences of opinion. The Northern Ireland Government has attached to the Home Office a responsible member of their Civil Service so that close liaison may be maintained both with the Home Office and with other departments of the United Kingdom Government. The Home Office has found this arrangement most helpful.[49]

Charles Brett, a Northern Ireland Labour Party leader who in the mid-1960s made considerable efforts to persuade the Labour government to adopt a more active reformist position on Ulster, recorded: 'The Home Office officials were not only unhelpful, they were downright obstructive, and we had grounds for believing they were secretly furnishing Stormont with reports to Labour ministers.'[50]

This situation seems to have prevailed as late as 1971. According to Joe Haines, a senior civil servant assisting Wilson and himself on a trip to Northern Ireland had never been to the South. Such visits were 'not encouraged' by the Home Office.[51]

Not only was Northern Ireland economically and politically marginal for Britain, but Britain had done much to keep it so. The forces for retaining such a relationship were powerful, outside and inside the government. It would have required a major strategic departure to implement or even formulate a reformist strategy for Ireland.[52]

A third general determinant of British strategy were the political objectives of contemporary British governments.

Initially the Labour government of 1964 declaimed reformist intentions of a general sort. Labour rhetoric envisaged considerable structural change, particularly in the economy, where its programme was one of energetic modernisation. This was supposed to involve 'putting teeth' into planning (with a National Plan), blunting what was perceived as the excessive influence of the Treasury and the City (through the Department of Economic Affairs), regional development, industrial reorganisation and insistence that growth in incomes should be tied to advances in productivity. The objectives of modernisation and a higher growth rate naturally required a favourable economic climate, however. As the government saw it, the most obvious solution was devaluation. But devaluation was held to involve unacceptable political costs. Opposition came from the City, which believed the consequent reduction in sterling balances would damage its international position, and from the United States, which believed it would lead to a run on the dollar. Both advanced the rather curious argument that calls for devaluation were inspired by de Gaulle, who saw it as a means of weakening Anglo-American influence.[53] Structural reform was sacrificed to this opposition.[54] By 1966 the rhetoric of reform was abandoned. The Labour government became obsessively cautious in all its actions. Its response to crises was managerial and institutional – problems were invariably met by setting up new bodies, usually involving the same individuals and invariably lacking the impulse or power to implement departures in policy.

The Heath government, elected in 1970, had by the spring of 1972 reached the same position, though from a different route – that of the so-called 'Selsden' policies, which were as rhetorically radical as Wilson's, but in a neo-liberal sense. They involved a commitment to substantially reducing the role of government, cutting the level of public expenditure, having wider recourse to the market and attacking the trade unions. In so far as these policies were implemented, they gave rise to a quite remarkable degree of political conflict, but after the fiasco of a defeat by the miners in February 1972 Heath's government was obliged to return to the same managerialist path trodden by Labour for most of the period between 1966 and 1970.

The general managerialist strategy of the Labour government disposed it towards a 'minimal' Irish position. So did that of the Conservatives, from spring 1972 at any rate. Before then they inclined to neo-liberal solutions, which would have had much the same effect.

Yet if the determinants of government strategy all point to non-intervention, events like the dispatching of troops, the Downing Street declarations, the Hunt Committee and Direct Rule seem inexplicably reformist as they were sold to the British public. Either they were reformist, and the general determinants of government strategy were suspended, or they were not reformist at all and had other objectives.

Enough is known today about at least some of the interventions to make the second answer the more plausible. Its coherence depends upon the validity of a preliminary distinction, however – one which the Unionists *en bloc* failed to make: between the subjective views of Harold Wilson and actual government policy.

As anyone who reads his memoirs will perceive, Harold Wilson was much concerned with historical immortality. As his policies were thoroughly nondescript, he became susceptible to a certain adventurism which he liked to confuse with statesmanship. It should not be thought that this reflected any particularly interesting psychological trait – on the contrary, it expressed and sometimes even fulfilled the Labour Party's need for some identifiable public achievement. Securing a negotiated peace in Vietnam was, of course, the jewel in the diplomatic crown of the 1960s, but despite frantic efforts the 'special relationship' alone made it unlikely that any of the parties to the conflict would take him seriously as a potential mediator. Ireland was a different matter entirely. Here were two dependent states, still within the receding British sphere of influence ripe for persuasion, if not bullying – that is, for statesmanship. Even before becoming Prime Minister, he had shown himself disposed to make diplomatic gestures on Ireland. From a Unionist viewpoint the most alarming such gestures occurred between 1964 and 1966 and they will be discussed in the next section. Others followed regularly, and their flavour may be appreciated from an incident in 1966. Shortly before the Westminster election that year he made a speech to the NILP which was reported to be about 'abhorring sectarianism'. A few days later, however, a rumour circulated that Wilson had privately suggested transferring the functions of the twelve Unionist MPs at Westminster to a joint Eire-Ulster committee with a British chairman.[55] Publicly and semi-publicly he urged a united Ireland, preceded by interim tripartite arrangements. He continued to push this line, to the horror of other members of the Cabinet, even after the crisis had begun to take shape in 1968. Crossman reported being told by Denis Healey in May 1969,

> You have no idea what it was like before you came on the [Northern Ireland] Committee [of the Cabinet]. The PM was always demanding active intervention early on, with this crazy desire to go over there and take things over, that we side with the RCs and the Civil Rights movement against the government, though we know nothing at all about it.[56]

Wilson must have been overruled, since the 'crazy desire' was not fulfilled in the course of the Labour government. Nor indeed did anything come of his other suggestions. Two months after the 1966 speech he was faced with a demand by Fitt for a commission to investigate the discrimination he had condemned. Wilson rejected the idea, commenting blandly,

'There are allegations and counter-allegations on both sides.'[57]

Charles Brett has recalled what he regards as the majority viewpoint: 'This is the twentieth century, not the seventeenth, and it is just not possible to believe that the religious divisions of Ireland could lead to violence ever again.'[58] He had added: 'A dozen times since then I have been reproached by friends in the British Labour Party: "Why ever didn't you warn us of what was coming?" I have never yet succeeded in finding words adequate to reply to that question.'[59] Brett is particularly eloquent in his condemnation of the inactivity of the Home Secretaries, Sir Frank Soskice and Roy Jenkins.

The *Sunday Times* 'Insight' team's work,[60] Crossman's diaries, Chichester-Clark's review of Wilson's memoirs[61] and other accounts[62] all suggest that British intervention in August 1969 was planned and executed as the minimum possible form of intervention by the British state. The Downing Street declarations, and to some extent the Hunt Committee, embodied the same principle, modified by a cosmetic tinkering with the institutions of government and, as will be seen, a severe miscalculation on the part of the Unionist Cabinet.

Every effort seems to have been made to forestall military intervention, and then to minimise and terminate it. The main tactic had been to threaten the Northern Ireland government that to call upon troops would bring about Direct Rule.[63] The Unionists were encouraged instead to use first CS gas and then the B Specials against rioting Catholics.[64] By mid-August 1969, when it became obvious that the Northern Ireland government would have to call in troops whatever the consequences, the British Cabinet made it known that no strings would be attached to their use after all, provided Chichester-Clark could dispense with them quickly.[65] To facilitate this, they were initially sent only to Derry. Callaghan sat in the Home Office listening to reports of the killings in Belfast and waited for a further specific request before he ordered them there the next day.[66] In any case, so few troops were made available that they had little immediate impact. All this took place in the Cabinet's full knowledge that it could not escape a legal obligation to provide troops in the long run. The point had been established in April 1969 at the latest, and was made somewhat revealingly by Crossman:

> I went through all the papers. I found the committee had already come to the conclusion that it was *impossible to evade* British responsibility if there was a civil war or widespread rioting. Strictly speaking the police in Northern Ireland or the government can ask for British troops to come in.[67]

The troops having been dispatched, and it being established by 19 August that they could not be immediately withdrawn, discussion took place on what policy to present to Chichester-Clark. The main concern seems to have been to discover a means by which orderly military disengagement might take place. Differences arose over the conditions under which this could be achieved. Some, including Callaghan, felt that institutional changes (stopping short of giving Catholics a share of power) were necessary. Others, notably Healey, felt that 'they must push Chichester-Clark only as far as he wanted to go'.[68] The latter view seems to have been accepted, and all that was anticipated from Chichester-Clark's visit was a new head of the RUC and a promise of a review of the position of the B Specials and the local authorities.[69]

Chichester-Clark's perception of the needs of the situation – specifically the need to pacify Wilson – led him to propose a more radical course of action: a complete British take-over of security and a full-scale inquiry into the police and B Specials.[70] The Cabinet could hardly reject it, and pondered the implications. The most obvious was that the B Specials, who were responsible only to themselves, would have to go. Wilson, who had wanted this all along, promptly announced their impending dissolution – without informing Chichester-Clark, who was under the impression that they would come under military control.[71]

Within five weeks, the Cabinet had decided these measures were insufficient. On 11 September:

> [Callaghan] said life was very bleak ... there was no prospect of a solution. He had anticipated the honeymoon wouldn't last very long and it hadn't. The British troops were tired and were no longer popular and the terrible thing was that the only solutions would take ten years, if they would ever work at all ...[72]

The Cabinet agreed on the necessity of administering another bout of cosmetic institutional reform. This was the background of the Hunt and post-Hunt reforms. It was considered, however, that further serious change would repel Protestant support and hence postpone military disengagement. The reforms of 1969 were to be the last. By mid-1970 a consensus had emerged between Labour and Conservative leaderships that the road to a solution lay elsewhere.[73]

The necessity of avoiding a confrontation with the Protestants, with its implication of greater military involvement, appears to have become by 1970 the major influence upon government policy. After the election of that year the Conservatives were also anxious to re-insulate the whole question from British political life. The army was given tactical control over the situation and a convention was evolved to keep the army satisfied: it would have the power of veto over suggestions by the Stormont-dominated Joint Security Committee.

Despite a number of diplomatic blunders the army settled relatively well into its authoritarian position. It was unable to prevent the growth of the IRA, however, and its 'long haul' aim of 'reducing the IRA's capacity to conduct terrorist warfare' fell considerably short of Unionist expectations.[74] Once Brian Faulkner became Prime Minister and a bolder Unionist policy was adopted towards London, Unionist rhetoric began to have an effect on the British Cabinet. In the general context of a substantial increase in IRA activity, not to say a continued wariness about introducing Direct Rule, the notion of engineering a swift conclusion to the troubles began to appear attractive. It could be achieved, according to Faulkner, by a strategic shift to a short-run policy of aggression.

From August 1971 to February 1972 Faulkner was given his head, and army, not to say Ministry of Defence, opinion was systematically overruled. This was certainly the case with respect to the introduction of internment in August 1971[75] and the toleration of the UDA,[76] and it seems likely also to have been behind the loosening of Ulster Defence Regiment recruiting standards and the reorganisation of the force on local lines.[77] It should not be thought that the new policy reflected merely the personal weakness of Reginald

Maudling, as Callaghan suggests in his book. On the contrary, some powerful figures supported it, among them Cecil King[78] and the former champion of reform, Sir John Hunt.[79] At the time it was widely said to be supported by Callaghan, though later, when it had demonstrably failed, he was to argue that his backing had been conditional upon its accompaniment by a 'political initiative'.[80] Strictly speaking, of course, it was.[81]

As his gamble collapsed, Faulkner became reduced to increasingly desperate measures. The decision that live rather than rubber bullets should be available during the Bloody Sunday operation was his direct responsibility – one that was to cost him dearly. The events of that day inspired the Catholic population to go further over to the offensive. By February 1972 it was clear that far from creating the conditions for British disengagement, Faulkner was creating a minor Vietnam.

Direct Rule was received as an abandonment of 'temporary' considerations of minimisation. Some even believed it to be the prelude to integration. But if the idea of integration was ever entertained it was only in the context of a review of various long-term strategies. In February 1972 a Northern Ireland Cabinet minister voiced a more realistic appraisal: 'Look, let's face it. Ted Heath regards us as his doorstep Cyprus. Don't be surprised by anything that happens – I won't.'[82]

The same month marked the onset of Heath's phase of 'U turns', most notably on incomes policy. The impetus for these changes came from the Central Policy Review Staff, adapted by Heath to act as a Prime Ministerial department, and the CPRS enabled him to climb down on a number of issues. Northern Ireland was among those it considered, and Direct Rule was its suggestion.[83]

It is clear from the literature on the subject that the CPRS's suggestions were intended as interim rather than final solutions for urgent problems.[84] In view of this it seems likely that Direct Rule was recommended on account of its potential for opening up new possibilities rather than as an end in itself.

British political thinking about 'ends in themselves' concerning Ireland had not come far since 1964. The major development was that more British politicians were coming round to Wilson's views on unity. Figures as mainstream as Roy Jenkins, Peter Carrington and William Whitelaw were now said to be espousing this line. Certainly the Labour Party had been discussing it seriously (under the melodramatic code name 'Algeria'[85]). The reasoning seems to have been that the IRA was strong enough to make any other solution unworkable. This was confirmed in Wilson's mind (and possibly Heath's, since he was kept informed) by a secret meeting he held on 13 March 1972 with leaders of the Provisionals. Wilson came away impressed both by David O'Connell and by the Provisionals' claim to be in a position to step up their campaign.[86]

Clearly the British government was not about to capitulate to the IRA, but it now had every reason to develop a policy that would make withdrawal and a united Ireland possible.[87] Despite London politicians' contempt for those in Dublin, it was widely accepted that if such a solution were adopted the southern government could deliver the Provisionals.[88] The army and the Ministry of Defence favoured a policy of this kind, since in their view southern collaboration had to be secured if they were to handle the IRA in the North.[89]

Support for a policy that would make withdrawal feasible also came from the United States, which at this time began to exert strong pressure upon Heath. 'London has not had an easy time with overseas governments, including some of Britain's principal partners in the world, since the engagement of British military forces in Northern Ireland,' observed the *Times*.[90] Demands for drastic action apparently quickened after the burning of the British embassy in Dublin following Bloody Sunday. M.J. Killeen, managing director of the Irish Industrial Development Association and a frequent spokesman for American interests, was reported to have said,

> The burning of the British embassy had particular significance. The Americans regard embassies as symbols of stability. They could not believe it when an embassy was burned in a peaceful country like Ireland.'[91]

The day Direct Rule was introduced Whitelaw told Cecil King that, 'In the end the answer must be a united Ireland.'[92] At the time it looked as if Direct Rule was actually the interim solution that Wilson had been talking of for so long. Whilst the Protestant reaction was feared, withdrawal meant that ultimately it would be somebody else's problem. In the meantime the reaction could be contained by Ian Paisley, whom Whitelaw was said now to be calling 'the future leader of Northern Ireland'.[93]

In the event few real steps towards a united Ireland were actually taken and Whitelaw pursued instead the Sunningdale strategy, which was itself fated to collapse within a year. Sunningdale was remarkable in *being* a strategy, however: it was the first identifiable set of constructive British goals to emerge since 1922. This is not to agree with King and Haines that there was no consistent policy on Ireland throughout the period. There was one – one, indeed, which was bipartisan. Though it was the organising principle for British action, its nature meant that it was disclosed only in times of crisis like 1969. The policy, which was manifest in every twist and vacillation described above, was to minimise British involvement politically and militarily. Action was taken only where the alternative appeared ultimately to entail a greater degree of involvement. It was always designed as a short-term stop-gap unavoidable if the status quo ante in British-Ulster relations was to be restored. In reality there were no long-term commitments to integration or to unity, since either implied the probability of a temporary or permanent increase in engagement. The underlying continuity of British strategy was an absence of active desire to do anything at all, except to avoid getting further ensnared. Even the sort of disengagement that was favoured was limited, since a more comprehensive variety had unpredictable elements.

While the durability of this policy obviously had much to do with Ireland's declining importance for British economic interests, it was clearly also to some extent self-perpetuating. The deliberately insulatory measures undertaken by both the Unionists and the British in the 1920s generated a mutual ignorance of each other's political arena. Absorbed by the Home Office, probably one of the least energetic departments of state, consideration of Northern Ireland was insulated even from the limited diplomatic knowledge and strategic thinking in the Foreign Office.[94] Under these conditions it was impossible for any informed Irish policy to emerge at all. Specific crises – especially where they could be assimilated to what Crossman called 'messy' history – served only to reinforce the tendency towards minimising involvement, since, as Healey remarked, 'we know nothing at all about it'. Short of total Unionist loss of control or the intervention of 'powerful allies', there was no way in which this circuit could be broken and no guarantee that even if it was anything novel would happen.

Minimal involvement had, of course, an ambiguous effect on Northern Ireland. For fifty years it preserved the state from certain pressures for change and allowed the Unionists to maintain a particular kind of autonomy. In the long run, however, it meant that the government had little or no recourse to British support. Obligations were admitted (as in 1949 by Attlee) only when they seemed to forestall events which would have disrupted the condition of mutual insulation. When times changed obligations were modified and redefined. The lability of 'loyalism' once more found itself mirrored in the lability of British solidarity.

Unionist Divisions: The Role of New Industry

We have already examined the 'orthodox' view of the nature of divisions within Unionism. Backwardness and sectarianism are seen as expressions of declining traditional industry while newly arrived international companies are held to play a progressive, modernising and non-sectarian role. We have explored the reductionism implicit in this approach and also the apparent decline of traditional industry. It is nevertheless worthwhile focusing on the nature of international companies drawn to Northern Ireland as a way of examining the dissolution of Unionism. Take, for example, four aspects of the newly established businesses.

Firstly, international businesses drawn to Northern Ireland could not be said to be in any way homogeneous. Certainly many multinational companies set up or acquired branches in the Six Counties during the 1950s and 1960s. Dupont, Enkalon, Michelin, Courtauld's, ICI, Goodyear, Hoechst, ITT, Molins, Baird and Monsanto all did so. There is no doubt either that some of these enterprises made very substantial investments. With its roughly pound-for-pound investment grant policy, Stormont paid out over £200 million between 1945 and 1972 for 'new projects'. Total investment in them therefore amounted to £400-£450 million.[95] American holdings made up £125 million of this; Dupont's contribution alone came to about £25 million.[96] Other major multinational investments included Courtauld's £13 million plant at Carrickfergus[97] and Hoechst's £10 million plant at Limavady.[98] But such large-scale projects were exceptional. Many of the multinational operations were small and corporately marginal enough to be painlessly terminated during the recession of the early 1970s.[99] Different companies had very different levels of economic and political commitment to Northern Ireland.

Secondly, international companies accounted for only a *part* of the 'new capital' invested. The average contribution of enterprises themselves to new projects was well under £1 million (more than £200 million spread over about 250 projects).[100] About one in ten of the new projects was attracted by some existing link with an enterprise already based in Northern Ireland.[101] In this sense 'new' capital was no more unambiguously external than pre-1945 capital (linen excepted) was unambiguously local. Some of the largest investments involved industrial entrepreneurs. For example, from 1955 Cyril Lord, a Lancashire carpet firm which was put in the hands of the receiver in 1968, obtained £900,000 in grants, a free purpose-built factory at Carnmoney and further grants and loans of £2.8 million towards plants at Donaghadee and Rathgael.[102]

Thirdly, international companies' dissolution effect on traditional businesses apparently continued to be limited. Objections to new industry by local business interests recurred, particularly from linen manufacturers in small towns, whose profit margins were tied tightly to low wages.[103] As a rule, though, they remained rare. While evidence suggests a progressive and relative local disinvestment in traditional industry,[104] the economic statistics indicate that on the whole local capital was reproduced at least at its former rate during the 1960s and early 1970s. A general decline in its fortunes appears to have occurred in the 1964-69 period, but a recovery had at least compensated for this by direct rule.

The blunting of the 'dissolution effect' was due to a number of factors. The Ministry of Commerce 'consciously avoided aiming primarily at attracting labour-intensive

Table 4 *Quinquennial Averages, 1950-74, of Northern Ireland Joint-stock Company Registrations, Formations, Liquidations and Paid-up Capitals*

	1950-54	1955-59	1960-64	1965-69	1970-74
Total registered companies	3,327	3,771	4,809	5,851	6,775[a]
Average paid-up capital	£20,218	£22,618	£28,799	£27,338	£29,444[b]
Average new registrations p.a.					
Public	0.8	0.6	1.0	1.2	1.0
Guarantee	2.2	3.8	7.8	10.4	5.2
Private	135.8	196.6	343.6	300.6	534.6
Average no. of liquidations p.a.	22.6	30.0	46.6	63.6	53.2

a 1970-73
b 1970-71
Source: Government of Northern Ireland, *Digest of Statistics*, Belfast annual.

concerns'[105] The maintenance of high direct and indirect subsidies to traditional industry was important; the shipyard, upon which much of the engineering industry of east Belfast relied, received a staggering total of £70 million from the state up to 1973.[106] Some new projects had their own multiplier effects. Dupont, for example, was said in 1963 to purchase goods and services from 130 Ulster firms.[107] In any event, the dissolution of old industry – though continuing – was slowed. In 1970 some 60 per cent of the manufacturing and 86 per cent of the total workforce were still employed outside the new projects.[108] Although no direct comparison is possible, the figures suggest a slower rate of dissolution than in other development areas, such as Scotland.[109]

Fourthly, there is little evidence that representatives of new industries sought any political system other than the established Stormont one. Some dissatisfaction was expressed with local government on the score of physical planning.[110] Also, according to Callaghan, 'major industrialists' approved his 1969 reforms when directly asked.[111]

Hitherto no pressure for reforms was ever evident from this source. A good many new businesses conformed without protest to old practices. In 1965, when new industry provided about 60,000 of 190,000 manufacturing jobs, the first Development Plan complained that only 10 per cent of new vacancies were being filled through labour exchanges.[112] Evidently Orangeism was becoming absorbed into the new workplaces.

New industry actually had as much interest as old in an undisturbed continuation of Stormont. The advantage for both was described as early as 1953 by a senior civil servant, L.G.P. Freer:

> Senior officials of the various departments are known personally to those with whom they have dealings to an extent which would be impracticable in a larger area of administration ... Administrators in Northern Ireland find it easier to assess what the results of any particular line of action are likely to be, and when action has been taken, to correct more quickly any untoward consequences which may appear likely to arise.[113]

Consciously or unconsciously, this point is the essence of Lawrence's defence of Northern Ireland.[114] It was most succinctly recapitulated by Terence O'Neill, who himself supported Stormont's existence to the end:

> A small area with a regional or provincial government can take administrative decisions and can take them quickly within the limits of its powers ... *incoming industrialists are delighted to be able to deal with a small, local and intimate government.*[115]

Industrialists of all species benefited from the sympathetic attention of the Ministry of Commerce, whose generosity was unchecked by Whitehall or by the Ministry of Finance. Among the consequences was that in Northern Ireland each job cost roughly twice as much to create as in Wales or Scotland.[116] With eggs like this, few recipients were interested in the colour of the goose.

This is not to imply unanimity in the political elite. Divisions existed – but not on one fundamental. Recognising this is of vital importance to understanding the nature of the divisions that did occur. There was no specifically economic force which wanted to see Stormont removed. Stormont's development funds seemed inexhaustible, and whatever its other deficiencies it represented the best possible political arrangement. Divisions revolved around the question of how to maintain it.

The main political problems confronting the elite were to this extent common problems. At the beginning of the 1960s they had concerned the defection of Protestant working-class support in Belfast to the NILP. By 1964, though, O'Neill was on the road to resolving this difficulty. In the mid-1960s a far more serious difficulty arose. In various forms it was to divide and redivide Unionists and finally to ensure the collapse of the state. It was the problem of developing a policy to meet what was perceived as a transformation, or potential transformation, of traditional London-Belfast relations.

Substantially increased dependence on British subsidies, and centralised control in Belfast over their distribution, was one aspect of this transformation which was to give rise to tensions. More fundamental was the change of British government that brought Harold Wilson and the Labour Party to power in 1964. The effects on Catholic politics have been described. Among Unionists it generated considerable apprehension. This was not simply because Labour governments, unlike Conservative ones, had actively to 'demonstrate [they were] as staunch friends of Ulster as were the Labour leaders of twenty years ago'.[117] There was also the question of Harold Wilson's surrogate Irish nationalism.

Concern about Wilson's politics was created not only by his various off-the-cuff pronouncements in favour of a united Ireland, or gestures like his return of the remains of Sir Roger Casement to the southern government,[118] but by a specific commitment he appeared to have entered into shortly before the 1964 General Election. On 5 October the *Newsletter* published a letter from him to Patricia McCluskey, who was shortly to found the Campaign for Social Justice in Northern Ireland. It promised, should Wilson be elected, to implement large-scale changes in Northern Ireland.[119] While this incident had only a tenuous connection with Britain's actual Irish policy, it seemed to make development of a 'Wilson strategy' imperative to Unionism.

Although O'Neill had encountered resistance in the

execution of his strategy against the NILP, it did not last long. The reduction in local government powers and certain infrastructural decisions caused brief furores,[120] but opposition to them failed to coalesce. As has been demonstrated, those on the right of the party specifically failed in their endeavours to assist the process.

This relative success inspired O'Neill to undertake what must have seemed at the time a relatively daring 'Wilson' strategy. He embarked on a series of progressive-looking public gestures towards the South and towards public opinion in Britain. Such gestures – the invitation to Lemass to visit Stormont in January 1965, for example – would convince Wilson of Unionism's reforming intentions and thus induce him to keep at bay what were thought of as the Labour Party's wilder counsels. The timing of the meeting with Lemass might even have been regarded as somewhat cautious: the *Newsletter* had chided O'Neill in November 1964 for refusing to meet the Southern premier when he came to Belfast to speak at Queen's University.[121]

O'Neill was careful to indicate the bounds of this strategy, however, and in particular to distinguish it from a secularisation of the state machinery. He went out of his way to point out that no changes were contemplated in the field of discrimination. In February 1964 he strongly rebutted accusations of 'apartheid' in Northern Ireland. In March 1966 he described such accusations as 'facile'. In January 1967 he advised his supporters to 'forget jargon words like community relations', while in April 1967 he described the views of the Campaign for Democracy in Ulster as 'baseless and scurrilous'.[122]

The opposition to O'Neill found a voice in Brian Faulkner. Faulkner advanced the view that the only way of handling Wilson was to recreate 'lost' Unionist unity around the party's traditional positions. This would call Wilson's bluff and force him to abandon his reformist pretensions. Gestures such as the invitation to Lemass simply whetted his nationalist appetite. Support for Faulkner's view came when, three months after Lemass's visit, Wilson called for tripartite talks on the future of Ireland.[123]

Even after this O'Neill's position remained relatively firm, however. It was certainly firm enough to enable him to seek, in his future efforts at conciliating Wilson, to damage the right-wing critics endeavouring to unify opposition to him. His first and most serious attack upon the right was on the then extra-parliamentary wing of the party, Paisleyism. Ian Paisley and his supporters, who were the most vocal supporters of the notion that there was a general undesirable anti-Unionist streak in all O'Neill's policies, laid themselves open to attack by embarking upon a 'strategy of tension' during the spring and summer of 1966. According to the Belfast correspondent of the *Economist,* O'Neill welcomed the opportunity to 'lance this boil of simmering nastiness'.[124] After incidents outside the Presbyterian General Assembly in June he called the Paisleyites 'Nazis', practitioners of 'obscenity and sedition' using 'the sordid techniques of gangsters'.[125] After the Malvern Street murders by Protestant extremists styling themselves on the Ulster Volunteer Force, he banned the UVF, which he said was associated with Paisley, commenting, 'This [is] an evil thing in our midst … a very dangerous conspiracy [which] … we cannot and will not tolerate … one cannot touch pitch without being defiled.'[126] When Paisley was imprisoned for his part in the trouble outside the Assembly his supporters demonstrated in Crumlin Road. The RUC dispersed them using baton charges, armoured personnel carriers and – for the first time – water cannon.[127]

O'Neill's opponents now tried to link this policy to his general gestures of reform and his alleged anti-Unionism. Faulkner claimed the Assembly had been used to disseminate an inaccurate report on discrimination, and that the Paisleyites had been provoked.[128] Moreover, 'Mr Paisley in prison is more an embarrassment to the government than an asset.'[129] Brookeborough agreed:

> Many of us do not like the way things have been going of late … may I offer a grave warning at this time – never at any time can we Unionists afford to forget that in unity and unity alone rests all our strength.[130]

Despite such powerful opposition, O'Neill was still strong enough to add to his gestural attacks on the right by dismissing Harry West in April 1967. Faulkner continued to articulate opposition: 'The Unionist party inside and outside of parliament is tired of crises which serve only to disrupt and divide.'[131] A few days later he was once more condemning as 'nonsense' O'Neill's view that fascist extremism was a force in Ulster politics.[132]

O'Neill's position was not, of course, wholly determined by the Wilson problem. The strategy of reformist gestures accorded with his earlier outflanking of the NILP, and was accompanied by an ideology of modernisation. In most instances his policies were successful, too. This served to diminish opposition and to forestall its unification.

But his situation was a precarious one. An independent political factor was working for the unification of opposition to him. Most of his policies had as a necessary consequence the reduction of different aspects of the state's relative autonomy. The threat from the NILP, the importance of reducing unemployment, the desire for indicative planning and the need to control Paisleyism all involved centralisation. This trend should not be exaggerated, since the populist discriminatory core of the state's autonomy remained intact. The consolidation of O'Neill's position turned on whether the distinction could be maintained. Until the emergence of the civil rights movement in 1968 the problem did not arise.

The crisis provoked by the arrival on the scene of the civil rights movement was therefore not restricted even to the great fundamental issue of discrimination. Involved with this basic problem were all the tensions raised by earlier crises of the 1960s.

For O'Neill the dilemma was excruciating. On the one hand, placating the civil rights movement was likely to mean consolidation of the opposition to him. On the other, failing to do so would probably lead – in his eyes at least – to British intervention and a complete dissolution of local autonomy. O'Neill chose the road of minimal appeasement (the five-point programme of November 1968[133]), emphasising that Wilson had made it 'absolutely clear that if we did not face up to our problems, the Westminster Parliament might well decide to act over our heads'.[134]

From that moment he was probably doomed. Even a purely placatory line towards Catholics proved difficult to implement with the machinery at his disposal, while dissatisfaction with the way it was put into effect further cemented opposition to him. This was most sharply illustrated in the question of the civil rights movement's 'freedom to march'. From the beginning the right to hold marches was not recognised by a substantial number of Unionists and this feeling was shared by at least a segment of the police and B Specials whose reluctance to grant such a right coincided with popular Protestant views. These were in any case well represented in the bodies concerned: for example, over a quarter of the RUC were former B Specials,[135] a further 300 Specials were fully mobilised into the force in 1968-69,[136] and 80 of these were to be found in the Reserve Force or riot squad.[137] Sections of the judiciary saw matters in a similar light. Judge Topping, a former Minister of Home Affairs who in 1947 had declared, 'The enemy today is no different from what it had been 257 years ago,'[138] and who was said in parliament to have appointed himself Recorder of Belfast in 1959 (an event exceptional even by Unionist standards), was a particular target of criticism.

As the civil rights movement continued its progress, both the heightening of tensions in the organs of state which it provoked and the increasing efforts to centralise control over them which this inspired served to coalesce previously disparate forms of opposition to O'Neill and to isolate him within both the state apparatus and the party leadership. As a result O'Neill began to appear weak and impotent. It seems likely that it was grounds such as these, rather than a 'revulsion against violence' or the development of class opposition to his 'aristocratic' qualities, that were the basis of the collapse of O'Neillism as a popular position.

Its collapse was fairly dramatic, as during 1968 O'Neill seems to have been far from isolated within the Protestant community as a whole. After his 'Ulster at the crossroads' speech of 9 December over 150,000 letters or telegrams of support were received, while another 120,000 newspaper coupons supporting the speech were returned. By the 1969 Stormont election this support appears to have diminished, although it was still substantial.

Boal and Buchanan have shown that definite voting trends were discernible among the Protestant community at this election, although they probably misinterpret them.[139] Pro-O'Neill votes tended to be highest in suburban greater Belfast, anti-O'Neill votes most substantial along the border and in working-class Belfast constituencies. It has been argued in explanation that since these regions contained a concentration of deprived Protestants, and since the opposition to O'Neill frequently employed anti-establishment rhetoric, class antagonism underlay popular preference for O'Neill's opponents.[140]

While a rhetoric of class did consistently surface in the contest, a simpler explanation is available.[141] As Boal and Buchanan themselves point out, both on the border and in working-class areas of Belfast Protestant communities were in close proximity to zones of high Catholic concentration. In both, the Unionist elite had historically been obliged to extend the relative autonomy of the state from its control in order to maintain its dominance. Likewise, these were areas of high workplace exclusivism. Although it was articulated along anti-'big house' lines, opposition to O'Neill seems to have been most obviously founded on the question of the state's relations to the mass of the Protestant population. Anti-O'Neill areas were those which had earlier been bastions of populism and were therefore most sensitive to its erosion – a phenomenon popularly known as 'Lundyism'.

While the O'Neill grouping's greatest successes were in the kinds of area where there was suburban middle-class support for modernisation, O'Neill's colleagues also did surprisingly well in working-class and rural constituencies (except Bannside) where they were opposed by Paisleyites.[142] Indeed, a striking feature of the election was the remarkably good performance of official Unionist candidates, whether pro- or anti-O'Neill. In 22 contests where they faced unofficial Unionist opposition (of whatever variety) only two resulted in official Unionist defeat (Bangor and Willowfield, where pro-O'Neillists were returned). In eight constituencies where moderate official Unionists were opposed by unofficial Unionists or Paisleyites, moderates won on each occasion. In the fourteen constituencies where official anti-O'Neill Unionists stood against unofficial pro-O'Neill opponents, all but the two mentioned won. Official Unionism, whatever its colour, bestowed a high probability of success on its bearer. A large part of both the pro- and anti-O'Neill camps appear to have been traditional – might one say deferential – in their attitudes.

In this sense 'pure' O'Neillism represented only a part of an artificially inflated 'popular' O'Neillism. As alternative centres of official Unionism emerged these trends became distinct. In April 1969, four days after a series of explosions which seemed further evidence of O'Neill's weakness, he resigned. His succssor, Chichester-Clark, was to face identical difficulties.

If anything, the situation confronting Chichester-Clark and his successor, Brian Faulkner, was even more acute than that which had defeated O'Neill. Both necessarily had to resolve the question of the nature of the state in Northern Ireland, and both faced the question – in a much sharper form than O'Neill had – of handling the British. In August 1969, with the greatest reluctance, Chichester-Clark called in British troops. Subsequent events were overshadowed by the apparent imminence of Direct Rule.

Chichester-Clark and his supporters evidently took the position, like O'Neill, that the threat of Direct Rule was the major imperative governing policy and that questions about the shape of the local state must temporarily be dictated by it. For Chichester-Clark, as for O'Neill, Stormont's autonomy was the major issue. In order to preserve it the various reforms Britain was expected to demand should be pre-empted. Later the traditional form of the state could be retrieved by stealth.[143] Chichester-Clark volunteered to transfer security decisions to the army and to set up a commission of inquiry into the RUC;[144] he accepted, without argument, proposals for investigations into housing, local government and community relations. As for public order, he institutionalised distinct RUC and army jurisdiction.

Not only was gestural appeasement reproduced in identical form, but so was its opposition, which continued – as under O'Neill – to argue for party unity and the calling of Britain's bluff, coupled now with the demand for restoration of control over security.

So too, in an intensified form, were its effects. The 'gestural' changes of 1969 and after were to prove far from minimal. As Poulantzas has pointed out, one of the most significant characteristics of exceptional states is their rigidity and brittleness.[145] The cumulatively destabilising effect of reforms, especially when they reached the security forces, increased in geometric progression. Efforts to improve and centralise control, prior to 1972 at least, were to prove unsuccessful and disruptive. The RUC in particular suffered from an almost total loss of efficacy between 1969 and the imposition of Direct Rule. Other parts of the state apparatus seem to have assumed an informal or unofficial guise: the B Specials in paramilitary organisations, local government in the loyalist Vanguard movement, etc. As a result, Chichester-Clark's and later Faulkner's isolation was to be far more complete than even O'Neill's. Both became extremely susceptible to increases in Catholic militancy. Chichester-Clark's fall was directly precipitated by the first dramatic signals of the Provisional IRA's offensive. In consequence both, but especially Faulkner, were to be driven to desperate attempts to preserve their credibility in the face of accusations of weakness. Chichester-Clark pressed the Falls curfew on the army and then proposed that a 'third force' of civilian volunteers should be re-formed.[146] Faulkner's initiatives were more dramatic – an ill-prepared internment operation and Bloody Sunday. The point had been reached at which the repercussions began to impinge directly on British politics, provoking Direct Rule.

To interpret the significance of these events in relation to the history of the state as a whole we must consider for a moment one of this final period's most extraordinary features. In view of the nature of much of its original support and its isolation from the security forces, it is not surprising that the party's 'centre' collapsed and failed, later reappearing in the form of the Alliance Party. Much more remarkable was the failure of the right to take advantage of the centre's unpopularity. It was surprisingly timid throughout the period, for reasons which at the time were not altogether clear. It was even more timid when Direct Rule was actually introduced – the threatened holocaust dissolved into a series of peaceful rallies. In fact the right (and even then this did not include much of the parliamentary right) was not to launch a real offensive until the Ulster Workers' Council strike of 1974.

A clue to this curious conduct, which in a sense provides a key to the period, was provided by William Craig in an interview in 1976. Questioned about the significance of Chichester-Clark's resort to British troops, he explained, 'At that point in time I was convinced that it was only a matter of time until the parliament of Northern Ireland was abolished … once the army came in and the way they came in … here could be only one end to it.'[147] The statement has both immediate and longer-term implications.

In terms of immediate implications, Craig provides a reason for the right's quiescence. It was due not to an ideological crisis about 'ultimate loyalties' but to a calculation that the British government had the will to take the loyalists on. Militarily this would almost certainly have meant that the loyalists would be crushed. Paisley continually echoed this argument in the winter of 1971-72 in his declarations that another 1912 was not on. His own opportunistic solution was full integration – another form of words for the anticipated Direct Rule, although when this came he opposed it. Paisley's and Craig's vacillations essentially reflected not only their need to take account of the hostility of the Protestant working class to Chichester-Clark and Faulkner, but their conviction that they would soon be required to treat with whatever instrument of Direct Rule Westminster selected. Hence the constant jockeying for position within rightist politics, which made a mockery of all calls for unity. Hence too the somewhat eccentric dove-like positions[148] adopted (presumably for British consumption) by Paisley's Democratic Unionist Party shortly after its formation.

If this view held by the right, which was presumably shared by the centre too, is related to the motives behind O'Neill's movement towards general placation in 1964, a compelling continuity appears. There was a common conviction throughout Unionist politics and throughout the eight years preceding Direct Rule that a substantial British intervention in Northern Ireland was a significant probability.[149]

Any such intervention would obviously present a grave threat to the two key aspects of the Unionist position. On the one hand, it appeared to put in question the status of Northern Ireland with respect to the Republic – this was particularly evident in Wilson's earlier years. On the other, and probably more directly, it threatened Northern Ireland's independence from the rest of the United Kingdom.

Insistence on autonomy had at first been based on Britain's unreliability as an ally, evident between 1918 and 1922. Its consequences were the establishing of the B Specials, the creation of a predominantly populist political regime and the extension to an exceptional degree of the state's relative freedom from central control. Henceforth the

Unionist regime was to absorb these characteristics indelibly and to acquire a high degree of rigidity where they were concerned.

One aspect of this rigidity was a certainly inflexibility over reform, whose effects have already been described. Unionist leaders more perceptive than Chichester-Clark recognised that an end to Unionism's autonomy within the United Kingdom was undesirable because it would very likely make reformist demands upon a state too inflexible to cope with them. Hence the preference for the disastrous course of gestural, than actual, reform.

The question remains of what gave birth to a widespread belief in the likelihood of British intervention, which was contrary both to historical indications and the reality of British strategy. The fact is that this universal misperception arose from precisely the situation which Unionists sought to preserve – the autonomy of the local state. This autonomy, welcomed as it was on both sides of the water, was associated, as has been noted, with a progressively distancing of the political life of Britain and Northern Ireland. From time to time the insulation was weakened, by the war or the rise of the 'regional problem'. These difficulties failed to touch at the heart of the state, however. Unionism managed to contain them, and to reaffirm a general insulation. Partly it consisted in a mutual ignorance of the strategic realities of British and Irish political life. While Crossman could confuse St Patrick's Day with 12 July, O'Neill, Craig and Paisley could confuse the rhetoric of British politicians with their actual intentions.

This structural misperception, arising out of a specific form of inter-state relations, was the source of Ulster politics' fatal irony. In order to safeguard Northern Ireland's autonomy from what was regarded as the near inevitability of British intervention, a section of the Unionist Party actually began to dismantle the populist structures whose preservation was a large part of the regime's *raison d'être*. Directly and indirectly the move led to conditions under which the populist alliance at last began to founder and break up. The state's autonomy was designed to preclude a united Ireland and reduce dependence on an unreliable ally. Success depended on creating an alliance which would perpetuate that autonomy. Yet autonomy failed to endow

Unionists with a realistic perception of the prospects of securing external assurance that it would continue. In consequence they embarked on a strategy which not only removed its motive force but in so doing destroyed the state's autonomy itself.[150]

Notes

1. Michael Farrell, *Northern Ireland: The Orange State*, London 1975, p.291.
2. Bernadette Devlin, *The Price of My Soul*, London 1969, p. 143.
3. *Belfast Newsletter*, 3 January 1972.
4. The following two paragraphs rely on the final chapter of E. Rumpf and A.C. Hepburn, *Nationalism and Socialism in Twentieth-Century Ireland*, Liverpool 1977.
5. *Irish Times*, 3 February 1965.
6. Rumpf and Hepburn, *Nationalism and Socialism*, p. 191.
7. *NIHC*, Vol. LXX, c. 507-8.
8. Government of Northern Ireland, *Disturbances in Northern Ireland*, Cmnd 532, Belfast 1969 (hereafter 'Cameron'), p. 15.
9. The nearest approximation to such support comes from Eamon McCann's figures on enrolment at the major Catholic boys' grammar school in Derry, which increased from 725 in 1959 to 1,125 in 1967, *War and an Irish Town*, London 1974, p. 212. Michael Morgan, 'The Catholic Middle Class in Northern Ireland: Myth or Reality?', *L'Irlande Politique et sociale*, 1987, Vol. 1, No. 3, tends to support our scepticism about a 'new' Catholic middle class.
10. E.A. Aunger, 'Religion and Occupational Class in Northern Ireland', *Economic and Social Review*, 7 (1975).
11. No comparison is possible for the Catholic middle class as a whole.
12. The authors are obliged to J.H. Whyte for this point.
13. See appendix, p. 265.
14. Aunger convincingly argues that there was probably little overall change between 1961 and 1971 for this population.
15. cf., e.g., G. Routh, *Occupation and Pay in Great Britain*, Cambridge 1965, Table 1.
16. Routh's figures show that in Britain expansion in the upper white-collar sector was most rapid in the period 1931-51 (ibid.).
17. cf. F.S.L. Lyons's argument in *Ireland Since the Famine*, London 1971.
18. Campaign for Social Justice in Northern Ireland, Dungannon 1969.
19. Fermanagh Civil Rights Association, Enniskillen 1969.
20. *Irish Times*, 3 June 1965.
21. Ibid., 26 May 1966.
22. Farrell, *Orange State*, p. 240.
23. McCann, *War*, p.213 (speech by Patrick O'Hare).
24. *NIHC*, Vol. LXVIII, c. 1270. Later, apparently after press comment, the matter was taken up by O'Reilly, Diamond and Fitt (ibid., c. 1344-7).
25. *NIHC*, Vol. LXIX, c. 782.

26. *NIHC,* Vol. LXVIII, c. 1140.

27. The position of the NILP was far from a militant one, however. Agitation was directed only at securing reforms 'from above', and in any case diminished in conviction after an embarrassingly unsuccessful visit by Paul Rose in 1967 (J.A.V. Graham, 'The Consensus-Forming Strategy of the NILP', unpublished MSc thesis, Queen's University, Belfast, 1972, p. 187).

28. *NIHC,* Vol. LXVII, c. 1445.

29. McCann, *War,* p. 44.

30. Just a few weeks before the civil rights explosion the northern correspondent of *Hibernia* described the lack of discussion among northern Catholics of a recent papal encyclical on contraception. He commented, 'It must be accepted that there has not yet evolved in the north the type of middle-class liberal intellectual society which might be expected to participate [in this] controversy.' (*Hibernia,* September 1968).

31. McCann, *War,* p.47.

32. It is evident that many Catholics, even in this period, resisted mobilisation. Some of these probably retained the support for O'Neillist Unionism apparent in the surveys of R. Rose, *Governing Without Consensus,* London 1970, and I. Budge and C. O'Leary, *Belfast: Approach to Crisis,* London 1973.

33. Government of Northern Ireland, *Violence and Civil Disturbances in Northern Ireland in 1969,* Cmnd 566, Belfast 1972 (hereafter 'Scarman'), p. 27.

34. In Derry in July 1969, according to D.I. McAtamrey (RUC), 'stopping somebody in the street and asking him what religion he was' became common. 'If he gave the wrong answer, he would be assaulted' (ibid., p. 31).

35. 315 of 88,379 Protestant households were also evacuated (ibid., p. 248).

36. cf. Devlin, *Price,* p. 193.

37. For the authoritative description of the SDLP's formation, see I. McAllister, *The Northern Ireland Social Democratic and Labour Party,* London 1977, pp. 29-34.

38. Ibid., p. 101.

39. As McAllister has shown, this achievement was practically realised in a purely negative way, through the SDLP's inability to generate any concrete policies prior to Direct Rule (ibid.).

40. C. King, *Diary, 1970-74,* London 1977, p. 80; J. Haines, *The Politics of Power,* London, 1977, p. 112.

41. M. Barratt-Brown, *After Imperialism,* London 1963.

42. 'According to McGilligan's statement at the Imperial Conference in 1930, Irish capital in British industry was estimated at £90 million, and British capital in Irish industry at only half that amount.' E. Burns, *British Imperialism in Ireland,* Dublin 1931, pp. 63-4.

43. Giles Merrit, 'Britain's Poor Relation', *Financial Times,* 22 November 1976.

44. The offer was made in the course of a letter to Roosevelt, who was evidently in touch with de Valera. The letter is reprinted in W.S. Churchill, *The Second World War,* Vol. II, *Their Finest Hour,* London 1949, pp. 498-9.

45. H. Calvert, *Constitutional Law in Northern Ireland,* London 1968, pp. 95-6.

46. R.H.S. Crossman, *The Diaries of a Cabinet Minister,* Vol. III, *1968-70,* London 1977, p. 187.

47. They should have read L. O'Nuallain, *Ireland: The Finances of Partition,* Dublin 1952.

48. F. Newsam, *The Home Office,* London 1954, pp. 168-9.

49. Ibid., p. 170. Confirmation of this position is provided by Brian Faulkner: 'The relationship between Stormont and Westminster [in 1960] makes an interesting contrast with the one which developed later. As Minister of Home Affairs I was in charge of the counter-terrorist measures. Westminster was helpful and co operative at all times, providing troops when they were needed for a particular operation and making various representations to Dublin ... its role was very much a supportive one, standing aside from day-to-day decisions ...' B. Faulkner, *Memoirs of a Statesman,* London 1978, p. 24.

50. C.E.B. Brett, *Long Shadows Cast Before,* Edinburgh and London, 1978, p. 135.

51. Haines, *Politics,* pp. 121-2.

52. Southern Ireland shared both in this insulation and in an anomalous and obscure set of inter-state relations with Britain (see below also). J. Peck, *Dublin from Downing Street,* Dublin 1978, pp. 16, 26, 44-5, 116.

53. Callaghan, then Chancellor, voiced this argument with characteristic banality: 'The whole thing was a wicked French plot to bring down the dollar by bringing down the pound first and making Paris the financial capital of the world' (King, *Diary, 1965-70,* London 1972, p. 83).

54. According to John Steven, Treasury representative in Washington, 'Johnson made it quite clear to Wilson that the pound was not to be devalued' (ibid., p. 78). In fairness it should be pointed out that there is considerable doubt whether the National Plan and Wilson's structural reforms had sufficient credibility to be worth gambling on anyway. cf. A. Budd, *The Politics of Economic Planning,* Manchester 1978, pp. 115-8.

55. *Irish Times,* 25 and 29 March 1966.

56. Crossman, *Diaries,* Vol. III, p. 478.

57. *Irish Times,* 27 May 1966.

58. Brett, *Shadows.*

59. Ibid., p. 139.

60. *Sunday Times* Insight Team, *Ulster,* London 1972.

61. *Belfast Newsletter,* 27 July 1971.

62. e.g. R. Maudling, *Memoirs,* London 1978, and Faulkner, *Memoirs.*

63. Insight Team, *Ulster,* pp. 84-5, 110.

64. Ibid., pp. 109,111-12; Crossman, *Diaries,* p. 601.

65. Insight Team, *Ulster,* p. 121.

66. Ibid., p. 137.

67. Crossman, *Diaries,* pp. 463-4; emphasis added.

68. Ibid., pp. 621-3.

69. Ibid.; Insight Team, *Ulster,* p. 144.

70. Crossman, *Diaries; Belfast Newsletter,* 27 July 1971.

71. Insight Team, *Ulster*, p. 146; *Belfast Newsletter*, 27 July 1971.

72. Crossman, *Diaries*, p. 636.

73. Nor was encouraging a shift to a two-party British-style political system the answer, although it was at one time favoured both by James Callaghan, *A House Divided*, London 1973, pp. 151-2, and Quintin Hogg.

74. *Times*, 17 March 1972.

75. Insight Team, *Ulster*, p. 265.

76. The unqualified opposition of Carrington and Tuzo was reported in the *Belfast Newsletter*, 2 October 1971.

77. *NIHC*, Vol. LXXXII, c. 877-8, 1258, 1283.

78. King, *Diary, 1970-74*, pp. 99-100.

79. *Belfast Newsletter*, 15 March and 9 July 1971. (Baron Sir John Hunt should not be confused with Sir John Hunt, shortly to become Cabinet Secretary.)

80. Callaghan, *A House*, pp. 168, 174.

81. The obvious corollary of British support for this policy was British pressure on the southern government to cut the supply lines of the IRA and – when necessary – to introduce internment themselves. However, this policy was pursued ineptly and half-heartedly. Lynch was asked if he would introduce internment in the south, but not until twelve hours after it was actually implemented in the North (Peck, *Dublin*, p. 127).

82. *Belfast Newsletter*, 4 February 1972.

83. J. Leruez, *Economic Planning and Politics in Britain*, London 1975, p.238. However, in his memoirs Maudling himself claims responsibility for this recommendation, together with power-sharing and appointing Whitelaw as Secretary of State (p. 185). This seems somewhat unlikely, since, according to Faulkner, Heath had a low evaluation of Maudling's contribution to Irish strategy (*Memoirs*, p. 129).

84. H. Heclo and A. Wildavsky, *The Private Government of Public Money*, London 1974, p. 320.

85. Haines, *Politics*, p. 114.

86. Ibid., pp. 125-9.

87. On 8 February 1972 Cecil King met Whitelaw at the House of Commons. 'Whitelaw was ... very frank. Things cannot possibly be allowed to go on as they are; Stormont will have to be closed down; confidence in Faulkner has gone. They have looked at the possibility of incorporating Northern Ireland in the UK [*sic*] ... They have also considered moving the border. To both policies there are insuperable objections ... the plain impression left was that they had decided on a united Ireland ...' (King, *Diary, 1970-74*, p. 178).

88. *Times*, 28 March 1972.

89. Ibid., 17 March 1972.

90. Ibid., 28 March 1972.

91. *Irish Times*, 8 March 1972. Pressure from France seems to have been strong too (Faulkner, *Memoirs*, p. 140). There is evidence also that the Foreign Office by this time were beginning to argue that further 'drift' might irreparably destabilise southern politics (cf. Peck, *Dublin*, pp. 4,12).

92. King, *Diary*, p. 81.

93. Ibid., p. 188. King and Hugh Fraser, MP, had for some time led a campaign for the rehabilitation of Paisley. King himself found Paisley 'nearly as tall as I am ... an honest man and a nice man. It is not clear to me why Tory Ministers regard him as a sort of pariah' (p. 138). It should be pointed out that King, an easily puzzled man, was equally baffled by the unpopularity of Mosley.

94. To make matters worse, the Foreign Office only took charge of relations with southern Ireland in October 1968 as a consequence of the merger of the Foreign and Commonwealth Offices. Until Peck's arrival as ambassador in Dublin in 1970 it concerned itself only with the 'butter wrangle' and provided no intelligence for London on southern politics. Peck appears to have remedied this situation, but in 1971 responsibility for Irish affairs was shifted within the Foreign Office to a desk whose concern was defence and liaison between the FO and the Ministry of Defence. This meant that intelligence from Dublin was subsequently evaluated only militarily. (Peck, *Dublin*, pp. 45-6,116.)

95. M. Blades and D. Scott, *What Price Northern Ireland?*, pamphlet, London 1970.

96. *Fortnight*, 17 September 1971.

97. *Economist*, 6 May 1972.

98. Ibid., 2 March 1968.

99. Ibid., 23 February 1974.

100. Government of Northern Ireland, *Industrial Development in Northern Ireland*, Belfast 1973, p. 8.

101. P.D. McGovern, 'Problems of Industrial Dispersal in Northern Ireland', unpublished PhD thesis, London University 1963, p. 38.

102. *NIHC*, Vol. LXX, c. 2136. Lord's repaid a total of £768,000 before they went bankrupt. In this and other cases it was claimed that incoming firms and their directors had received additional undisclosed perquisites.

103. Government of Northern Ireland, *Development Programme, 1970-75*, Belfast 1970, p. 15.

104. Estate duty: analysis of property (proprietary shares or debentures in joint-stock companies (thousands of pounds) selected years ending 31 March):

Companies	1952	1957	1962	1967	1972	1974
NI private	1,007	754	549	879	781	985
NI public	536	324	792	941	355	282
GB private	1	4	4	4,404	6,568	7,446
GB public	2,350	2,556	4,493	4,404	6,568	7,446
Foreign	329	383	475	530	689	621

Source: Government of Northern Ireland, *Digest of Statistics*, Belfast annual.

105. G.P. Steed and M.D. Thomas, 'Regional Industrial Change in Northern Ireland', *Annals of the Association of American Geographers*, 61 (1971).

106. *Economist*, 27 July 1974.

107. McGovern, *Problems*, p. 41.

108. V. Simpson, 'Population, Employment and Urbanisation Trends

in Northern Ireland', *Journal of the Statistical and Social Inquiry Society of Ireland*, 33 (1976).

109. cf. J. Foster, 'Capitalism and the Scottish Nation' in Gordon Brown (ed.), *The Red Paper on Scotland*, Edinburgh 1975.

110. *Development Programme, 1970-75*, p. 24.

111. Callaghan, *A House*, p.88.

112. Wilson,p.80.

113. L.G.P. Freer, 'Recent Tendencies in Northern Ireland Administration' in D.C. Neill (ed.), *Devolution of Government: The Experience of Northern Ireland*, London 1953.

114. R.G. Lawrence, *The Government of Northern Ireland*, Oxford 1965.

115. T. O'Neill, *Autobiography*, London 1973, pp. xi-xii. An almost identical formulation may be found in Faulkner's *Memoirs*, p. 31.

116. Blades and Scott, 'What Price?' Whereas public anxiety was rife in the 1920s about the closeness of government and people in Northern Ireland, it re-emerged in the 1960s about the proximity of government and incoming industry. An admission by Faulkner does nothing to dispel this anxiety: 'Goodyear was another "blue chip" American firm which came to Ulster in 1966 after long negotiation ... I was led to understand at the conclusion of these ... that if I ever decided to get out of politics the Chairman of Goodyear would have a job waiting for me.' (*Memoirs*, p. 31) As it turned out, he did.

117. *Belfast Newsletter*, 30 March 1965.

118. H. Wilson, *The Labour Government, 1964-70: A Personal Record*, London 1971, p. 75.

119. *Belfast Newsletter*, 5 October 1964.

120. The most notable of these concerned the siting of the new University of Ulster and Craigavon New Town. In the case of the university Warnock observed, 'a very reluctant Unionist party was compelled to vote against its intentions' (*Irish Times*, 13 May 1965). Craigavon's siting was opposed by North Armagh farmers (ibid., 17 December 1965). In order to deflect opposition to the university proposal, O'Neill moved his Minister of Development (William Craig) to Home Affairs (ibid., 1 May 1965).

121. In a leader the *Newsletter* argued that such a meeting in no way threatened the constitutional position (20 November 1964).

122. The first three speeches referred to are to be found in T. O'Neill, *Ulster at the Crossroads*, London 1969. The last was reported in the *Irish Times*, 20 April 1967. A similar sentiment was expressed in an interview with Mervyn Pauley in the *Newsletter*, 12 January 1965.

123. *Irish Times*, 18 March 1965.

124. *Economist*, 2 June 1966.

125. *Irish Times*, 16 June 1966.

126. Ibid., 29 June 1966.

127. Ibid., 23 July 1966. The vehicles carrying water cannon had been adapted to this function only shortly before; cf. Scarman, p. 7.

128. Ibid., 20 June 1966.

129. Ibid., 29 August 1966.

130. Ibid., 24 September 1966.

131. Ibid., 1 May 1967.

132. Ibid., 8 May 1967.

133. *Belfast Newsletter*, 23 November 1968.

134. Ibid., 10 December 1968.

135. *NIHC*, Vol. LXXIII, c. 1454.

136. Scarman, p. 7.

137. Ibid., p. 19.

138. Quoted in *NIHC*, Vol. LXXXIV, c. 48.

139. F.W. Boal and R.H. Buchanan, 'The 1969 Northern Ireland General Election', *Irish Geography*, VI (1969).

140. One of the present authors argued similarly some years ago, cf. P. Gibbon, 'Ulster: The Dialectic of Religion and Class', *New Left Review*, 55 (1969). Boal and Buchanan's interpretation is close to this: 'These are slender indications of change within the Unionist Party yet ... they reveal basic differences relating to class and region ... which could be exploited by a party concerned more specifically with policies of economic and social development' ('The 1969 Election').

141. 'It is a long time since the word "class" has been bandied about so freely [here]' – R. Porter (O'Neillist), *Times*, 18 February 1969.

142. e.g. Victoria: Unionist 9,249, NILP 2,972, Paisleyite Unionist, 2,489; North Antrim: Unionist 9,142, Paisleyite Unionist 3,241.

143. This was Callaghan's interpretation in *A House*, p. 96.

144. Ibid., p. 51;*Belfast Newsletter*, 27 July 1971.

145. N. Poulantzas, *Crisis of the Dictatorships*, London 1976.

146. *NIHC*, Vol. LXXVI, c. 1988-2000.

147. R. Deutsch, interview with William Craig, *Etudes Irlandaises*, 1 (1976), p 163

148. e.g. its calls for dissociation of the Orange Order and Unionist Party, or, more remarkably, Paisley's interview on RTE in November 1971 (*Irish Times*, 29 November 1971).

149. cf. Faulkner on Callaghan: 'It was soon clear that Callaghan was determined to use any military involvement to allow him to intervene decisively in the political situation ...' *Memoirs*, p. 62). The unreality of this judgement is itself acknowledged in the next sentence: '... though he did not put to us anything he thought we ought to be doing but were failing to do.' (ibid.).

150. Faulkner effectively acknowledges this argument in his autobiography: '... we were too absorbed in our own affairs. The only real contacts with Westminster were ministerial. There was precious little other contact because Westminster was not interested in Northern Ireland and similarly Northern Ireland was not interested in Westminster. The important place politically was Stormont. And I think that was a mistake, a weakness. It led politicians in Northern Ireland into illusions of self-sufficiency, of taking part in a sovereign parliament. It created separatist tendencies. It also meant that the crisis of 1969 hit an unprepared Westminster between the eyes. Both sides must accept responsibility for that situation.' (*Memoirs*, p. 26). On this whole period, see Ken Bloomfield's illuminating *Stormont in Crisis: A Memoir*, Belfast 1994, especially chapters 5 and 6.

6 The Twilight of the Union?
1972–1993

The nature of the classical Unionist regime had been determined by the perception of Britain as an unreliable ally to be guarded against by the construction of a regional structure of government with a predominantly populist and sectarian flavour. The regime had disintegrated in the 1960s as O'Neill and his successor calculated that reforms were necessary to stave off a feared British intervention which would end autonomy and re-open vistas of more fundamental constitutional change. As the state apparatus had represented the consolidation of a particular type of communalist alliance, its disintegration faced Unionism with the formidable, in fact insurmountable, task of constructing another set of alliances on which to refound a local regime.

But the conditions under which this task was to be accomplished were radically different from those of the period between 1918 and 1920. At that time, whatever reservations sections of the British government may have had about military and financial support for the emergent regime in Belfast, it was able to accomplish this and diminish its own direct involvement in Northern Ireland by relying on the ability of the Unionist Party to deliver a relatively stable if not altogether legitimate regime. The very fact that after August 1969 the British were again involved in the direct governance of the North meant that from a British point of view Unionism's usefulness had radically diminished. As return to a Stormont-type regime was now ruled out, Unionism was faced with a politically impossible task: that of maintaining its monopolistic control of the Protestant electorate while denied the possibility of establishing its own structures of government in Northern Ireland.

The dominant logic of Unionist political argument had been that the only secure defence of the Union was the existence of the particular type of exclusivist political regime. The anti-populist concerns about the ultimately destabilising effects of this approach had never resulted in an alternative strategic conception for defending the Union. It had simply warned that populist extremism could undermine the state by forcing British intervention. Now that the institutional basis for the populist alliance had been removed with the end of Stormont, Unionist politics inevitably entered into a period of ideological and institutional flux. For the first time anti-populist impulses had a distinct institutional form – Faulknerite Unionism – which argued that the preservation of the Union and its increasingly crucial material subvention meant unheard-of political compromises with reformist nationalism.

This, however, was a strategy that implicitly made the maintenance of the Union dependent on a process of political bargaining with a political force, the Social Democratic and Labour Party, that had adopted a policy, 'Towards a New Ireland', calling for a British declaration in favour of eventual Irish unity and for an interim system of 'joint sovereignty' involving Britain and the Republic.[1] Faulknerite Unionism, led as it was by a former opponent of O'Neillism and the architect of internment, was a less than enthusiastic convert to a strategy of accommodation and was strongly challenged by those sections of the Unionist Party linked to William Craig's Vanguard movement with its paramilitary appendages that mimicked the mass Unionist mobilisations against Home Rule. The Provisional IRA's adoption of an intense bombing campaign in the spring of 1971, the resulting disastrous decision to introduce internment in August 1971 and the consequent spiralling of deaths created hankerings for former glories which were little more than embattled nostalgia. Thus the *Belfast Newsletter* claimed that IRA violence had recreated the pan-class unity of the period of Carson and the UVF:

> They [the Provisionals] have brought together with one mind and one purpose all sections of pro-government opinion, from the humble labourer to the clergyman in his pulpit, from shipyard technician to surgeon in a hospital.[2]

In fact, despite the intensification of IRA violence and the evidence that British governments would not exclude the possibility of negotiating with the Provisionals, it was increasingly obvious that the vision of Unionist unity was a chimera. The Protestant right was clearly divided over how to respond to Direct Rule. Paisley, not for the last time, would demonstrate an unwillingness to confront the British state directly, and to the discomfort of many of his supporters argued for full integration of Northern Ireland into the Westminster system. William Craig's Vanguard movement most clearly allied itself with the emerging paramilitary organisations and was prepared to contemplate an independent Ulster if that was the only way of defending it from republicanism and what was described as 'a Conservative party, tired, even bored with Irish politics from which they wish to extricate themselves'.[3]

Five separate Unionist parties and groupings were represented in the Northern Ireland Assembly elected in June 1973. The British government's Green Paper, *The Future of Northern Ireland*, published in October 1972, and the subsequent White Paper, *Northern Ireland Constitutional Proposals*, published in March 1973, made clear that any new settlement must be based on some form of executive 'power-sharing' and would have an 'Irish dimension': 'new institutional arrangements for consultation and co-operation on an all-Ireland basis'.[4] William Craig's failure to persuade the Ulster Unionist Council to reject the White Paper outright led to his leaving the Unionist Party and the formation of the Vanguard Unionist Progressive Party (VUPP). The right inside the Unionist Party, which cultivated the Vanguard movement with its paramilitary supporters as a means of establishing dominance, was not about to cede control to Faulkner and, just as it had resisted earlier attempts by Paisley to form a new party, stayed inside and mobilised opinion against 'capitulation' to Britain's 'pro-republican' stratagems.

In the campaign for the Assembly election prominent Unionists refused to pledge support for the party's manifesto, which provided grudging acceptance of the White Paper. The extent of Unionist Party resistance to the Faulkner position was understated in the election outcome as many Unionist voters' traditional loyalty to the party delivered a reluctant vote to Faulknerite candidates. The new anti-White Paper coalition of dissident Unionists, Paisleyites, VUPP and loyalists clearly predominated in the Protestant electorate, with 35.4 per cent of the total vote to the Faulknerites' 26.5 per cent: 27 seats to 23. The Faulknerites were reduced to warning that the alternative to the White Paper was 'widespread disorder' and that their opponents were 'flirting with a new brand of Sinn Feinism'.[5]

Table 5 *Northern Ireland Assembly Election Results, 1973*

	Votes			
	Number	Percentage of total	Number of cands.	Number of seats won
Anti-White Paper				
Unionists	89,759	12.4	15	11
DUP	78,228	10.8	17	8
Vanguard	75,759	10.5	25	7
Other loyalists	11,660	1.6	8	1
Total loyalist	255,406	35.4	65	27
Faulkner Unionists	191,729	26.5	41	23
Alliance	66,541	9.2	35	8
NILP	18,675	2.6	18	1
SDLP	159,773	22.1	28	19
Republican Clubs	13,064	1.8	10	0
Independents/Others	17,053	2.4	13	0
Total non-loyalist	466,835	64.6	145	51

Source: Richard Rose, *Northern Ireland: A Time of Choice*, London 1976, p. 30.

The central problem for the section of the Unionist Party prepared to accommodate the British government was that its argument that the Union could not be secured except through the mechanisms in the White Paper ignored the degree to which the Union itself had for many become identified with the strategy of populist Protestant control of the state. The communalist assumptions that underlay the political culture of the North meant that a Union which could be only cemented by sharing power with the SDLP and giving some form of institutional recognition to the 'Irish dimension' was not going to enthuse its supposed beneficiaries.

Such a radical shift in deeply rooted assumptions was made all the more unlikely given the frenetic levels of violence which were convulsing Northern Ireland in 1972 and 1973, years in which the collapse of the Unionist regime gave rise to the most unrealistic of expectations and the most paranoid of fears. The crescendo of killings was never to be repeated: the two years account for over a quarter of all deaths from political violence between 1969 and 1990.[6] Although the Unionist right put the defeat of the IRA at the top of its demands on the British government, and the two years saw the most intense republican onslaught on the police and the army, the largest group of casualties was Catholic civilians.[7] These 241 deaths were the starkest indication of the increasingly rampant and autonomous logic of Protestant paramilitarism.

Just as the construction of the state apparatuses in 1919-21 had involved the incorporation of unofficial Protestant violence, Direct Rule, coming as it did after a period in which the state's security apparatus had lost all efficacy, meant that the Unionist Party was riven between those who were prepared to accept that repression could no longer be directly controlled and those who hankered after a return to untrammelled control by 'Ulstermen'. The party that was to benefit most from the fissures within the Unionist Party was the Democratic Unionist Party (DUP). From its performance in the Assembly elections in 1973, when it won 10.8 per cent of the vote, only slightly more than Craig's VUPP, it quickly emerged as the only significant competitor for a Unionist Party which had jettisoned its 'compromisers'. The DUP's progress, however, should not be allowed to obscure the more fundamental dilemmas of all varieties of Unionism after the abolition of Stormont and the clear indication from Britain that it would never be resurrected.

These are apparent even at the high-point of Unionist revanchism, the destruction of the power-sharing Executive by the Ulster Workers' Council (UWC) strike in the spring of 1974. The continuing slippage of Faulknerite Unionism was clear in November 1973 when a resolution opposing power-sharing was almost passed at the Ulster Unionist Council.[8] The members of the new power-sharing Executive met the British and Irish governments at Sunningdale Civil Service College in Berkshire in December 1973. All hope for accommodationist Unionism evaporated when to the cross of power-sharing was added the new affliction of a vaguely defined Council of Ireland which the SDLP, to the exultant choruses of the Unionist right, depicted as a crucial mechanism for easing the transition to a united Ireland.

In January 1974 Faulkner resigned from the Unionist Party after being defeated at a meeting of the Ulster Unionist Council on a vote on the Council of Ireland.[9] His new Unionist Party of Northern Ireland was routed in the February General Election when the various components of the Unionist right won eleven of the twelve Northern Ireland seats. The right had won 51 per cent of the total vote to 13 per cent for the Faulkner Unionists. It had successfully depicted power-sharing as an integral part of a 'republican' agenda and not as a means of consolidating the state. (A National Opinion Polls survey carried out a month after the election found that 78 per cent of Catholics strongly approved of power-sharing but only 28 per cent of Protestants did so.[10]) The fact that the various parties supporting power-sharing had fielded opposing candidates increased the impression of disarray and deepened the rout.

The whole power-sharing structure had become untenable. Apart from its clear separation from the bulk of Unionist opinion, it was internally divided over the unfinished business of Sunningdale, the exact structures and powers of the Council of Ireland. In April the recently formed UWC demanded fresh elections within a month or threatened to call a strike.[11] The UWC had developed out of an earlier organisation, the Loyalist Association of Workers, established early in 1970 in some of the key concentrations of Protestant workers spanning traditional bastions like the shipyard and aircraft factories but also including power stations and the branch plants of 1950s and 60s inward investment.[12] The strike began in the middle of May after a loyalist motion calling for the rejection of

Sunningdale was defeated in the Assembly.[13] Within a fortnight it had brought the internal divisions in the Executive and between it and the Labour Secretary of State, Merlyn Rees, to such a level that Faulkner and the Unionist members of the Executive resigned when Rees refused to listen to their pleas that he should meet the UWC.

The UWC had clear links with the main Protestant para-military organisations, the Ulster Defence Association and the Ulster Volunteer Force, and its success was clearly dependent on the intimidatory tactics of these organisations in the strike's earliest stages and on the support of groups of key workers in the power stations. Nevertheless the claim made by the SDLP, at the time and ever since, that the strike could have been defeated by a resolute response from the Wilson government ignored the degree to which Harold Wilson and some of his key advisers had decided that the Executive had been fatally wounded by the results of the February election and its own deep divisions over the Council of Ireland issue. There was no inclination to challenge the advice coming from the army command in Northern Ireland that it would be counter-productive to use force against the strikers to defend a regime that would collapse because of its own acute internal divisions. A British general serving in Northern Ireland at the time has subsequently revealed that the military evaluation was that the Executive was 'doomed before the strike ever began'. He went on to comment on Rees's conduct during the strike:

> I think it was a mercy that Merlyn Rees was there at the time. He didn't make any decisions of any kind. If you'd had a decisive man who arrested the strikers on the first day it would have created chaos and brought the province to the point of no return.[14]

Unionism After the Strike: Bombast Versus Minimalism

The UWC victory was to prove a pyrrhic one. Those leading loyalist politicians like Paisley, Craig and the Unionist Party leader, Harry West, who had collaborated with the UWC in the early resistance to the Executive had initially been opposed to the idea of a strike and had only come round when they were presented with a *fait accompli*. Indeed, Paisley had chosen to be in Canada on pastoral business in the early days of the stoppage. The implicit fear of a radical British response based on exasperation was a reasonable one. Harold Wilson's provocative television broadcast in which he referred to the strike as a 'rebellion' and the loyalists as 'spongers' was no prelude to strong action – in fact it solidified support for the strike.[15] But Wilson's decision not to support the Executive with the army did not indicate any desire to accommodate loyalist demands and he returned to his impulses of 1971 and the belief that no solution was possible except in the context of withdrawal. A Cabinet sub-committee which he chaired held meetings from the end of the strike into 1975. A number of options including withdrawal and repartition were considered. Wilson's own inclination was certainly for withdrawal and he appears to have given it up reluctantly only after the Irish government responded to rumours of it with total consternation.[16] Loyalists' euphoria in the aftermath of the strike blinded them to the fact that, although they could defeat an initiative which depended on Unionist involvement, they could not dictate their own terms to the British government. Their demands for fresh elections to the Assembly were ignored and the Westminster consensus remained firm that there could be no legislative devolution without power-sharing.

The strike also pushed the SDLP in a more nationalist direction. Although the Executive had been increasingly crippled by its own internal divisions, the fact that the *coup de grâce* was delivered by the strike was to have unfortunate long-term consequences for the chances of any internal settlement. An important sector of the party was left permanently embittered by the manner in which the Executive had been brought down and convinced itself that if the British government had 'faced down' the loyalists in the early days of the strike the Sunningdale package could have been saved. Although such resolve would most likely have brought the Executive to a bloody end rather than a collapse, the long-term effect of rampant loyalism was to increase the weight within the SDLP of those who increasingly looked outside the province for the source of political progress.

The second half of the 1970s saw a strong Paisleyite challenge to the Official Unionist Party's predominance in Protestant politics. Tactically astute, Paisley focused on the

increasing evidence of interval divisions as the Unionists
attempted to adjust to life without a local state apparatus to
exploit. Still reeling from a recent history of bitter internal
divisions, the Unionist Party appeared a less than formidable
opponent. It was faced with a major strategic dilemma with
regard to the DUP challenge. The party's post-strike
leadership had waged a common struggle with the DUP and
Vanguard against the 'compromisers' led by Faulkner. They
expressed the common loyalist outrage at the end of
Stormont and at any British proposals to reconstitute
governing institutions on a non-majoritarian basis.
Ideologically, therefore, it appeared that there was little to
differentiate them from the DUP. This inevitably advantaged
the smaller party as its leader had an established reputation
as a vigorous opponent of any reforms and this gave it the
initiative when the larger party's recent history had been one
of inner turmoil on reform. It was easy for the Paisleyites to
depict themselves as the force that had 'saved Ulster' from
the compromising vacillations of the Unionist Party. As long
as the Unionists committed themselves to the impossiblist
demand for majority-rule devolution, therefore, they fought
on a ground intrinsically favourable to the DUP.

Yet, unattractive as this may have been to the more astute
members of the party, the alternatives were equally fraught
with difficulties. During the period of the Northern Ireland
Convention, elected in May 1975 and seen by the British
government as a means of keeping local political forces
harmlessly occupied whilst consideration was given to a
possibility of some new departure in policy, the Vanguard
leader proposed the idea of an 'emergency coalition' which
would include the SDLP. Craig's iconoclasm reflected the
febrile conditions of the time when the year-long British
'truce' with the IRA produced both an intensification of
sectarian killings and a widespread belief that it had decided
on withdrawal.[17] Fear that such a stratagem would be
justified by reference to loyalist intransigence was what
underlay this conversion to accommodation. Nevertheless,
such calculations were anathema not only to the bulk of
Unionist Convention members and the DUP but also to a
majority of his own party. The idea was repudiated,
destroying Vanguard and effectively denying Craig any
future role in Unionist politics. He lost his East Belfast seat to

Peter Robinson of the DUP in the 1979 General Election.

But, if the Unionists clove to the majority report of the Convention which rejected power-sharing as an unwarranted departure from British standards, they were then faced with the clear rejection of this by the British government. This left them vulnerable to DUP charges that they were unwilling to take the 'resolute' action necessary to 'restore democracy'. The main Unionist party increasingly shifted to a constitutionally minimalist position best articulated by its leader at Westminster, James Molyneaux.* This shift was characterised by its rather negative and implicit nature and assisted by the more bombastic excesses of a DUP which was 'dizzy with success' in the mid-1970s.[18]

The DUP had been the force behind the creation of a United Unionist Action Council (UUAC) whose purpose was to end Direct Rule and implement the Convention Report. The UUAC, which also included the anti-Craig elements of Vanguard and the remnants of the UWC, aimed to use strike action to force British acceptance of majority rule and even tougher security policies. The strike launched on 3 May 1977 had failed miserably within ten days. The UUAC had claimed that the government was 'attempting to destroy the traditional Unionist conception of the Union',[19] but there was clearly no Protestant unity over demands to confront a British government to restore majority rule. Unionist Party opposition to the strike on the basis that it threatened the Union and was motivated by a desire for an independent Ulster clearly struck a chord amongst a Protestant community, all sections of which were well aware of the increasingly crucial role of the British financial subvention in maintaining their incomes and employment.

It was becoming increasingly clear that while there was a substantial constituency for a politics of demagogy and confrontation, it had no hegemonic capacity precisely because of many Protestants' reservations about confrontation with the British state. The Unionist Party benefited from an increasing Protestant willingness to live with Direct Rule as a basic framework of governance. Although in the short term this was a sustainable position, it held major strategic problems.

Wilson's resignation and the disappearance of the Callaghan administration's parliamentary majority in early

* See Biographical Note on p. 261.

1977 produced a conjunctural strengthening of the Unionist Party and of the political line supported by Molyneaux. Although much in awe of the new Unionist MP for South Down, Enoch Powell, and his overly cerebral support for integration as a means of removing the constitutional uncertainty that was supposedly the main motivating factor behind the IRA campaign, Molyneaux knew the depth of distrust of Westminster politics in his party made full-blown integrationism a recipe for internal strife. His means of reconciling devolutionists and integrationists in the party was the notion of a form of administrative devolution which could be sold either as a staging point to full-blooded legislative devolution or as part of a process of democratising Direct Rule, i.e. as a crypto-integrationist measure. Although Molyneaux was able to detect the fatuity of the pro-devolutionist optimism of the party's declining leader and Stormont left-over, Harry West, his own position failed to engage with the deeply held consensus in the British political elite that Direct Rule was temporary and that some form of local political compromise had to be achieved.

The embattled Callaghan administration, dependent on Unionist support at Westminster, increased the number of Northern Ireland seats in the House of Commons to seventeen, thus convincing the SDLP that both the major British parties were working on an integrationist agenda. The result was an acceleration of the party's shift away from demands that the British implement the Sunningdale package, a clearly impossible task given the absence of any substantial Unionist party interested in power-sharing, towards a focus on the need for a fundamental recasting of Anglo-Irish relations over the heads of the Unionists. By the time of its 1978 conference a motion calling for British disengagement was passed with only two dissenters.[20] However the traditionalist tone of the motion reflected the temporary pressure on the SDLP of the newly formed and fundamentalist Irish Independence Party and the party's rising star, John Hume, was determined that it should not be pushed back into what would be perceived outside Northern Ireland as the rigid obverse of Ulster Unionism. Hume's developing strategy of enlisting British involvement through inter-national pressure, not for withdrawal as traditionally conceived but for a recasting of Anglo-Irish relations which would force a fundamental re-evaluation of Unionist positions, would prove a formidable long-term threat to Unionist minimalism.

Molyneaux's variety of Unionism, while it was well-placed to extract advantage from the necessities of a declining Labour government, was bereft of the ideological and political resources to guarantee its influence on British governments in the longer term. Unable, and most likely unwilling, to challenge the deep reluctance in the party to any form of co-government with the SDLP, its only 'strategy' for dealing with Northern Ireland Catholics was not to challenge the benefits of Direct Rule by a flagrant yearning for the return of Stormont. Against the devotees of the old Stormont regime it was prepared to see a radical diminution of Protestant political power in Northern Ireland, not as the necessary effect of some type of political accommodation with the SDLP but rather through the denial of substantive legislative powers to any new representative institution. But even if a settlement based on the purely negative appeal of the absence of capacities for Protestant rule over Catholics had been acceptable to the SDLP, which it clearly was not, the shift towards a Unionist strategy dependent on cultivating support at Westminster was less than reassuring to many members of Molyneaux's own party who shared with the DUP a deep distrust of 'English' politicians.

Molyneaux's Unionism clearly recognised the reactionary utopianism of demands for a return to majority rule and went with the grain of a predominant Protestant inclination to find Direct Rule the best possible shell for 'business as usual'. Its blind spot was the almost total absence of any accommodation to the political forces represented by the SDLP, not to mention the increasingly sharply delineated reservoir of support for revolutionary nationalism. Unable to break from the reactive loyalist reflexes of the late 1960s which had depicted all demands for reform as the thin end of a nationalist wedge, his type of Unionism continued to reduce SDLP politics to its nationalist dimension, establishing to its own satisfaction that this made any form of partnership government impossible. While it may have been true that a consociational solution to communalist conflicts is extremely difficult when the state whose power is to be shared is not accepted as legitimate by one of the key communities, Official Unionism represented a soothing refuge in doctrines of national identity and sovereignty which ignored more fundamental realities of relative social and political power.

The civil rights mobilisations, the collapse of the state and the subsequent restructuring of nationalist politics into much more effective constitutional and increasingly formidable paramilitary forces were processes that no longer-term British strategy for Northern Ireland could ignore. From the Green Paper in 1972 some sort of role for the Irish government in the management of the problem was clearly envisaged. Initially it was thought that a largely gestural Irish dimension and power-sharing would be sufficient to get the type of settlement which would allow the devoutly desired reduction of direct involvement. The blow dealt this approach by the UWC strike did not prove terminal and until the early 1980s, in so far as a strategy existed, it was based on devolution, power-sharing and some institutional expression of the 'Irish dimension'. But whatever intellectual or moral substance this strategy had was increasingly attenuated in the late 1970s. With a Unionist political universe split between minimalism and bombast and the SDLP increasingly looking outside the North for the catalyst of change, British attempts at political movement looked more and more like a triumph of hope over experience. Ironically, it was the political leader in whom Molyneaux invested most hope for the realisation of his agenda who would radically break with the consensus on power-sharing devolution, but only to embark on a path far removed from his minimalism.

As leader of the opposition Margaret Thatcher had appointed her friend and close political ally Airey Neave as spokesman on Northern Ireland. His clear scepticism about the possibility of power-sharing and his sympathy for Molyneaux' s minimalism led many observers, including an increasingly frustrated SDLP leadership, to expect a pro-Unionist administration when the Conservatives came to power in 1979. Molyneaux had played a key role drawing up the Northern Ireland section of the Tory manifesto which contained one significant innovation: 'In the absence of devolved government we seek to establish one or more elected regional councils with a wide range of powers over local services.'[21] Neave's murder by the INLA during the General Election campaign was not the fundamental reason why the new government quickly turned its back on these minimalist and integrationist assumptions in favour of another attempt to launch a devolutionist initiative. Two factors, security policy and US pressure, would have crucial effects on Thatcher's approach and pushed her towards taking the initiative.

Ultimately, events like the IRA's murder of Lord Mountbatten and the separate killing of eighteen British soldiers on the same day, 27 August 1979, determined Thatcher's radical break first with minimalism and then with the whole devolutionary approach. As her autobiography makes clear, her 'profoundly Unionist' instincts did not prevent a fundamental incompatibility of approach emerging with even her closest Unionist allies.[22] She points out that, 'I did not believe that security could be disentangled from wider political issues.'[23] One of these issues was her conviction – in no way an iconoclastic one in the policy area – that, 'Much depends on the willingness and ability of the political leaders of the Republic to co-operate effectively with our intelligence, security forces and courts.'[24] She also accepted that a key element in dealing with the IRA 'requires that the minority should support or at least acquiesce in the constitutional framework of the state in which they live'.[25] Her major problem was that neither collaboration with the south in the security area nor a tying of a substantial majority of the Catholic population to the state could be obtained by the minimalist legacy of the Neave approach, whilst she does appear to have shared his deep scepticism concerning the possibility of achieving a power-sharing compromise.

It was this combination of a felt need for action, initially, if only to respond to US pressure, together with a less than wholehearted commitment to devolution, that inevitably impelled her towards an inter-governmental approach first manifest in her Dublin summit with Charles Haughey in December 1980. For Molyneaux such a deviation was to be explained by a Prime Minister too involved in other affairs of state adequately to resist manipulation by those in the Foreign Office and their allies in the Northern Ireland Office whose goal was to use devolution and improved relations with the Republic as a means of ultimately dissolving the Union.

Molyneaux's prolonged presence at Westminster had not significantly undermined the narrowing influence of an Ulster perspective on his view of Thatcher. The very factor that encouraged Unionist faith – her attachment to an absolutist conception of sovereignty – blinded them to her capacity to agree, once she satisfied that legal sovereignty was maintained, to contemplate radical institutional innovations in the way Northern Ireland was governed within the Union. Her radicalism of approach to many central issues in the British polity appears not to have encouraged any apprehension in her most enthusiastic Ulster supporter.[26]

The void at the core of Unionist minimalism should be clear. If it was, to a degree, successful in providing an alternative to the impossiblist dream of a return to Stormont and the accompanying Paisleyite bombast and theatricality, it was nevertheless an inadequate position to cement a union with a ruling class that, if it had any coherent position on Northern Ireland, believed fervently in doing whatever was necesary to minimise its own involvement. The post-1968 mobilisation and organisation of the Catholic population demanded institutional expression, even if the basic objective was, like Thatcher's, the defence of the Union.

'As Much as Can Be Achieved in One Generation'

Thatcher's decision to have her first Secretary of State for Northern Ireland, Humphrey Atkins, launch another political initiative in November 1979 was above all a response to the intensification of pressure from the United States orchestrated by Speaker O'Neill and Senators Kennedy and Moynihan. Using the Carter administration's stated concern to link foreign policy to concern for human rights, the campaign had persuaded the State Department to suspend the sale of hand-guns to the RUC in August 1979. As Adrian Guelke has noted, 'This was an alarming development for the British government.'[27]

Airey Neave's residual influence was clear in the ruling out of any discussion of the 'Irish dimension', which provoked a split in the SDLP and the resignation of its leader, Gerry Fitt, who favoured dialogue with the Unionists, even under restrictive conditions, and the choice of Hume as his successor. The erratic progress of the talks was ample testimony for those on the Tory right who scorned the whole consociational consensus at Westminster. The main Unionist party refused to participate, claiming that the talks were a 'gimmick', with Powell warning that they were designed to separate Northern Ireland from the rest of the UK.[28] Atkins was forced to retract the exclusion of the 'Irish dimension', but although the SDLP then participated and Paisley adopted a publicly supportive posture, the chasm between his party's continued support for majority rule and the minimum acceptable to the SDLP ensured the effective collapse of the initiative by November 1980.

Thatcher had already been encouraged by Charles Haughey, at their first meeting in May 1980, to adopt a radically pro-active role:

> He kept on drawing the parallel, which seemed to me an unconvincing one, between the solution I had found on the Rhodesian problem and the approach to be pursued in Northern Ireland. Whether this was Irish blarney or calculated flattery I was not sure.[29]

The collapse of the Atkins talks came just after the beginning of the first hunger strike by republican prisoners demanding political status, and with growing international pressure an attempt was made to minimise the effects of this by a largely gestural concession to an inter-governmental approach to the conflict. The 'historic' Dublin summit of December 1980, the first Prime Minister-led delegation of British ministers to the Irish capital since partition, was subsequently judged by Thatcher to 'have done more harm than good'.[30]

In the joint communiqué after the talks Thatcher acknowledged Britain's 'unique relationship' with Ireland; she permitted the formation of joint study groups to find ways of expressing this relationship in 'new institutional structures'. The reference in the communiqué to the 'totality of relationships within these islands' which was to be considered at their next summit was exploited by Haughey to imply that constitutional issues would be discussed. As Thatcher bitterly notes, 'It was a red rag to the Unionist bull.' Paisley, who had trounced the two Unionist Party candidates in the 1979 European election, taking 29.8 per cent of the total vote compared to their 21.9 per cent,[31] and having failed to get a devolutionary set-up through a temporary 'statesman' pose, now returned to his more effective role as harbinger of imminent betrayal, launching a major mobilisation of disorientated loyalists that combined paramilitary histrionics and bathetic attempts to recreate the spirit of previous mobilisations, the so-called 'Carson Trail'. The only significant effect of this was to predispose the government to demonstrate its toughness to the loyalists by showing a hard face to the demands of the republican hunger strikers.

As Thatcher notes of the effects of the hunger strikes: 'This was the beginning of a time of troubles. The IRA was on the advance politically.'[32] The advance reflected in part the growing weight of a northern leadership cadre in the republican movement centred on Gerry Adams. Adams had been arguing since the mid-1970s that there was a need for more than a military machine to obtain republican objectives. An 'armed struggle' without a significant political dimension risked increasing isolation and ultimate defeat. Adams was interested in a shift in the relative weight of the political and military wings of the republican movement, which would see Sinn Fein develop as a serious political force on both sides of the border.[33] His prescriptions had increasing influence for two main reasons. One was the effect of the disastrous 'truce' of 1974-75 in discrediting the southern-dominated leadership of the movement, which had been predicting an imminent British withdrawal. When it became apparent that the British government had used the 'truce' to embark on a strategy of 'criminalisation' manifest in the removal of political status for those convicted of terrorist offences, the old leadership was discredited and the way was clear for the IRA's adoption of a 'long war' strategy by which a slimmed-down and restructured paramilitary organisation would be complemented by a more assertive political wing.[34] Both were prepared to accept that 'victory' might not come for decades and would demand a more sophisticated combination of violence and politics than the Provisionals had until then been capable of mounting. The second factor was the hunger strikes which developed out of the republican prisoners' refusal to accept the removal of political status. These created the conditions for a political breakthrough more rapidly than republican modernisers could have hoped for.

The first wave of hunger strikes petered out before the end of 1980. A second, more determined wave led by Bobby Sands, the Provisionals' commanding officer in the H-Blocks of Long Kesh prison near Belfast, began in March 1981. As early as November 1980 the Provisional-led campaign in favour of political status was turning out parades comparable in size to the great civil rights marches. The hunger-strikers and their supporters, as Richard Kearney put it, 'articulated a tribal voice of martyrdom, deeply embedded in the Gaelic, Catholic nationalist tradition'.[35] Thatcher and her advisers were well aware of the potentially radical effects of the deaths of the hunger-strikers and she even declared her admiration for the courage of Sands and his comrades.[36] 'Lines of communication' which had existed between British governments and the Provisionals since the early 1970s were re-opened with Thatcher's authorisation and there was a period of 'frenzied contact' aimed at a settlement.[37] But as Thatcher had ruled out any concession which could be represented as granting political status, deaths, ten in all, were inevitable.

The new possibilities for the Provisionals were first manifest when Sands won a by-election for the Westminster constituency of Fermanagh-South Tyrone on 9 April 1981, the fortieth day of his hunger strike. This major propaganda victory was soon complemented by the election of two other hunger-strikers in the Republic's General Election in June and, after Sands's death, of his election agent for the Fermanagh-South Tyrone constituency. Despite Thatcher's claim that the end of the hunger strikes in October 1981 was 'a significant defeat for the IRA',[38] the rapid political progress of Sinn Fein told another story. James Prior's 'rolling devolution proposals' provided the first mechanism for a registering of its new-found political weight in the North's Catholic community. Banished to Northern Ireland in the reshuffle of September 1981, the idea of yet another attempt at a devolutionary settlement was very much Prior's own initiative. Thatcher, after intervening to cut out a chapter in the White Paper dealing with relations with the Republic, still let it be known that she thought the venture was worthless.[39] In fact Prior's scheme had unintended effects that would prove much worse, rather than merely worthless, from Thatcher's perspective. A Sinn Fein vote of 64,191 first preferences,

10.1 per cent of the total, in the October 1982 Assembly elections compared favourably with the showing of a demoralised and worried SDLP which did comparatively poorly with 118,891 first preferences, 18.8 per cent of the total poll.[40] Fears of the imminent demise of constitutional nationalism became commonplace in London and Dublin.

By creating the conditions for the first significant political registering of what a subsequent Secretary of State called 'the terrorist community', the hunger strikes shifted Thatcher from a largely negative and reactive relation to the existing policy consensus on Northern Ireland at Westminster. Sir David Goodall, who had recently been seconded from the Foreign Office to the Cabinet Office, provides a precise point of departure:

> One evening in December 1982, after a dinner at 10 Downing Street ... I found myself improbably talking over a post-prandial whisky to Mrs Thatcher, about Ireland, and the sad fact that the only place in the world where British soldiers' lives were being lost in anger was in the United Kingdom. 'If we get back next time,' she said, 'I think I would like to do something about Ireland.'[41]

'Something' meant a decisive turn towards the development of the existing framework of inter-governmental relations which had been formalised in the creation of an Anglo-Irish Inter-governmental Council at a summit with Garret FitzGerald in November 1981. At that time Unionist hostility to something that Thatcher had conceived as little more than an embellishment of existing ministerial and official contacts[42] had produced her never to be forgotten, if much misquoted, statement in the House of Commons: 'Northern Ireland is part of the United Kingdom – as much as my constituency is.'[43] Haughey's return to power, the sharp down-turn in Anglo-Irish relations following the Falklands War and Prior's internalistic initiative all served to halt any further development of the inter-governmental framework. But the emergence of an apparently dangerous level of political support for republicanism and Haughey's replacement at the end of 1982 by the more accommodating FitzGerald created the circumstances for a radical departure in British policy.

One key to the ambiguities of the agreement which

resulted from the qualitative intensification of intergovern-
mental communications from 1983 was Thatcher's
well-established policy style of deep scepticism of established
institutional interests, policy communities and mentalities in
those areas where she decided to exercise what Riddell has
termed 'her executive compulsion to act'.[44] For Northern
Ireland this meant suspicion of the Northern Ireland
Office's wedding to devolution plus power-sharing as the way
forward. The republican surge in 1980-81 had already
convinced the *Sunday Times* and James Callaghan that the
existing policy consensus was barren, both turning towards
'independence' as a way of extricating Britain from the
warring of two ungrateful Irish tribes.[45]

Thatcher, whose commitment to the Union, if not the
Unionists, formed the stubborn outer limit of her many
policy reversals and compromises, was clearly not going
down such an uncharted route. Nevertheless, if devolution
was ruled out and a radical initiative demanded while she
rejected integration for its disruptive effects on Anglo-Irish
relations, some sort of development of the Anglo-Irish
framework was inevitable.[46]

Various accounts, including the most detailed by
FitzGerald, have attached great importance to the role of the
Cabinet Secretary, Sir Robert Armstrong, in persuading
Thatcher to sign the Agreement. FitzGerald refers to him as
'a man with a sense of history and a deep commitment to
Anglo-Irish relations'.[47] Armstrong gave the impression that
he was motivated by a desire to make amends for Britain's ill-
treatment of Ireland over the centuries.[48] The sincerity of
these effusions is doubtful, and it is more probable that they
reflect that, for those who might be termed the 'maximalists'
within the British elite, there was no perceived conflict of
interests with constitutional nationalism whilst there
certainly was a clash with both revolutionary nationalism and
loyalism. Even the Provisionals had come to accept that by
the 1980s Britain had no material interest in the North,
which was a significant and growing burden on the
Exchequer. The effects of Thatcherism, from which
Northern Ireland was to a degree insulated, still accelerated
the decline of local industry and increased dependence on
the public sector. While the continuation of the republican
campaign ensured the deepening of the Westminster

consensus that there could be no 'capitulation to the men of violence', the maximalists concerned themselves with ways in which the Provisional surge could be stemmed whilst at the same time achieving a distinct institutional distancing of Northern Ireland from the rest of the United Kingdom.

While Thatcher's fetishised view of sovereignty put an outer limit on what could be achieved, the core official negotiators on the British side, Armstrong and Goodall, were able to exploit both her desire to act decisively and her distrust and distaste for the power-sharing/devolution strategy to get her committed to a process of intergovernmentalism which developed a dynamic from which she would find it difficult to withdraw. They were also, like FitzGerald, able to exploit the widespread, if misplaced, alarm after the 1983 General Election in which Gerry Adams won West Belfast for Sinn Fein and the party polled over 100,000 votes in the province, 13.4 per cent of the total, to the SDLP's 17.9 per cent. It was assumed in many quarters that the surge to Sinn Fein was now irresistible.[49]

It was in this context that the negotiations 'began very tentatively and privately between the British and Irish governments in the second half of 1983, the initiative [coming] from the Irish side'.[50] As Goodall indicates, the negotiations were carried on in great secrecy and confined to a small group of officials working under the two prime ministers. The Irish position is accurately and shrewdly summed up by Goodall:

> Dr FitzGerald was prepared drastically to lower nationalist sights on Irish unification in the interests of promoting stability in Northern Ireland and halting the political advance of Sinn Fein. This meant trying to reconcile nationalists to the Union rather than breaking it; but ... this could only be done if the Republic were associated in some institutionalised way with the government of Northern Ireland.[51]

As he indicates subsequently, the lowering of sights was from something that FitzGerald had long rejected as a realisable or desirable goal, the achievement of a unity against the wishes of the Protestants, to an objective that, while it was sure to produce an angry Protestant response, was conceivably realisable. Goodall comments that Irish expectations about the lengths to which the British would go to enlist Irish assistance in dealing with the Sinn Fein/IRA challenge were 'unrealistically high' as they involved some form of joint sovereignty. That it took some considerable time for these expectations to be lowered was a reflection of the ambiguities and divisions on the British side. Here the 'maximalists', Armstrong, Goodall and the Foreign Secretary Geoffrey Howe, saw no reason not to go to the limit of impressing an integral Irish dimension on the structures of government in Northern Ireland. Apart from its immediate advantage of enlisting Dublin's assistance in dealing with the Provisionals, it had the longer-term advantage of emphasising the distinctiveness of Northern Ireland, its semi-detached status within the UK.

Thatcher's visceral rejection of anything that could be represented as joint sovereignty was clearly a major constraint on this willingness to engage with the Irish position. This was amplified by the inclinations of the NIO, whose Principal Permanent Secretary, Sir Robert Andrew, was a sceptical voice from the beginning. His reservations reflected what he regarded as the heavy long-term responsibilities of his department. Its co-head, Sir Kenneth Bloomfield, also head of the Northern Ireland Civil Service, was as a 'native' and former servant of the Stormont regime totally excluded from the negotiating process.[52] However Andrew's concern reflected what Armstrong and Goodall regarded as an undue quietism.[53]

Thatcher's central concerns – to get a settlement that would stand some chance of weaning nationalists away from Sinn Fein; to secure better co-operation in the security field from Dublin; and to retain US support, deflating international criticism of British indifference – overrode her genuine fears about possible Unionist response, which echoed those of the NIO. Originally she had talked of a 'basic equation': Dublin's acknowledgement of the Union through repeal of Articles 2 and 3 of the Irish constitution, with their territorial claim to Northern Ireland, in return for some Irish involvement in the government of Northern Ireland which would have particular emphasis on security but stop short of joint authority.[54] However she soon realised that a referendum on the Irish constitution would only be forthcoming in return for more radical British concessions – joint authority – and retreated from the demand.[55] The

result was the Anglo-Irish Agreement signed by the two Prime
Ministers at Hillsborough Castle in County Down on 15
November 1985.

From the Irish point of view the Agreement was considerably less than what was needed radically to alter Catholic
attitudes to the northern state. From their point of view the
core of the Agreement was the establishment of an Anglo-
Irish Inter-Governmental Conference jointly chaired by
British and Irish ministers and serviced by a permanent
secretariat including Irish officials and based at Maryfield on
the outskirts of Belfast. The Conference was to deal on a
regular basis with political, security and legal matters
including the administration of justice and the promotion of
cross-border co-operation. This was more than consultation
but fell short of joint authority, and FitzGerald would
subsequently comment that it gave the Irish responsibility
without power and meant that 'nothing substantive had
changed'.[56] For the British, the possibility of significant
improvements in the manageability of the situation in
Northern Ireland was hemmed in by the decision not to
press for a referendum on Articles 2 and 3. The stridency of
Unionist opposition and what was regarded as Irish 'foot-
dragging' on the security front produced rapid
disenchantment on Thatcher's part: 'Our concessions
alienated the Unionists without gaining the level of security
co-operation we had a right to expect.'[57] She was, perhaps,
doubly frustrated given Garret FitzGerald's refusal to accept
that anything substantial had changed.

However such short-term disenchantment does not
detract from the strategic significance of the Agreement.
One of its architects pointed to two 'important and
irreversible' changes in the 'Anglo-Irish landscape'. The first
was the concession of a role and responsibility to the
Republic in the affairs of Northern Ireland and the second
the putting a halt 'to the idea that any government in the
Republic could or would seek to incorporate the North into
a united Ireland without the consent of a majority of the
population of the Province'.[58] The second shift is certainly
more disputable than the first. While Thatcher and other
ministers would try to reassure Unionists that the Agreement
reinforced their position through Article 1, which affirmed
that any change in the status of Northern Ireland would only

come about with the consent of a majority of its people, they ignored the degree to which the vision of constitutional nationalism had itself transcended the imperatives of the Republic's constitution.

Thus John Hume depicted Article 1 as a radical change in the British attitude to the Union. He focused on clause C of Article 1:

> If in the future a majority of the people of Northern Ireland clearly wish for and formally consent to the establishment of a United Ireland, they will introduce and support legislation in their respective parliaments to give effect to that wish.

Hume claimed that this is an implicit British declaration that they have no interest of their own in staying in Ireland:

> The British government is neutral in that it is no longer pro-Union. There is nothing therefore to stop the British government from becoming pro-Irish unity in their policies. The SDLP's task is to persuade the British to go in that direction and to use all their considerable influence and resources to persuade the Unionist people that their best interests are served by a new Ireland.[59]

While the institutionalisation of a southern role in the governance of the North was undeniable, the ratification of the existing constitutional position was much less sure. As one sympathetic observer noted, while the Agreement speaks of no change in the status of Northern Ireland, it nowhere defines what that status is, precisely to avoid a clash with Article 2 of the Irish Constitution: 'The very skill of the draftsmen had made the first article so ambiguous that it was no surprise if it caused suspicions of doublespeak over the entire accord.'[60]

The ambiguity stemmed in large part from the differing and inconsistent dispositions on the British side. For Thatcher it was primarily a device to win greater security co-operation from Dublin, for some of the key officials involved and for Geoffrey Howe it was a first step in the process of gradually reducing the British stake in Northern Ireland. The fact was, and remains, that it is difficult to see why Britain has any material interest in strengthening the

Union – Northern Ireland is a drain on Britain's political and economic resources.

Thatcher makes clear that despite her 'profoundly Unionist' instincts she never had an easy relationship with the Ulster Unionists and explains this by reference to the essentially 'Irish' nature of the Northern Ireland conflict: 'What British politician will ever fully understand Northern Ireland?' This incomprehensibility reflected the strength of primordial passions:

> In the history of Ireland – both North and South … reality and myth from the seventeenth century to the 1920s take on an almost Balkan immediacy. Distrust mounting to hatred and revenge is never far beneath the political surface. And those who step on it must do so gingerly.[61]

Conventional in her repetition of the mentality of a succession of prime ministers both challenged and ultimately frustrated by what Nigel Lawson called 'The Curse of Ulster',[62] her pro-Unionism was predominantly negative – the 'terrorists' could not be allowed to win. The Unionists were sympathised with as victims of the IRA, but their own discriminatory past was noted, as was the fact that their patriotism was real but 'too narrow'.[63] From her point of view the Union turned out not to be a seamless entity. Whilst its core component, the other island, could be damaged by a radical concession on sovereignty, the 'otherness' of the Irish component would allow a significant institutionalisation of the interest of another government in its structures without this having damaging implications for the basic structures of the British state.

So while she had not approached the negotiations from the point of view of lessening the British stake in Northern Ireland, and her determination that 'sovereignty' would be safeguarded meant the disappointment of Irish ambitions, she was responsible for a major strategic departure. This was described by one of the British negotiators:

> It was an attempt to redress the balance of power … by giving the nationalists a voice in the affairs of Northern Ireland through the Dublin government. Although the Agreement paid lip service to devolution, it was really an admission that power-sharing in Northern Ireland had not worked and the

nationalist interest could only be protected by Dublin.[64]

From this perspective the logic of the Agreement was in fact joint authority, for without this it was possible to argue that all that had been achieved was responsibility without power – 'direct rule with a green tinge'.

The depth of Unionist opposition, increasing frictions with the South on the security front (particularly after Haughey's return to power in 1987), increased levels of violence and all the evidence of continuing support for Sinn Fein led Thatcher to shift back towards a more traditional approach in the search for a new and more widely based agreement which began under Peter Brooke, who became Secretary of State in 1989. However the Agreement had fundamentally altered the context in which any future initiative was launched: there could be no return to the approaches adopted in the first dozen years of Direct Rule.

Howe had referred to the Agreement as perhaps 'as much as could be achieved in one generation'.[65] For him the achievement was the framework which could conciliate constitutional nationalism, marginalise Sinn Fein and weaken Unionism by holding it at arm's length and keeping it in a reduced and demoralised condition. There was the perspective of the gradual and peaceful extension of the hegemony of Irish constitutional nationalism over the whole island. This approach would register one notable success, but a key failure would provoke a re-assessment of the best means of dealing with Sinn Fein.

Direct Rule with a Green Tinge

The argument had surfaced from the Irish side in the negotiation of the Agreement that one positive effect of the accord would be to 're-educate' Unionism by making it clear that only by accepting power-sharing devolution could it minimise the role of the Dublin government in the affairs of the North. This thesis had been doubted by the British but it was in fact borne out, even though changes in the disposition of the SDLP made it of dubious significance.

The early life of the Agreement was dominated by the theme of confrontation: Paisley versus Thatcher. It soon became clear, however, that the Unionist campaign against the Agreement – in its most intense form including strikes and attacks on the homes of members of the RUC for alleged 'collaboration' – lacked the resources to win. In particular the widespread sense of material dependence on the UK Exchequer was profoundly debilitating and prevented mass militancy. The Agreement's fundamental unpopularity with Protestants was to remain one of the core facts of Northern Irish political life, but this was to co-exist with a growing awareness that the Agreement was a more-or-less permanent fixture in the governance of Northern Ireland. In January 1986 the mass resignation of Unionist MPs, by far the most striking of the anti-Agreement strategies, had led to only a slight increase in the Unionist vote in the subsequent by-elections.

Another notable feature of the post-Agreement landscape was the weakening of the DUP, which appeared powerless in the face of the Agreement. Indeed the DUP's intransigence could be credibly presented as part of the reason for the imposition of the accord itself. The DUP's practice of resistance to relatively marginal concessions to the Catholic community was in any case rendered futile when such a substantial concession as the Agreement was already in place. The party entered hesitantly into a pact with the OUP from which it emerged in a weakened state, shorn of some of its best-known leaders. In the 1992 General Election it achieved a mere 13.7 per cent of the poll, though its decline stabilised somewhat at 17.2 per cent in the May 1993 local government elections. (At one key point in 1981, with 26.6 per cent, it actually outpolled the OUP's 26.5 per cent.[66]) The DUP's difficulties went hand-in-hand with a steady rise in Protestant paramilitarism: loyalist paramilitaries killed only two people in 1984, but by 1991-92 they were more active agents of death than the IRA.

While the Agreement led to a significant increase of support for integrationist ideas amongst the Protestant middle class, James Molyneaux advocated a strategic minimalism based on twin perceptions of the need to maintain OUP unity and of increasing Conservative disenchantment with the Agreement. Aware of the weakening in the Unionist position which the Agreement had so graphically established, and whilst deeply averse to the more traditional NIO objective of power-sharing devolution, Molyneaux was nevertheless determined that mainstream Unionism would not be imprisoned within a public posture of inflexibility: if the British were to moot the possibility of a new and more broadly-based agreement, the OUP would not adopt a rejectionist stance.

But if there was to be increasing evidence of a new-found Official Unionist flexibility, it could not disguise the profound divisions that still existed with constitutional nationalism. This was only partly because the leadership of the OUP still found it publicly unpalatable to talk of power-sharing devolution. For the SDLP had, by 1988, shown clear signs of having moved decisively beyond the demands of Sunningdale. This was, in part, the result of the failure of the Agreement to marginalise Sinn Fein. For although that party's support had peaked before the Agreement, it had consolidated at around 11 per cent of the electorate. While the Agreement had accelerated those tendencies which made Direct Rule the 'best possible shell' for an expanding Catholic middle class, it had delivered neither the final decisive defeat of Unionism nor the concrete economic benefits for impoverished urban Catholic ghettos which might have reduced republican support in a more substantive way. It was also a reflection of the failure of Hume's own belief in the early phase of the Agreement – from November 1985 to mid-1987 – that the Unionists would accept power-sharing devolution within the framework of the Agreement: he predicted that Unionists would negotiate with him by the end of 1986. The failure of the prediction produced, with the lack of a Sinn Fein melt-down, a radical turn away from the vista of Sunningdale – a marginalisation of the 'men of violence' through a coming together of constitutional nationalism and Unionism.

The first sign of this was the seven-month-long dialogue with Sinn Fein in 1988. This was facilitated by Sinn Fein's well established desire to avoid the political isolation and marginalisation which was the objective of the Agreement. Despite the political breakthrough of 1982 and 1983, Gerry Adams recognised that as long as the Sinn Fein vote was contained at around 30-40 per cent of the Catholic electorate – as seemed likely – the impetus of the 1982 electoral surge might well dissipate. To deal with this, and also with the narrow limits of Sinn Fein support in the Republic, the organisation's leadership was keen to create conditions for a broader 'nationalist coalition', including Fianna Fail and the SDLP, aimed at mobilising domestic and international opinion against the 'British presence'. The SDLP/Sinn Fein meetings were abruptly terminated by Hume after the accidental killing by the IRA of two of his Catholic constituents. In the documents which the parties then released, the main issue of contention, apart from violence, was Hume's claim, rejected by Sinn Fein, that the Agreement demonstrated Britain's neutrality on the question of partition.

As the republican movement both intensified its military campaign and gave public hints of a new-found flexibility over the next five years, British policy assumed an increasingly pro-Union public posture while at the same time giving substantive private signs of an interest in republican revisionism. Secretary of State Peter Brooke had launched the search for a new agreement through inter-party talks in January 1990 and managed by the eve of the 1992 General Election to initiate some talks. A largely spurious suspension of the Agreement proved enough to ensure Unionist participation. After the election the talks continued in a more serious vein with a new Secretary of State, Sir Patrick Mayhew. The Unionists approached the talks in a slightly more confident frame of mind: their proposals were certainly considerably more advanced and elaborate. Under John Major, who had succeeded Thatcher in late 1990, the government gave even more explicit signs that it wished to reduce the Unionist sense of isolation and anxiety. The Foreign Secretary, Douglas Hurd, told the 1991 Conservative Party conference that the debate on partition was over. The Anglo-Irish inter-parliamentary tier in early 1992 was presented with a critical British analysis of the working of the Agreement. In the run-up to the election in April 1992 a Tory Prime Minister rediscovered the Union as a political theme. After the election there was the appointment of a team at the NIO which was just about as Unionist as the then Conservative Party could produce.

However the talks process foundered on the rock of the SDLP's refusal to depart from its original and leaked paper which argued for a form of joint authority with an added European dimension. It was clear during the talks that the NIO was impressed with the flexibility of the Official Unionists. Although they had originally insisted on an agreement in 'strand one', which dealt with the internal structures of the North's governance before the start of 'strand two', dealing with north-south relations, they proved willing to make the crucial transition without agreement having been reached in 'strand one'. The unprecedented willingness to go to Dublin to discuss north-south relations was made possible by a private letter from Mayhew to Molyneaux, indicating the former's lack of enthusiasm for the SDLP document. Nevertheless, Dublin's apparent unpreparedness to respond to the Unionist flexibility, together with Hume's refusal to budge from the original document, led to the collapse of the talks.

British frustration with Hume was typically myopic. Deeply ingrained distrust of Unionist motivation and an acute awareness of the potential republican challenge to a 'sell-out' to anything smacking of an 'internal solution' strongly impelled the SDLP against an historic compromise with Unionism. The Anglo-Irish Agreement had created a context in which it became logical, almost compellingly so, for constitutional nationalists and the British Labour Party to argue for a form of joint authority. British dissatisfaction with the Agreement's domestic failures – nobody questioned its international success in fire-proofing British policy in Northern Ireland – produced the usual frenetic tactical ingenuity, but this simply served to obscure the fundamental shift in terrain which the Agreement had produced. Even if a Sunningdale-type agreement was now possible, it was too 'internalist', too dependent on Unionist goodwill, to be attractive from the SDLP's point of view. Constitutional and revolutionary nationalism were profoundly convinced that the Agreement was the clearest indication that the tide of history was running their way. It was the first semi-constitutional recognition of longer-term structural shifts – economic, social, demographic and ideological – which were consigning Unionists to the category of defeated peoples.

The failure of the talks and Major's increasingly precarious position in the House of Commons and the Tory Party buoyed up the Official Unionists as, dependent on their votes at Westminster, the public tone of government statements intensified in their Unionism. Yet the failure of the talks also pushed the government back towards an inter-governmental approach and into the intensification of private communications with the republican movement which had been restarted in October 1990.[67] The initial sounding out of Sinn Fein in 1990-91 produced a number of public indications of a new-found republican flexibility on some of their more fundamentalist postures – particularly that Britain should withdraw in the lifetime of one parliament. A 'scenario for peace' emerged in which an IRA ceasefire might be forthcoming for a British commitment to withdraw in a 'generation' whilst in the interim structures of joint authority would operate. Ultimately it appears that, despite the intensification of IRA activities in Ulster and Britain in 1991 and 1992, it was republican rather than Unionist flexibility which was found most impressive.

Only the impact of serious intelligence work can explain the willingness to wager on 'new thinking' in the republican leadership in the midst of a major intensification of IRA violence. In the year before the Warrington bombs which killed a three-year-old and a twelve-year-old boy on 20 March 1993,[68] the IRA had waged its most sustained military campaign in Britain since the Troubles began – killing five people and causing over £1 billion of damage.[69] A month later the campaign culminated in a devastating car-bomb attack in the City of London causing damage estimated at over £1 billion.[70] In Northern Ireland it had shifted operations towards a series of massive car-bomb attacks on Belfast and a number of other, largely Protestant, towns. On 23 March the British government representative was able to tell his republican contact just how much republican interest in the 'healing process', a term used by John Hume and now recycled by Sinn Fein, had impressed the government:

> Mayhew had tried marginalisation, defeating the IRA etc. That's gone ... Mayhew is now determined. He wants Sinn Fein to play a part not because he likes Sinn Fein but because it cannot work without them. Any settlement not involving all of the people North and South won't work. A North/South settlement that won't frighten Unionists. The final solution is union. It is going to happen anyway. The historical train –

Europe – determines that. We are committed to Europe.
Unionists will have to change. This island will be as one.[71]

Earlier that month Mayhew had made a speech in Bangor
in which he had tried to calm Unionist fears aroused by a
speech he made in December 1992 in Coleraine – supplied
in advance to Sinn Fein – which had been widely read as a
strong rendition of Britain's 'neutrality' on partition. Now
he assured his listeners:

> The reality is that if Northern Ireland's position as part of
> the UK is ever going to change it will only be by the will of a
> majority of its people ... We are not indifferent, we are not
> neutral in our resolve to protect and deliver the people of
> Northern Ireland from terrorist violence. We are not neutral
> in defending the right of Northern Ireland people to
> democratic self-determination.[72]

The relation between public and private discourse is not as
starkly opposed as might appear, however queasy one might
feel about the tone of the post-Warrington effusions from
the British representative. For the whole 'novelty' of Hume's
post-Agreement strategy, the potential efficacy of which he
appears to have convinced Adams, was to accept that
Unionists were the main opposition to a united Ireland and
that they could not be coerced into one. Instead they were
to be persuaded and educated over a period of years – a
process of peaceful attrition in which the British would play
a central role. Thus it was possible for Mayhew both to try to
placate Unionists by acknowledging their democratic right
to self-determination while others held out to republicans
the notion that fundamental historical processes – and basic
British inclinations – were working in their favour.

Such a balancing act is clearly not sustainable for long.
Suspicious of Britain after the experience of the previous
negotiated 'truce' in 1975, the IRA insisted on a public
adoption by Britain of the role of persuader and a
specification of the 'mechanisms' by which an 'agreed
Ireland' would be reached. The British dilemma was clear. It
was now deeply committed to an inter-governmental
approach which had massive advantages internationally and
more disputable advantages on the security front. These
advantages were bought at a price, which some on the

British side, and Thatcher in particular, had not calculated. Constitutional nationalism north and south found 'direct rule with a green tinge' the very minimum recognition of a fundamental shift in the balance of power on the island. Unionism was perceived as a waning force and the Conservatives as most reluctant Unionists. The very fractiousness of Unionists in their ultimately futile opposition to the Agreement led apologists for the accord, like Michael Lillis, who had been one of the chief Irish negotiators, to argue that the process of 'educating' them would have to continue for some time.[73] It is little wonder that the air was soon to be rent with cries for 'clarification' of the intentions of the British government.

Notes

1. Martin Wallace, *British Government in Northern Ireland*, London 1982, p. 94.
2. *Belfast Newsletter*, 2 September 1971.
3. Ulster Vanguard, *Ulster a Nation*, Belfast 1972.
4. Wallace, *British Government in Northern Ireland*, *p.* 94.
5. David Hume, *The Ulster Unionist Party in an Era of Conflict and Change 1972-1992*, 1985, p. 14, unpublished PhD thesis, University of Ulster 1993, p. 83.
6. John McGarry and Brendan O'Leary, *The Politics of Antagonism*, London and New Jersey 1993, p. 30.
7. Kevin Boyle and Tom Hadden, *Ireland: A Positive Proposal*, London 1985, p. 14.
8. Paul Bew and Henry Patterson, *The British State and the Ulster Crisis: From Wilson to Thatcher*, London 1985, p. 64.
9. Hume, *The Ulster Unionist Party*, p. 85.
10. Richard Rose, *Northern Ireland: A Time of Choice*, London 1976, p.31.
11. Hume, *The Ulster Unionist Party*, *p.* 87.
12. Steve Bruce, *The Red Hand: Protestant Paramilitaries in Northern Ireland*, Oxford 1992, p. 82.
13. The two serious accounts of the strike are Robert Fisk, *The Point of No Return: The Strike which Broke the British in Ulster*, London 1975, and Don Anderson, *14 May Days: The Inside Story of the Loyalist Strike of 1974*, Dublin 1994.
14. *Irish Times*, 15 May 1984.
15. Brian Faulkner recorded that he was 'surprised and alarmed' when he read a copy of the text: 'It merely seemed to lump everyone in Ulster together as reprobates and insult them to no purpose.' Brian Faulkner, *Memoirs of a Statesman*, London 1978, pp. 275-6.
16. Bew and Patterson, *The British State and the Ulster Crisis*, pp. 76-7.
17. Ibid. pp.78-88.
18. An ex-member of the DUP claims that by early 1977 the inner

circles of the party had a 'high conceit' of themselves, particularly as the destruction of Craig and the VUPP made them the sole political voice of resolute loyalism: Clifford Smyth, *The Ulster Democratic Unionist Party: A Case Study in Political and Religious Convergence*, unpublished PhD thesis, Queen's University, Belfast, 1983, p. 117.

19. Bew and Patterson, *The British State and the Ulster Crisis*, p. 103.

20. *Irish Times*, 6 November 1978.

21. Bew and Patterson, *The British State and the Ulster Crisis*, p. 111.

22. Margaret Thatcher, *The Downing Street Years*, London 1993, p. 385.

23. Ibid., p. 387.

24. Ibid., p. 384.

25. Ibid.

26. See his interview with Padraig O'Malley in the latter's *The Uncivil Wars: Ireland Today*, Belfast 1983, pp. 161-2, where his faith in the Unionist decencies of Thatcher, which he sees as obscured by Foreign Office intrigues, is clear.

27. Adrian Guelke, 'The American Connection to the Northern Ireland Conflict' in *Irish Studies in International Affairs*, Vol. 1, No. 4, 1984, p. 34. His arguments appear in expanded form in his book, *Northern Ireland: The International Perspective*, Dublin 1988.

28. Paul Bew and Gordon Gillespie, *Northern Ireland: A Chronology of the Troubles 1968-1993*, Dublin 1993, p. 137.

29. Thatcher, *The Downing Street Years*, p. 388.

30. Ibid., p. 390.

31. Bew and Gillespie, *Chronology*, p. 132.

32. Thatcher, *The Downing Street Years*, p. 391.

33. Henry Patterson, *The Politics of Illusion: Republicanism and Socialism in Modern Ireland*, London 1990, pp. 170-1.

34. Ibid., p. 163.

35. *Myth and Motherland*, Field Day Pamphlet No. 5, Derry 1984, p. 12.

36. Thatcher, *The Downing Street Years*, p. 391.

37. The phrase is taken from Sinn Fein's published account of the communications, *Setting the Record Straight: A Record of Communications Between Sinn Fein and the British Government October 1990-November 1993*, Belfast 1994, p. 11.

38. Thatcher, *The Downing Street Years*, p. 393.

39. James Prior, *A Balance of Power*, London 1986, p. 197.

40. See Bew and Gillespie, *Chronology*, p. 165.

41. Sir David Goodall, 'The Irish Question', Headmaster's Lecture given at Ampleforth, November 1992, *Ampleforth Journal*, Vol. XCVIII Part 1 (Spring 1993).

42. Thatcher, *The Downing Street Years*, p. 393.

43. The correct version is from Bew and Gillespie, *Chronology*, p. 158.

44. Peter Riddell, *The Thatcher Decade*, Oxford 1989, p.3.

45. See the leader in *Sunday Times*, 16 August 1981 – a powerful, if despairing, plea for a renunciation of British sovereignty in favour of an independent state, for Callaghan, see his speech in House of Commons, *Hansard*, Vol. 7 col. 1049, 2 July 1981.

46. Thatcher, *The Downing Street Years*, p. 386.

47. Garret FitzGerald, *All in a Life*, Dublin 1991, p.469.

48. Sir Robert Armstrong, 'Ethnicity, the English and Northern Ireland: Comments and Reflections' in D. Keogh and M. Haltzel (eds), *Northern Ireland: The Politics of Reconciliation*, Cambridge 1993, p. 205.

49. Bew and Patterson, *The British State and the Ulster Crisis*, p. 124.

50. Goodall, 'The Irish Question'.

51. Ibid.

52. Ken Bloomfield, *Stormont in Crisis: A Memoir*, Belfast 1993, pp. 253-5.

53. The issue here is a complex one. The NIO might reasonably claim that it too wanted an agreement but that, as the department of government concerned with trying to implement it, the NIO was more realistic about its long-term viability.

54. FitzGerald, *All in a Lifr*, p. 495.

55. Thatcher, *The Downing Street Years*, pp. 399-400.

56. Ibid., p. 415.

57. See his contribution to *Northern Ireland: A Challenge to Theology*, Edinburgh: Centre for Theology and Public Issues, 1987.

58. Goodall, 'The Irish Question'.

59. See his interview in Padraig O'Malley, *Northern Ireland: Questions of Nuance*, Belfast 1989, p. 17.

60. Anthony Kenny, *The Road to Hillsborough*, Oxford 1986, p. 17.

61. Thatcher, *The Downing Street Years*, p. 385.

62. The title of the section on Northern Ireland in Nigel Lawson, *The View from Number 11*, London 1992, p. 669.

63. Thatcher, *The Downing Street Years*, p. 385.

64. In a personal communication.

65. Goodall, 'The Irish Question'.

66. Figures from Bew and Gillespie, *Chronology*, p. 149.

67. Sinn Fein, *Setting the Record Straight*, p. 12.

68. Bew and Gillespie, *Chronology*, p. 292.

69. *Irish Times*, 22 March 1992.

70. Bew and Gillespie, *Chronology*, p. 298.

71. Sinn Fein, *Setting the Record Straight*, p. 28.

72. Quoted in Bew and Gillespie, *Chronology*, p. 290.

73. See his 'New Coalition Must Work the Anglo-Irish Accord as if Starting Anew', *Irish Times*, 30 December 1992.

7   Ceasefire and Peace Process, 1994–2001

The British and Irish governments reiterate that the achievement of peace must involve a permanent end to the use of, or support for, paramilitary violence. They confirm that, in these circumstances, democratically mandated parties which establish a commitment to exclusively peaceful methods and which have shown that they abide by the democratic process, are free to participate fully in democratic politics and to join in dialogue in due course between the governments and the political parties on the way ahead.

Joint Declaration, Downing Street, 15 December 1993

Ceasefire: A New Strategy or a Necessary Illusion?

The decision of the IRA leadership to announce a 'complete cessation' of military operations on 31 August 1994 came as a surprise to many. At its Letterkenny conference on 24 July Sinn Fein had spoken in predominantly fundamentalist tones. Even a few days before the announcement senior republicans had been talking in terms of a temporary 'ceasefire'.[1] The broader context is, however, clear. A key development had been John Hume's controversial but eventually vindicated decision to renew intensive dialogue with Gerry Adams in 1993. A dialogue which became known as the Hume-Adams 'peace process' was built around a fundamental proposition: 'We accept that the people of Ireland as a whole have a right to self-determination.' In parliament in November 1993 John Major had praised Mr Hume's 'courageous efforts', but noted that this formulation was not compatible with the principle of consent which was

219

central to the British government's Irish policy. Indeed, in response, the British and Irish governments together issued the Reynolds-Major principles or 'Six Points' which acted as the forerunner to the Downing Street Declaration:

1. The situation in Northern Ireland should never be changed by violence or the threat of violence;
2. Any political settlement must depend on consent freely given in the absence of force or intimidation;
3. There can be no talks between the two governments and those who use, threaten, or support political violence;
4. There can be no secret agreements or understandings between government and organisations supporting violence 'as a price for its cessation';
5. Those claiming a serious interest in advancing peace in Ireland should renounce for good the use of or support for violence;
6. If and when a renunciation of violence has been made and sufficiently demonstrated, 'new doors could open' and both governments would wish to respond 'imaginatively' to the new situation which would then arise.

The Downing Street Declaration proved to be a document of considerable originality and sophistication. For Unionists it formalised a distasteful message, albeit one already sent by Peter Brooke in 1990: 'The Prime Minister ... reiterates on behalf of the British government that they have no selfish strategic or economic interest in Northern Ireland.' As we saw earlier, however, only for a brief period in the aftermath of the Second World War had belief in a 'selfish strategic interest' really existed in Whitehall. The real novelty of the Downing Street Declaration lay elsewhere. It is necessary at this point to consider the complex language of the Joint Declaration's fourth paragraph:

The Prime Minister, on behalf of the British government, reaffirms that they will uphold the democratic wish of a greater number of the people of Northern Ireland on the issue of whether they prefer to support the Union or a sovereign united Ireland. On this basis, he reiterates, on behalf of the British government, that they have no selfish strategic or economic interest in Northern Ireland. Their primary interest is to see peace, stability and reconciliation established by agreement among all the people who inhabit the island, and they will work together with the Irish government to achieve such an agreement which will embrace the totality of relationships. The role of the British government will be to encourage, facilitate and enable the achievement of such agreement over a period through a process of dialogue and co-operation based on full respect for the rights and identities of both traditions in Ireland. They accept that such agreement may, as of right, take the form of agreed structures for the island as a whole, including a united Ireland achieved by peaceful means on the following basis. The British government agrees that it is for the people of the island of Ireland alone, by agreement between the two parts respectively, to exercise their right of self-determination on the basis of consent, freely and concurrently given, North and South, to bring about a united Ireland, if that is their wish. They reaffirm as a binding obligation that they will, for their part, introduce the necessary legislation to give effect to this, or equally to any measure of agreement on future relationships in Ireland which the people living in Ireland may themselves freely so determine without external impediment. They believe that the people of Britain would wish, in friendship to all sides, to enable the people of Ireland to reach agreement on how they may live together in harmony and in partnership, with respect for their diverse traditions, and with full recognition of the special links and the unique relationship which exist between the peoples of Britain and Ireland.

After the Downing Street Declaration Hume-Adams phraseology continued to dominate the political scene, but its content was dramatically altered. One of the most effective slogans of Irish nationalism had been given a new, decidedly softer conceptual content – and this had been done by a Fianna Fail government. The self-determination of the Irish people was conceded by Britain, but only on the basis that the Irish government wished to operate that principle in favour of Irish unity with the support of a majority in the North. Superficially, the rhetoric of the Hume-Adams process had been conceded but, in essence, the process had been stripped of its content in a quite dramatic way. The British, it is true, were now 'facilitators', but for an agreed Ireland rather than for Irish unity, and an 'agreed' Ireland, by definition, could not be a united Ireland until there was majority consent in the North:

> The role of the British government will be to encourage, facilitate and enable the achievement of such agreement over a period through a process of dialogue and co-operation

based on full respect for the rights and identities of both traditions in Ireland.

Yet while making clear its commitment to the principle of consent, the Irish government continued to support the Hume-Adams-inspired peace process, eventually investing so much in it that the IRA leadership felt compelled to reciprocate by issuing the dramatic statement of 31 August, a statement – with a decidedly valedictory tone as far as violence was concerned – which announced the birth of a new purely political strategy embracing Irish America, the Irish government and the SDLP, designed to achieve Irish unity.

In the 1790s Edmund Burke spoke polemically of 'a species of men, to whom a state of order would become a sentence of obscurity', adding it is 'no wonder that, by a sort of sinister piety, they cherish in their turn, the disorders which are the parents of all their consequence'.[2] In the 1990s, however, matters were to be organised in a different fashion. It has been arranged both by John Hume and the Irish premier, Albert Reynolds, that the Adams leadership was given the option not of obscurity but of much public applause in Dublin and the United States; as a result they may be able to leave behind the 'disorders' which are the 'parents' of all their 'consequence'. The republicans were not to be deprived of the oxygen of publicity, as Mrs Thatcher had wanted, but instead were invited to overdose on it. Perhaps unsurprisingly, a modern Burkean, Conor Cruise O'Brien, Edmund Burke's most empathetic biographer,[3] remained defiantly sceptical of the peaceful intentions of the Provisional leadership. He insisted:

> The IRA has accorded a complete cessation of military operations but it has refused to define that cessation as permanent – and its political representatives reiterated that refusal this week. In the circumstances, to equate the present ceasefire with peace is irresponsible ... The private army of whose pacifist intentions the Irish government is apparently convinced is still in being, heavily armed and organised within our territory, in defiance of our laws. It disposes of approximately one hundred tons of arms, ammunition and explosives.[4]

On this basis, and clearly not without reason, O'Brien continued to argue that the widespread media optimism concerning the prospect for lasting peace was unjustified. The republican movement's unrelenting agenda had not changed in O'Brien's view.

Yet if the agenda remained unchanged, the possibility of implementing it seemed to be greatly reduced. All the principal substantive political developments in the month after the ceasefire seemed to weaken, rather than strengthen, the republican position. The obviously cagey reaction of the British government to the ceasefire announcement; the resolve of the US government to be 'even-handed' and, indeed, to make a strictly limited financial commitment to Northern Ireland; the observation made by the Irish premier that Irish unity might take one generation, or even longer; and the decision of the new British Labour Party leader, Tony Blair, to move his party's position closer to that of the government and dilute some of his party's traditional pro-nationalist rhetoric.[5] The notion of 'joint authority' seemed to lose a little of its intellectual respectability, although the possibility remained that Unionist opinion might be severely jolted by the new framework document on which the two governments were working. The British government gave itself a safety net here by insisting that any new settlement would have to survive the test of a Northern Irish referendum. As Anthony McIntyre, writing from an independent republican perspective, put it:

> Talking to Sinn Fein, while initially distasteful for British officials, will be infinitely more pleasing to the ear than the thunder of IRA bombs at the Baltic Exchange. Given the Unionist veto, Britain is likely to take the cynical view that republicans in unarmed struggle are like birds without wings.[6]

The Adams leadership appeared to be locked into a purely political process announced by a dramatic series of media events, occasional backsliding remarks about the possibility of a renewal of IRA violence notwithstanding. Significantly, there appeared to be no alternative republican leadership. Much, however, would depend on the ability of the base of the republican movement to cope with these new developments. Republicanism, which had been fuelled by action and anger, would have to deal in the unfamiliar territory of positive rhetoric. In the longer view much would also depend on the ability of the local political class and the two governments to resolve on a new pattern of Unionist-nationalist relationships which, while based on the principle of consent, would foreclose forever the possibility of another armed conflict. The problems which had haunted the 1992 talks process still awaited their resolution. In a volatile, unpredictable situation, therefore, no one could say with certainty that such a point had been reached.

The Birth of Pro-active Unionism

The more fluid political circumstances created by the cessation of violence helped to provoke major changes in the political leadership of Ulster Unionism. On 28 August 1995 James Molyneaux resigned as party leader on the eve of his seventy-fifth birthday. Molyneaux's leadership had been mortally wounded in February when the British and Irish governments jointly commended the Frameworks Documents on the future of the province. The green rhetoric of these documents dismayed Molyneaux's supporters and indeed Molyneaux himself; as a result he was unable to argue – as he might have done with some credibility – that, at bottom, the Frameworks embodied a partitionist approach to the Irish question.[7] To the members of the Ulster Unionist Party it seemed that, like Brian Faulkner in 1974, Molyneaux had put his trust in a Tory premier and been sacrificed. Indeed, in Molyneaux's era this had happened twice, first with Margaret Thatcher and the Anglo-Irish Agreement of 1985, and then with John Major over the Frameworks Documents of 1995.

Molyneaux had excellent excuses. Margaret Thatcher was a highly unpredictable politician as far as Ireland was concerned, and as late as 30 October 1994 the nationalist Dublin *Sunday Business Post* was reporting that, 'Major hardly sneezes in the direction of the North without seeking Molyneaux's approval.' Molyneaux, always a stabilising force in Ulster politics, was not the only one to be surprised by the dilution in the British government's negotiating stance in the following few weeks, in particular Britain's failure to secure an explicit commitment from Dublin to lift the territorial claim in the event of an overall settlement – something which the British government had declared to be a *sine qua non* of any deal. Nevertheless, his party activists felt that he had failed to prepare the ground; others felt he should have resigned at once.

In March 1995 Lee Reynolds, an unknown 21-year-old student, obtained 15 per cent of the votes in an audacious leadership challenge to Molyneaux. In the summer his party lost the North Down by-election, a prime Unionist seat, to an arch Molyneaux critic, Robert McCartney, QC. The party leader found life increasingly uncomfortable in the Glengall Street headquarters, as activists and party officers made known their criticisms of his leadership.

What did he really believe in? Where did he stand in the debate which divided Ulster Unionism? As his biographer, Ann Purdy, makes clear, Molyneaux was at heart an integrationist rather than devolutionist. He told her that Stormont – 'a puppet parliament', he called it – did not strengthen the Union even when it was dominated by Unionists from 1921 to 1968; hardly surprisingly, he felt in the 1970s and 1980s that devolution was 'not worth the candle' if it involved accepting both the Anglo-Irish Agreement and power-sharing.

In an important speech to his party conference in 1989, Molyneaux added an intriguing gloss. He identified himself with a civil rights agenda by stressing the theme of equal citizenship within the UK, first advanced by Sir Edward Carson before the First World War. He strongly implied that the parochialising effect of Stormont had led Unionists into the error of supporting local privilege. In sombre tones Molyneaux observed:

> Unfortunately by 1969 Unionists had become detached from the touchstone of political wisdom … Had Unionism remained true to Carson, the flood waters of civil rights would have divided into separate streams, the genuine democrats and the closet republicans. That is the lesson of 1969 and all that.[8]

This was to be the height of Molyneaux's iconoclasm. It is worth recalling that his options were always rather limited.

As political Protestantism, a phenomenon embracing both nineteenth-century English parties, declined in the rest of the UK, Ulster Protestants appeared as an increasingly bizarre and vulgar parody of Britishness. Matters were made worse by the region's relative economic decline and the growing dependence on the centre after 1920. Only Irish neutrality in the Second World War allowed a brief Unionist return to popularity in London.

James Molyneaux, therefore, had never had the option of playing the 'heroic' Carson role. At times in the mid-1980s he seemed content merely to manage decline, though it is fair to say that in more recent years he harvested small but significant gains (a Northern Ireland Select Committee, for example) at every turn. He did, however, hold the ground which mattered and protected the British citizenship of his supporters.

To the surprise of many commentators, the Unionist Party elected David Trimble as its new leader following Molyneaux's resignation. Trimble, in turn, soon appointed John Taylor as his deputy leader. What were the implications of David Trimble's election?

Since the retirement of Garret FitzGerald and the death of John Kelly there has been a gap for the role of 'intellectual in Irish politics'. Trimble recalls both: he is as well read as FitzGerald while he also has some of the sharpness of John Kelly, a fellow academic lawyer and a Fine Gael politician. His forays into 'amateur' historical writing are not without subtlety and do not always adopt a pious attitude towards the Unionist past. It is a rather wry David Trimble who wrote so shrewdly about the Home Rule issue of 1912-14:

> There is a Unionist myth about the Ulster crisis. It is that gallant Ulster took a stand, armed itself for the fight and its opponents in London backed down and its enemies in Ireland were defeated.[9]

Much has been made of Trimble's involvement in the militant Vanguard movement which helped to bring down the power-sharing Executive in 1974. Less well known, however, is his heavy involvement in an unsuccessful attempt to put together a Unionist-SDLP coalition the following year.[10] For northern nationalists, of course, David Trimble will always be seen in the context of the sectarian emotion unleashed at the Orange march at Drumcree, Portadown, in the summer of 1995. They find it hard to take seriously his subsequent prospect of the modernisation of Unionism as exemplified in his move to transform the 'Orange' link. How could the Ulster Unionist party elect such a man, they ask? They had, after all, the choice of a 'liberal' in Ken Maginnis (otherwise the most popular Unionist politician with both Protestants and Catholics according to a *Sunday Tribune* poll) or the highly experienced John Taylor, whose more recent speeches have seemed to some to possess a certain statesmanlike quality. But the Unionists were hungry for an articulate and energetic leader to put their case – just as Fianna Fail was when it selected Charles Haughey even after the affair of the arms trial.

Trimble set a cracking pace. The first leader of Ulster Unionism to meet with a Taoiseach in twenty years, he has also been to the White House. In the short term his realistic objective is not to make the Unionist Party attractive to Catholics (this is a highly utopian project), but to make it more attractive for intelligent Protestants. This is the real reason why he has pushed the pace on weakening traditional links with the Orange Order – to the distaste of traditionalists like Martin Smyth and Willie Ross.

Much of 1995 was to be dominated by bitter arguments about the progress being made – or rather the palpable lack of it – towards all-party talks leading to a final settlement. Many were understandably obsessed by the fear of the return to violence. But, set against the weight of inter-communal bitterness – which in Ulster always threatens to carry all before it – there were significant changes in both sides' political rhetoric. Sinn Fein found it impossible to accept the principle of the necessity of Unionist consent to a united Ireland, even when pressed at great length to do so by the other nationalist parties at the Dublin Forum for Peace and Reconciliation in January 1996. Nevertheless, there was evidence of a melting of hard-core republican ideology. New territory was entered when Jim Gibney, a senior republican, talked of coming to terms with the 'positive aspects of the Britishness [of the Ulster Unionists]'. In May 1995 Gibney talked of a need for a new language of compromise. A united Ireland remained his preferred option but he added:

> There are other options. We will examine them carefully …
> We will consider any political model designed to accommo-
> date the special characteristics of the Irish people which
> history has handed down to us.[11]

The British government for its part moved to explain more

fully its vision of north-south co-operation in the Frameworks Documents. Michael Ancram, Minister of State at the Northern Ireland Office with responsibility for political development, explained that the watchword was 'carefully defined and clearly limited co-operation'. Any north-south co-operation must 'produce better results for the people of Northern Ireland than doing it unilaterally'.[12] This was clearly designed to reassure Unionists alarmed by the scale of the 'cross borderism' proposed in the Frameworks Documents. In two major speeches – one given in Dublin to the Irish Association in early 1995 and the other to his own constituency in January 1996 – John Taylor gave a response to both Sinn Fein and the British government's evolving position. He acknowledged that the Adams leadership was trying to move the republican leadership towards involvement in constitutional politics. Himself the victim of an IRA assassination attempt, he told the Irish Association: 'Having been on the receiving end of the IRA campaign, I know this will still be a bitter pill for Unionists to swallow, but [Sinn Fein's] effectiveness and ingenuity cannot be denied. Time is a great healer though.'[13] In the Strangford speech Taylor revealed that he was clearly prepared to accept significant cross-border co-operation provided that it was designed on strictly practical grounds. Yet for much of the time louder and more angry themes – the traditional ones of mutual recrimination – appeared to predominate, and indeed did so in a way which made it difficult to hold out any real hope for an accommodation.

In February 1996 the Mitchell Commission report on the arms issue commissioned by the British government suggested the waiving of the British government's precondition – clearly articulated and understood by the Sinn Fein leadership since late 1993 – for all party talks.[14] Brushing aside irritation with the report's concerned social-worker tone, Whitehall accepted its conclusions but, at the same time, embraced David Trimble's concept of an election as a necessary precondition for dialogue. The early reaction was one of dismay in the nationalist political class, North and South. Trimble was seen to have influenced the agenda in a way which was unimaginable in the Molyneaux era. A sterile bout of political slanging ensued, but underlying difficulties were to be of greater importance. The British government had hoped to make substantial progress on the arms issue and the territorial claim before all-party talks; it had to accept failure on both accounts. This was bound to make any subsequent settlement harder to attain, but the basic problem remained in essence a simple one. In his Strangford speech John Taylor had had the nerve to quote a passage from the strongly Orange and Unionist clergyman, the Revd William Shaw Kerr, written in the *Irish Church Quarterly* on the eve of the Easter Rising in 1916:

> Only by doing justice to the principles and ideals of both sides can any feasible attempt be made to compromise that may obviate the unalterable tragedy of a civil war. We have had the narrowest escape from such a catastrophe. Are we not to seize the interval to bring about a peaceful solution?

Much would depend on the answer to this question.

Writing in the January 1996 issue of *Parliamentary Brief*, Anthony McIntyre offered an ominous echo of his earlier analysis, given at the time of the original ceasefire, when he wrote pessimistically that, 'The dove of peace shall be mortally winged, hitting the ground with such speed that its breaking of the sound barrier may ring ominously like the last bomb at the Baltic Exchange.' So, sadly, it proved, as the IRA renewed its London campaign with a massive bomb at Canary Wharf on 9 February 1996. The changing balance of forces within the republican movement had been evident for several months; in particular, the establishment of an international body (the Mitchell Commission) to report on the decommissioning of paramilitary arms posed major problems for republican militants – Senator Mitchell was never likely to (and did not) accept the republican contention that arms should only be handed over *after* an agreed political settlement. Perhaps more than John Major's support for an election – after all, fighting elections involves no dropping of republicans' core principle – this convinced the IRA leadership that the peace process was simply too unrewarding. Any effort to re-establish the ceasefire would have to deal with this perception if it was to have any chance of success.

Despite the bombing of Canary Wharf, Trimble maintained that it would be disastrous for Unionists to retreat into a posture of resistance to dialogue. Neither London nor Dublin had given up on the republican movement, and a simple denunciatory response from Unionists would guarantee that they became the passive victims of political change. He could also point out that one of the main reasons for the republican relapse was anger at his success in persuading John Major of the need for elections as an alternative way into dialogue with republicans.

In the elections for a Northern Ireland Forum held in May 1996, the UUP received 24.2 per cent of the votes cast, a decline of 5 per cent compared to the 1993 local government elections, while at 18.8 per cent, support for the DUP had increased by less than 2 per cent.[15] The limited rise in the DUP's vote reflected inroads made into its support by the two parties linked to Protestant paramilitary organisations, the Progressive Unionist Party (PUP), associated with the UVF, and the Ulster Democratic Party (UDP), close to the UDA. Both organisations had responded to the IRA's ceasefire with one of their own declared on 13 October 1994. On that occasion the 'Combined Loyalist Military Command' had stated that assurances had been sought from the British government that no secret deal had been done with the IRA and that 'The Union is safe.' They also offered 'abject and true remorse' to the families of their many innocent victims.[16] Although members of both groups, particularly the larger and more fragmented UDA, would soon be involved in sectarian attacks on Catholics and, like the IRA, continue to use violence to defend their many profitable criminal activities from selling drugs to cross-border fuel smuggling, the loyalist ceasefire had the temporary effect of enhancing the credibility and political acceptability of the PUP and the UDP amongst working-class Protestants.

Concerned that politics should be seen to work for the loyalist paramilitaries, the Northern Ireland Office provided a mixed electoral system for the Forum, allocating an additional 20 seats to be filled on a regional list system that gave two seats to each of the ten parties with the highest votes. As a result, the PUP with 3.5 per cent, the UDP with 2.2 per cent and the Northern Ireland Women's Coalition with just 1 per cent of the ballot were all allocated seats. However the Forum elections also gave a major boost to

Sinn Fein, which won its largest ever share of the vote, 15.5 per cent. The narrowing of the gap with the SDLP and Sinn Fein's strong performance in the Republic's 1997 General Election made a second ceasefire very likely. At the same time it was clear that republicans were waiting for a General Election to the Westminster parliament to deliver a Labour government with a secure majority that they hoped would push forward with a settlement that could be portrayed as transitional to Irish unity.

Trimble had established good relations with elements in 'New Labour' and was untroubled by the prospect of a substantial Labour victory. Tony Blair had sacked Kevin McNamara, Labour's 'green' Northern Ireland spokesman, and replaced him with Marjorie ('Mo') Mowlam. Significantly, Blair's first official trip outside London as Prime Minister was to Northern Ireland where, on 16 May at Balmoral, he affirmed that Unionists had nothing to fear from his government: 'A political settlement is not a slippery slope to a united Ireland. The government will not be persuaders for unity. The wagons do not need to be drawn up in a circle.' He also declared that he valued the Union and that, 'None of you in this hall today, even the youngest, is likely to see Northern Ireland as anything but a part of the United Kingdom.'[17] Such sentiments were profoundly distasteful to republicans, yet they were soon given a very practical compensation when the government declared that a renewed IRA ceasefire would allow Sinn Fein to join talks within six weeks. The decommissioning precondition had gone.

From the earliest days of Blair's administration, the attractive and also the less palatable aspects of the deal on offer to Unionists were relatively clear. There was acceptance of the consent principle as central to any settlement. This was to be copper-fastened by full constitutional recognition of Northern Ireland by the Republic. There would be a return of devolution to the North in the context of Labour's commitment to constitutional change in the rest of the United Kingdom. This would spell the end of the Irish government's 'interference' in the governance of the North in the form of the Anglo-Irish Agreement. The price to be paid for these political and constitutional gains was an Irish dimension embodied in a North-South Ministerial Council and the determination of Dublin, London and the SDLP that republicans must be integral to any settlement.

The Good Friday Agreement

The IRA did not return to full-scale 'armed struggle' during the sixteen months between the Canary Wharf bombing and its declaration of a second ceasefire on 21 July 1997. This was little consolation for the families of Detective Garda Gerry McCabe, shot dead in June 1996 during an IRA robbery of a mail van in County Limerick, or Stephen Restorick, a British solider killed by a sniper in South Armagh in February 1997. Most IRA activity during this period occurred in Britain, with a series of bombs in London and the devastation of the centre of Manchester by a 3,500 pound lorry-bomb in June 1996. As the General Election approached, its attacks focused on disrupting road and rail networks. Such violence served a number of purposes. It reminded the British government that if a ceasefire were restored republican demands would have to be addressed seriously if the peace process were not to be put in crisis again. Gerry Adams's 'peace strategy' continued to have a coercive element. It maintained the unity of the republican movement by showing restive elements in the IRA that involvement in negotiations had not made them redundant. By keeping the level of violence low, and mostly outside Northern Ireland, it did little or no damage Sinn Fein's continuing electoral growth. In the General Election held on 1 May 1997 Adams regained West Belfast from the SDLP and Martin McGuinness won Mid-Ulster from the DUP's William McCrea. In the local government elections held three weeks later, Sinn Fein increased its vote to 17 per cent, reducing the margin between itself and the SDLP from 75:25 of the nationalist vote in the 1993 local government elections to 55:45 in 1997.[18]

But if republican violence, or the threat of it, continued to perform important functions for Adams's strategy, it was difficult to see it as more than a means of increasing the 'green' façade of what, it was becoming increasingly clear, was a partitionist settlement. Adams was now writing about 'renegotiating the Union' rather than ending it.[19] The new Taoiseach, Bertie Ahern, had already declared that

'Irredentism is dead,' and that it was neither 'feasible [n]or desirable to attempt to incorporate Northern Ireland into a united Ireland against the will of a majority there, either by force or coercion'. He also rejected joint authority as a realistic option.[20] It was possible for republican leaders to depict the north-south institutions as mechanisms for creeping integration, but there was no guarantee that their version of north-south links would be the accepted one.

Republican optimism was encouraged by the way the new Labour government played down the question of decommissioning. There was also a commitment to 'confidence-building measures' in areas like reform of the RUC and the strengthening of fair employment legislation. Although the government had initially proposed to deal with the arms issue along the lines of the Mitchell Report, with decommissioning taking place simultaneously with political negotiations, this was dropped after a flexing of IRA muscle. On 17 June two community policemen were shot dead by the IRA in Lurgan, County Armagh. Within days an Anglo-Irish paper on decommissioning made it clear that all Sinn Fein would have to do was agree to discuss the problem during the talks.[21] This approach, while it permitted the successful completion of the negotiations, could not prevent the question from returning to haunt the early life of the new devolved institutions.

Some on the Tory right had denounced the internationalisation of the search for a settlement with the British acceptance of Senator George Mitchell as chair of the talks process, claiming that American involvement would simply strengthen the nationalist cause.[22] In fact, for Mitchell as well as his sponsor, President Clinton, it was accepted that the talks could only be successful if, as well as bringing republicans in from the cold, they did not drive the majority of Unionists into the rejectionist camp. At the centre of Gerry Adams's pan-nationalist strategy there had been the over-optimistic assumption that Clinton's involvement would follow an Irish-American agenda. While there was no doubting the Democrat administration's emotional sympathy for nationalist Ireland, Clinton's substantive political interest was in achieving a deal that could be trumpeted as 'historic', and this necessitated keeping Trimble's party on board.

Ian Paisley and Robert McCartney had led their parties

out of the talks when Sinn Fein entered them in September 1997, thereby permitting the negotiation of an agreement.[23] While the Sinn Fein leadership claimed a victory over Unionist 'intransigence' and British 'prevarication', some members of the IRA, both at leadership and rank-and-file level, were increasingly apprehensive about the implications of the peace process for traditional republican objectives. To gain entry to the talks process Sinn Fein had to sign up to the 'Mitchell Principles', which bound them, amongst other things, to 'democratic and exclusively peaceful means of resolving political problems and to the total disarmament of all paramilitary organisations'. They were also committed to urge an end to punishment killings and beatings – the main rest and recreation activity of IRA volunteers on ceasefire – and to take effective steps to prevent them taking place.[24] Decommissioning was treated as an issue to be addressed during the talks and, although Unionist sceptics predicted that the question would be fudged, there were some in the republican movement who feared that the military integrity of the IRA would be sacrificed on the altar of Sinn Fein's electoral and governmental ambitions. To quieten such voices, a senior IRA spokesman had told *An Phoblacht* that the IRA 'would have problems with sections of the Mitchell Principles' and that the IRA was not a participant in the talks.[25] This was a fiction, as senior members of the political wing of the republican movement were also members of the IRA's Army Council, but it did reflect real tensions in the movement created by the political leadership's increasing involvement in the process of political bargaining.

Already the Continuity IRA, the military wing of Adams's former comrades who had seceded in 1986 to form Republican Sinn Fein, was attempting to attract disgruntled Provisionals with a series of car-bomb attacks on RUC stations. In November 1997 an attempt by Adams's supporters in the IRA to give control over the ultimate disposal of arms to the Army Council resulted in a scission when the IRA's Quartermaster General and a number of other senior figures in the border area resigned from the movement and formed the 'Real IRA'.[26] The dissidents established their own political wing, the 32-County Sovereignty Movement, which, although initially it had the support of only a few disillusioned members of Sinn Fein, made up for this in 'movement credibility' by having the support of a sister of Bobby Sands. Given the immense significance of the deaths of Sands and his comrades for the Provisional movement, it was acutely embarrassing for Adams to be condemned by Bernadette Sands-McKevitt for entering a talks process that could only result in a 'modernised version of partition'. As she witheringly put it, her brother did not die for the establishment of a cross-border tourism authority.[27]

If republicans were going to embrace a settlement which left the North as part of the United Kingdom for at least the medium term, and also accepted the principle of consent, or, to use the movement's traditional language, the 'Unionist veto', then it was important that it could be presented to their supporters as 'transitional'. Acceptance of new devolved structures of government at Stormont needed to be balanced by a set of strong, free-standing north-south institutions along the lines set out in the Frameworks Documents. But in January 1998 even these consolatory structures were called into question by the British and Irish governments' joint document entitled 'Heads of Agreement', which, in setting out their understanding of the likely parameters of any final deal, proposed north south institutions that would be mandated by and accountable to the Northern Ireland Assembly and the Irish parliament. A Belfast-based journalist knowledgeable about republicanism described Heads of Agreement as a triumph for Trimble and a disaster for republicanism.[28] In fact, as Trimble himself pointed out, the process of bargaining which led to an agreement and subsequently to the formation of an 'inclusive' government for Northern Ireland was a 'white-knuckle ride' in which an apparent victory for one side produced such a bitter response that the other camp was soon provided with a compensatory 'victory' of its own.

Republican displeasure was soon evident in another 'tactical use of armed struggle' in February 1998 when first an alleged drug dealer and then a prominent loyalist were shot dead. Although the violence resulted in Sinn Fein being temporarily excluded from the talks, it may have contributed to the Irish government's determination to press the British for a return to the bolder version of the cross-borderism of the Frameworks Documents. The result was a final frenetic four days of negotiation kick-started by George Mitchell's presentation to the parties of a draft of the agreement on 7 April. This included a section on strand two (north-south institutions) which returned to a maximalist version of the Frameworks vision. Mitchell himself recognised that this would be unacceptable to Trimble, and with the leader of the Alliance Party, John Alderdice, predicting disaster if the proposals were pursued, Blair and Ahern descended on Stormont shortly before Easter for three days and nights of what James Molyneaux disparagingly referred to as 'high-wire act' negotiations.

What became known as the Good Friday Agreement allowed Trimble to claim that the Union was not only safe but also stronger because of Unionist negotiating successes in strand two and on constitutional recognition. Unionist focus on strand two during the final days of the negotiations had achieved a result: the North-South Ministerial Council was not the free-standing body desired by republicans, and it was difficult for either republicans or Unionist rejectionists to portray the reduced list of 'implementation bodies' in areas like animal and plant health and teacher qualifications as 'creeping reunification'. For the first time in its history the Irish state had committed itself to the constitutional recognition of Northern Ireland, and all signatories of the Agreement were bound to accepting the principle of consent.

But the strongly-held belief of the two governments and the SDLP that republicans were essential to any final settlement inevitably meant that Unionists would have to pay a price for these victories. On devolution itself there was little attempt to defend the original Unionist Party position of administrative devolution with committee chairs allocated by the d'Hondt rule, a mathematical device normally used for the allocation of seats in legislatures under the additional-member system of proportional representation. The SDLP demand was for a power-sharing cabinet, while republicans, who were still ideologically opposed to devolution, had made no contribution to the negotiations in this area, although of course demanding 'inclusion' in whatever structures resulted. Robin Wilson described the result as 'Rather like the camel that emerged from a committee designing a horse, a power-sharing executive with positions distributed by d'Hondt was the outcome.'[29]

Unionists had agreed to what was in essence a compulsory coalition with republicans. If there was a calculation that this would be easier to sell to their supporters than a voluntary form of power-sharing, this was soon undermined by the lack of a clear linkage between participation in government and decommissioning. This allowed republicans to claim that IRA action on weapons was not a precondition for Sinn Fein's participation in government. It was this issue that led some of the members of Trimble's negotiating team, most notably the MP for Lagan Valley, Jeffery Donaldson, to refuse to support the Agreement. Ambiguity on the question of decommissioning was part of the price that Unionists had to pay to allow republicanism a soft landing, given that, as one of their leading strategists admitted, the Agreement had legitimised the British state in Ireland.[30] Another last-minute concession to republican unhappiness with the north-south and constitutional dimensions of the deal was the reduction from three to two years of the period before which prisoners belonging to paramilitary groups on ceasefire would be released. This and what Sinn Fein referred to as the 'Equality Agenda' – involving human rights legislation and safeguards, commissions on policing and criminal justice – and a British commitment to demilitarisation were to act as consolation for what a significant number of republicans considered an Agreement that enshrined the 'Unionist veto'.

It was these questions that dominated the intra-Unionist debate on the Agreement in the period leading to the referendums on 20 May when the electorates both north and south of the border were to express a judgement on what had been agreed on Good Friday. It soon became clear that while nationalists and republicans overwhelmingly supported the deal, Unionists were split. In the weeks leading up to the referendum in Northern Ireland attention focused not on the constitutional aspects of the deal and Trimble's success in domesticating the north-south institutions but on the more emotive issues of early prisoner releases, the presence of 'terrorists' in government and the supposed threat to the future of the RUC. Unionist rejectionists benefited from the spectacle of the triumphal reception given at a special Sinn Fein conference to recently released IRA men who had been involved in bombings and kidnapping in London in the 1970s. This event was, of course, designed to give the imprimatur of those who had killed and suffered two decades of imprisonment to a radically revised republican strategy, but it produced a predictable frisson of repulsion in the Unionist community and did major damage to the pro-Agreement cause.

The fact that a small minority of Unionists voted 'yes' in the referendum was in large part the result of Blair's frequent trips to the North during the final two weeks of the campaign, and his numerous reassurances, particularly on the issue of decommissioning. He was backed up by a cavalcade of British political leaders and international figures including Nelson Mandela. A strong sense of the 'historic' nature of the choice on offer was also encouraged by an unprecedented presence of the national and international media. A well-funded 'Yes' campaign run by Saatchi and Saatchi even teamed up the besuited and middle-aged figures of Trimble and Hume with the Irish 'mega-band' U2 at a rock concert in Belfast in the final days of the campaign.

The result was the mobilisation of the Protestant 'comfortable classes' in an unprecedented fashion. At 81 per cent, turn-out was the highest ever in Northern Ireland: 160,000 more people participated than in the previous Westminster election, but in the Republic a mere 56 per cent of the electorate bothered to vote.[31] This surge in participation was disproportionately drawn from the majority Unionist areas east of the Bann, where turn-out was traditionally the lowest. So although the 71 per cent 'yes' vote gave the Agreement a strong boost, its basis in the Unionist community was relatively precarious. As a leading member of the DUP observed of those who had broken the habit of a lifetime, 'They came out to vote for what they saw as peace and now they will return to political hibernation for another 30 years. But those who voted "No" are not so apathetic.'[32]

This prediction appeared to be confirmed a month later with the election for the new Northern Ireland Assembly on 25 June. Many of those Unionists who had voted 'yes' in May stayed at home and Trimble's party turned in its worst ever performance. The UUP received 21.3 per cent of the first preference votes to the SDLP's 22 per cent, while DUP achieved 18 per cent. Although pro-Agreement parties won 73 per cent of the vote and 80 of the Assembly's 108 seats, there was no disguising the precarious nature of Unionist support in the Assembly, where pro-Agreement Unionists held 30 seats while the 'antis' had 28. Nationalist and republican concern with the supposed danger of a Unionist majority abusing its position had led to mechanisms for cross-community validation on key decisions which required, as a minimum, the support of 40 per cent of each communal bloc. This was now an ever-present threat to pro-Agreement Unionism.

Movement by the IRA on the arms issue would have given a substantial boost to Trimble's position both within his own party and in the wider Unionist community. The political wing of republicanism had never seemed stronger. The Assembly elections had been a major victory for Adams's pan-nationalist strategy. The SDLP topped the poll with 22 per cent and, with a Sinn Fein vote of 17.7 per cent, the aggregate vote of the nationalist/republican bloc reached its highest ever level. The peace process had put Adams and McGuinness at the centre of national and international attention. Received respectfully in Downing Street, Leinster House and the White House, they were listened to deferentially when they continued to complain of being marginalised. They had before them the heady vision of being the first transnational party in the European Union, with representatives elected to the Dail, Stormont and Westminster, and the possibility of being in government in both Belfast and Dublin.

If the massive political benefits of flexibility, compromise and *realpolitik* were obvious, the dire futility of a return to armed struggle was made awfully clear on 15 August in Omagh when 29 people were murdered in a Real IRA car-bomb attack. This was worst single atrocity in Northern Ireland during the Troubles. In the words of a former IRA hunger striker, Omagh was 'the end of an era for a certain school of republican thought. What little sympathy was remaining for the physical force element evaporated on that dreadful Saturday afternoon.'[33] The Omagh atrocity offered the leadership of the republican movement the best possible conditions to address the arms issue. However nothing was done for another year and a half, by which time Trimble's position was substantially weaker within his party and the wider electorate.

In part this reflected Adams's long-standing caution in edging the movement in a more flexible and political direction while doing his utmost to prevent a split. It was also the case that the substantively partitionist nature of the deal which republicans had accepted made action on arms more problematic: giving ground on political fundamentals made even a gesture on arms more difficult to sell within the IRA. There was also a major obstacle in the strong element of solipsistic self-righteousness so strongly developed in the republican mentality. Seen from this perspective, republican violence was a legitimate response to state and loyalist violence. This belief exists despite the fact that of the 3,633 violent deaths during the Troubles, republicans were responsible for 2,139, almost 60 per cent of the total. In comparison, the reviled RUC, whose disbanding Sinn Fein put near the top of its post-Agreement demands, was responsible for just 52 deaths.[34] Only a tiny element of the most sophisticated in the republican leadership would even hint at the possibility that the armed struggle had made an independent and powerful contribution to making Northern Ireland in 1998 more polarised, more segregated and more embittered than it had been thirty years earlier. From this perspective, the ceasefire was the fundamental concession made by the IRA and pressure for it to move on decommissioning was an attempt to 'humiliate' an 'undefeated army'.

Gerry Adams had recognised that most Unionists 'quite rightly' would not feel any gratitude towards the IRA, yet he did expect them to understand that any action on weapons would have to wait until all the aspects of the Agreement had been implemented, particularly the provision for an international commission on policing. Until then the IRA would remain 'on the sidelines'.[35] It did not take a particularly negative cast of mind for many in the Unionist community to interpret this as 'the politics of threat.'

From June 1998 to December 1999 David Trimble maintained his refusal to form an administration that included Sinn Fein until the weapons issue was seriously addressed. A tactically ingenious 'sequencing' proposition was put forward by the two governments at Hillsborough in April 1999 by which a 'shadow executive' would be formed and within a month, during a 'collective act of reconciliation', some arms would be 'put beyond use on a voluntary basis' and powers devolved to the executive. Martin McGuinness rejected the proposals as an ultimatum imposed by David Trimble and the British military establishment.[36] With republicans talking of the danger of a split, Unionists came under intense pressure to make a 'leap of faith' on the basis of Downing Street's belief that there had been a 'seismic shift' in the republican position. Blair, buoyed up by his central role in the Kosovo conflict and keen to announce an Ulster deal to coincide with the inauguration of the Welsh and Scottish assemblies, set a deadline of 30 June. If Trimble had felt any inclination to oblige a prime minister with whom he had an extremely good personal relationship, this was undermined by another disappointing electoral performance. In the European elections held in June the Ulster Unionist Party received 17.6 per cent of the vote, its lowest ever share of the poll, and narrowly avoided finding itself in an ignominious fourth place behind Sinn Fein.[37]

Trimble's rejection of the two governments' new attempt at sequencing in 'The Way Forward' proposals in July led to the renewed involvement of George Mitchell in a review of the Agreement that started in the autumn. Despite an increase in IRA punishment beatings and killings during the summer, Mitchell achieved a breakthrough with an agreement by Trimble to recommend to his party that, in return for a commitment by republicans to address the decommissioning issue by the end of January 2000, an executive could be formed. However the souring of the atmosphere as a result of the publication of the Patten Report on policing in September made Trimble's offer conditional. The international commission headed by the former Governor of Hong Kong produced a report that, while it did not recommend the disbanding of the force, as republicans demanded, put forward proposals for radical restructuring. The most controversial proposals were for a change in the force's name and the insistence that its symbols should not reflect those of the British or the Irish state. Combined with a failure to recognise the sacrifice of more than 300 dead police officers, the report produced fierce denunciations from all shades of Unionism.

Believing that he might not win a majority in the Ulster

Unionist Council for his proposal to form a government including Sinn Fein, Trimble promised to recall the Council in February to report on what progress there had been on the issue of weapons and deposited a post-dated letter of resignation as leader of the party with its president. Adams now claimed that Trimble had added a new precondition to what had been agreed in the talks chaired by George Mitchell. The result was that while in January 2000 Northern Ireland had its first devolved government since 1974, it lacked even the rudiments of a common understanding on one of the province's central problems – after all, under the Good Friday Agreement the decommissioning of paramilitary weapons was supposed to be completed by May 2000. This experience of devolved government lasted less than two months. While Unionists had to accustom themselves to two republicans, one of them, Martin McGuinness, popularly believed to have been until very recently a member of the IRA's Army Council, running the departments of Health and Education, republicans appear to have calculated that once the institutions of government were functioning Unionists would be reluctant to bring them down.

With the support of a more sympathetic Secretary of State, Peter Mandelson, who had replaced Mo Mowlam in October 1999, Trimble did not hesitate to use his threat of resignation to force a suspension of the institutions in February. This hard-nosed approach steadied nerves in his own party and forced republicans to move on arms decommissioning. On 6 May an IRA statement committed it to put its arms 'completely and verifiably beyond use' in a manner that would be acceptable to the International Commission on Decommissioning headed by the Canadian General John de Chastelain. The return of devolution on 27 May 2000 took place after Trimble had received the support of 53 per cent of the delegates to the Ulster Unionist Council, the party's ruling body. His support in the council had fallen substantially from the 72 per cent of the UUC that had voted in favour of the Good Friday Agreement in April 1998. However neither nationalists nor republicans appeared to be particularly concerned about this attenuation of pro-Agreement Unionism. After a leading member of the African National Congress and a senior Finnish politician independently inspected two IRA arms dumps in June, there was little more of substance for General de Chastelain to report. Meanwhile, Sinn Fein and the SDLP criticised the British government for allegedly eviscerating the Patten Report, while Trimble used his powers as First Minister to ban Sinn Fein ministers from attending meetings of the North-South Ministerial Council and the implementation bodies.

With a senior republican claiming that Trimble's action and the failure of the British government to deliver on Patten and 'demilitarisation' (the closing down of British army installations in strategic border areas like South Armagh was particularly emphasised) was threatening the peace process,[38] 2001 began gloomily for pro-Agreement Ulster Unionists. The IRA had formally disengaged from contacts with the international decommissioning body and the UUP's continued involvement in government with Sinn Fein was a source of increasing intra-party conflict as activists faced a General Election with a high probability of losses to the DUP. Reacting to this pressure, Trimble lodged a letter with the Speaker of the Northern Ireland Assembly on 23 May resigning as First Minister with effect from 1 July 2001 if the IRA had not begun to decommission by then. Despite this, the UUP lost three seats in the General Election while the DUP gained two. If Trimble had not taken this step, it is possible that the UUP would have lost two more seats, his own in Upper Bann, where he was hard-pressed by a little-known DUP candidate, and East Antrim. The overall result – UUP, 26.8 per cent and six seats; DUP, 22.5 per cent and five seats; Sinn Fein, 21.7 per cent and four seats and the SDLP, 21.0 per cent and three seats – was interpreted by many commentators as a triumph for the extremes.[39]

This was an oversimplification. Such a judgement was based on a comparison with the 1997 election, thus ignoring the radical effects of the Good Friday Agreement on the political environment in Northern Ireland, particularly its destabilising influence on Unionism. A better comparison is with the 1998 Assembly elections, and here the picture for pro-Agreement Unionism was not quite so bleak. The UUP vote increased from 21.3 to 26.8 per cent. It was also the case that the loss of the Fermanagh-South Tyrone seat to Sinn Fein was a direct result of the intervention of a proxy DUP candidate, a victim of the IRA's 1987 Enniskillen bombing who stood as an anti-Agreement candidate. The DUP's victories were also accompanied by a shift in its discourse towards a subtler, less hysterical critique of the Agreement. This was most ably accomplished by the DUP victor in North Belfast, Nigel Dodds, who focused not on the influence of Dublin or the Vatican but on the allegedly unbalanced nature of the workings of the Agreement, which he argued was hollowing out the Britishness of the North. This took up emotionally powerful issues like the 'destruction of the RUC' and Sinn Fein ministers' refusal to allow the Union Jack to fly over their buildings.

If decommissioning had begun, it might have been easier to deal with these criticisms, particularly as the DUP was heavily involved in the institutions of the Agreement, sitting on Assembly committees with Sinn Fein and participating in the Executive although refusing to sit around the cabinet table with 'Sinn Fein-IRA' ministers. Yet senior republican figures were still telling the rank-and-file that there would be no decommissioning.[40] Attempts to justify republicans' refusal to move on arms pointed to a continuing campaign of pipe-bomb attacks on Catholic homes by elements of the UDA and the challenge posed by republican dissidents. These justifications were shown to be less than convincing when, in October 2001, the IRA began to decommission despite continuing sectarian attacks and the scorn of fundamentalists who claimed the Provisionals had finally surrendered. That the weapons question was at last addressed was a result of events in Colombia and the United States combining to put irresistible pressure on the Sinn Fein leadership.

Despite Irish fears that the new US president, George W. Bush, would adopt a more distant approach to Northern Ireland, US strategic concerns ensured an engagement that, for the first time since 1994, Irish republicans would find unwelcome. Sinn Fein was acutely embarrassed by the arrest of three its supporters in Bogota on 6 August. It was unable to give a satisfactory explanation to either the Bush administration or its wealthy Irish-American supporters in response to the claim by the Colombian authorities that the three Irishmen had been training FARC guerrillas. A month later the events of 11 September brought an excruciating and irresistible pressure on Adams to demonstrate, beyond contradiction, that Irish republicans were not part of the 'international terrorist network'. Despite the instinctive anti-imperialism of many republicans – manifest in an editorial in *An Phoblacht* in the immediate aftermath of the attacks on the Twin Towers and the Pentagon denouncing US policies in the Middle East and Latin America – the Sinn Fein leadership moved quickly to accommodate the White House and corporate Irish-America, and on 26 October the IRA announced that it had begun the process of decommmissioning.[41]

The IRA's action enabled Trimble to win the support of the UUC for a return to government and, with no elections due until 2003, pro-Agreement Unionists hoped that, having secured the principle of consent, the abandonment of the Republic's territorial claim and the beginning of a process that republicans had claimed would never happen, ground lost to the DUP could be regained. However the prolonged nature of the conflict over arms decommissioning and the lack of transparency involved in its beginning undermined its positive effects, as did the British government's acceptance that the process might take years to complete.

Protestant 'alienation' became a central theme in the speeches of NIO ministers, and it took a particularly ugly form in the blockade of a Catholic primary school in North Belfast where declining working-class Protestant communities in areas like Glenbryn and Tiger's Bay felt themselves to be losing out to in a zero-sum territorial conflict with Catholics. A much broader section of the Unionist community found it difficult to accept a republican presence in government despite increasing signs that there was little chance of the Provisionals going back to war. This did not stem, as some commentators claimed, from an unwillingness to accept equality with Catholics, but from a perception that the new dispensation was based on the steady dilution of the North's Britishness, as reflected in changes in the name and symbols of the RUC and disputes over the role of British royal insignia in the court system. It was also the case that republican and loyalist guns, baseball bats and iron bars continued to be used to impose the summary and brutal 'justice' of the paramilitaries in both Catholic and Protestant working-class areas.

Adams's achievement in burying the republican project – and with it the abandonment of armed struggle – has removed a major source of communal polarisation. However the vacuousness at the core of Sinn Fein's reunification project was compensated for by its militant pursuit of an agenda based on ethnic grievance within Northern Ireland. The Blair government's indulgence of this agenda became the single most important cause of Unionist disenchantment with the Agreement. Lord Saville's Inquiry into the Bloody Sunday killings, possible inquiries into allegations of security force collusion in loyalist killings of Catholics and the new Police Ombudsman's criticism of the activities of the RUC's Special Branch in relation to the Omagh atrocity all contributed to a souring of Unionist opinion. By the beginning of 2002 Northern Ireland had moved decisively from war to peace, but those political forces within nationalism and Unionism that were most capable of accommodation were on the defensive. Despite the effect of 11 September in banishing the possibility of another Canary Wharf, the British government still seemed unwilling to upset republican sensibilities. However, without a more robust defence of the Union from London it seemed all too likely that the 2003 elections would confirm the minority status of Trimble's strand of Unionism.

Even if the forward march of the DUP is halted, there is little possibility of the devolved institutions surviving if Sinn Fein maintains and consolidates its position as the largest nationalist party. The prospect of Gerry Adams as Deputy First Minister would be daunting for all but a small fraction of Unionists. An internal Sinn Fein document suggests that republicans believe a 'strategic alliance' for a united Ireland only needs the support of 10 per cent of Unionists.[42] However, as Adams more openly acknowledges the partitionist nature of the Agreement, Sinn Fein's real trajectory comes increasingly into conflict with its vestigial republicanism. Choosing to address the World Economic Forum in New York rather than the march to commemorate the 30th anniversary of Bloody Sunday in Derry, Adams proclaimed, 'I don't think we can force upon Unionism an all Ireland state which doesn't have their assent or consent.'[43]

As Sinn Fein becomes increasingly integrated into the Stormont system, the maintenance of the North's uneasy peace appears more certain. What is much less clear is the prospect for a politics which is more than a struggle for ethnic supremacy.

Notes

1. Hence the coverage in the September 1994 issue of the consistently well informed magazine *Fortnight*, which went to press on the eve of the ceasefire announcement.

2. Quoted in H.O. Arnold Forster, *The Truth About the Land League*, London 1883, p. 13.

3. Conor Cruise O'Brien, *The Great Melody: A Thematic Biography of Edmund Burke*, London 1992.

4. *Irish Independent*, 10 September 1994.

5. Paul Bew and Paul Dixon, 'Labour Party Policy and Northern Ireland' in B. Barton and P. Roche (eds), *The Northern Ireland Question: Perspectives and Policies*, Aldershot 1994.

6. 'Waking up to Reality', *Fortnight*, October 1994.

7. On this point see, notably, Prof. Keith Kyle's lecture on the framework documents published by the Institute of Conflict Studies in Coleraine, 1995.

8. *Irish Times*, 15 November 1989.

9. David Trimble, *The Foundation of Northern Ireland*, Lurgan 1991.

10. J.A. McKibben, *Ulster Vanguard: A Sociological Profile*, unpublished MSSc thesis, Queen's University, Belfast, 1990, pp. 172-208.

11. *Times*, 24 May 1995.

12. *Irish Independent*, 26 April 1995.

13. Ibid.

14. See the interview given by Mr Gerry Adams in the *Irish News*, 8 January 1994. 'Mr Mayhew goes on to say, "Well, the exploratory dialogue will be so we can discuss with Sinn Fein how the IRA will hand over their weapons." So I say to myself, "This is what they want. They want the IRA to stop so that Sinn Fein can have the privilege 12 weeks later, having been properly sanitised and come out of quarantine, to have discussions with civil servants on how the IRA can hand over their weapons." ' Mr Adams added, 'I hear that reiterated again and again by Douglas Hurd, John Major, by Patrick Mayhew.'

But this did not stop him writing in the *Irish Times* on 14 July 1995: 'For its part, the British government never made an issue of decommissioning in the run-up to the IRA cessation as it knew perfectly well that this was an unrealistic demand. London knew that there would not have been a cessation if this demand had been made a precondition for talks. Nowhere in public statements nor in the course of dialogue and exchanges between the British government and Sinn Fein over a two-year period prior to the IRA cessation was this made an issue either as a precondition or otherwise.'

15. Sydney Elliott and W.D. Flackes, *Northern Ireland, A Political Directory 1968-1999*, Belfast 1999, p. 580.

16. Paul Bew and Gordon Gillespie, *Northern Ireland: A Chronology of the Troubles 1968-1999*, Dublin 1999, p. 298.

17. The text of the Balmoral speech can be found in Paul Bew, Henry Patterson and Paul Teague, *Between War and Peace: The Political Future of Northern Ireland*, London 1997, pp. 217-24.

18. Elliott and Flackes, *Political Directory*, p. 594.

19. Henry Patterson, *The Politics of Illusion: A Political History of the IRA*, London 1997, p.289.

20. Speech to the Irish Association, 2 February 1995, reprinted in Bew, Patterson and Teague, *Between War and Peace*, pp. 225-31.

21. Paul Bew, 'Decommissioning' in Robin Wilson (ed.), *Agreeing to Disagree? A Guide to the Northern Ireland Assembly*, Norwich 2001, pp. 139-42.

22. 'But is There an Agreement on Northern Ireland?', *Daily Telegraph*, 17 April 1998.

23. 'Reaching an agreement without their presence was extremely difficult, it would have been impossible with them in the room.' George Mitchell, *Making Peace*, London 1999, p. 110.

24. Bew and Gillespie, *Northern Ireland: A Chronology of the Troubles*, p. 318.

25. Ibid., p. 348

26. Deaglan De Breadun, *The Far Side of Revenge: Making Peace in Northern Ireland*, Cork 2001, p. 74.

27. Ibid., pp. 84-5.

28. Ed Moloney, 'Triumph and Disaster', *Sunday Tribune*, 18 January 1998.

29. Robin Wilson, 'The Executive Committee' in Wilson (ed.), *Agreeing to Disagree*, p. 76.

30. Mitchell McLaughlin in an interview in *Parliamentary Brief*, May/June 1998, quoted in Thomas Hennessey, *The Northern Ireland Peace Process*, Dublin 2000, p. 171.

31. Richard Sinnott, 'Historic Day Blemished by Low Poll', *Irish Times*, 25 May 1998.

32. Suzanne Breen, 'United No Parties Set Their Sights on Assembly', *Irish Times*, 25 May 1998.

33. Tommy McKearney, 'There is no Support for IRA Physical Force Any More', *Sunday Tribune*, 15 August 1999.

34. Paul Bew, 'Reckoning the Dead', *Times Literary Supplement*, 28 January 2000.

35. 'Keep IRA on Sidelines, Says Adams', interview by Geraldine Kennedy, *Irish Times*, 20 May 1998.

36. *Irish Times*, 8 April 1999.

37. Frank Millar, 'No Way to Soften the Impact of Paisley's Defiant Triumph', *Irish Times*, 15 June 1999.

38. Anne Cadwallader, 'Peace Deal on its Last Legs, Says IRA', *Ireland on Sunday*, 24 December 2000.

39. For a good critique, see Jyrki Ruohomaki's analysis of the election results in a Democratic Dialogue discussion paper: http://www.democraticdialogue.org/working/Elect.htm

40. Jim Cusack, 'Decommissioning Pace Forced by IRA's Colombian Links', *Irish Times*, 27 October 2001.

41. Ibid. The behaviour of the Bush presidency contrasted with its predecessor; for an illuminating study of the Clinton administration's attitude to IRA gun-running from Florida after the second ceasefire, see Max Potter's article in the US edition of *GQ*, August 2001.

42. 'A Road Map to the Republic', Sinn Fein internal discussion document, January 2002.

43. Suzanne Breen, 'Words for a World Stage from Adams', *Newsletter*, 7 February 2002.

Biographical Notes

John Andrews, 1871-1956

Prime Minister of Northern Ireland. Andrews came from a family with substantial interests in flax-spinning and railways and was president of the Ulster Unionist Labour Association and of the Belfast Chamber of Commerce in 1936. He was Minister of Labour from 1921 to 1937, Minister of Finance from 1937 to 1940 and Prime Minister from 1940 to 1943. From a liberal family, Andrews took up senior office in the Orange Order at the relatively late date of 1941. As late as 1 August 1938 he wrote to a liberal friend: 'I am delighted to hear that you are sticking to the old ship and carrying the old flag which you so gallantly upheld all your life.' But three years later in August 1941 he insisted to the same friend, General Hugh Montgomery: 'I do not admit for a moment that, as a government, we in Northern Ireland have been intolerant ... May I repeat that if the minority here had acted as the minority in southern Ireland had done, the position might have been very different.' (PRONI D2661/6/1 A/1)

Sir Richard Dawson Bates, 1876-1949

A Belfast solicitor, secretary of the Ulster Unionist Council 1906 to 1921. Responsible for the organisation of the Ulster Covenant in 1912. Knighted 1921. Stormont MP for East Belfast from 1921 to 1929 and Belfast Victoria from 1929 to 1943. J.F. Harbinson (*The Ulster Unionist Party 1882-1973*, Belfast 1973, pp. 50-7) offers this description of Bates: 'A small man, physically and intellectually ... His great strength was his meticulous attention to detail ... he was the grey eminence of Ulster Unionism who remained in the shadow of Carson and Craig.' Bates was widely considered to be the least enlightened member of the Cabinet, though even he acknowledged, in private conversation, the serious 'menace' of the Ulster Protestant League. (PRONI D2661/C/1/M/11)

Sir Basil Brooke (Viscount Brookeborough), 1888-1973

Prime Minister of Northern Ireland. Educated at Winchester and Sandhurst, he was a scion of the 'fighting Brookes', a Fermanagh landowning family. The First World War cost him his religious faith, the Second took away two of his sons. In the early stages of both wars he was strikingly willing to consider an entirely new Irish dispensation (even unity) as a price of wholehearted Irish support against Germany. Although his considerable political skills did not desert him until his last years in office, he was a man of shrewish political temperament, haunted always by the bitter anti-nationalist rhetoric that flowed from his involvement in the Ulster Special Constabulary in the 1920s. His successor, Terence O'Neill, remarked famously of Brooke in his later years that, 'Those who met him imagined that he was relaxing away from his desk. What they didn't realise was that there was no desk.'

Sir Edward Carson, 1854-1935

Edward Carson was born in Dublin, educated at Portarlington and Trinity College, Dublin, and called to the Irish Bar in 1877. In 1893 he was called to the English Bar and became Queen's Counsel in 1894, receiving a knighthood in 1900. In 1910 he accepted the leadership of the Irish Unionists at Westminster and became the principal leader of the Unionist resistance during the third Home Rule crisis of 1912-14. To many he seemed to follow precisely those Parnellite principles – the combination of constitutional and unconstitutional activity – which he had so abhorred when practised by nationalists in the iSSOs. Somewhat ironically, in this context, he became Attorney-General in 1915; in 1916 he accepted the office of First Lord of the Admiralty and in

1917 entered the War Cabinet. In 1918 Carson abandoned his Dublin University seat for the Belfast Duncairn division, but refused the invitation to become Prime Minister of Northern Ireland in 1921. Carson tried to stand apart from the northern sectarian influences which have played such a role in Irish Unionism. He was almost sentimentally Irish: 'I was born and bred an Irishman and I'll always be one,' and was easily reconciled to John Redmond, the leader of constitutional nationalism in 1915. He was, however, always very bitter about the treatment of Southern Protestants by the independent Irish governments of the 1920s and '30s. Carson believed profoundly that all evils of British policy in Ireland pre-dated the Union and that the Union provided the ideal framework for the development and co-operation of the two islands.

Michael Collins, 1890-1922

Born in County Cork, worked as a clerk in London, fought in the GPO in 1916; interned and released in December 1916; organised intelligence operations against the British in the Anglo-Irish war. Was credited with evolving a 'new concept of guerrilla war'; Minister of Home Affairs, 1918 and Minister for Finance 1919-22, in the first Dail Eireann. Member of the Treaty delegation, December 1921; Commander-in-chief of the government forces in the Civil War; shot and killed in County Cork, 22 August 1922, not far from where he was born, in an ambush set by a former colleague in arms. His most recent biographer, Tim Pat Coogan, insists that Collins did 'everything in his power to destabilise the Northern State'.

Sir James Craig (Viscount Craigavon), 1871-1940

Prime Minister of Northern Ireland. During his premiership (1921-40) Craig successfully impressed his personality on the institutions of government in Ulster. In February 1921, shortly before becoming Prime Minister, he declared: 'The rights of the minority must be sacred to the majority ... it will only be by broad views, tolerant ideas and a real desire for liberty of conscience that we here can make an ideal of the parliament and executive.' But his political life was dominated by a fear of internal Protestant schism and unfortunately in his later and least impressive years he found it difficult to maintain this early spirit and his rhetoric and that of his ministers often caused offence within the Catholic community.

Craig was the son of a Presbyterian whiskey millionaire and educated at Merchiston in Edinburgh. In 1906 he won his parliamentary seat (for Down East, which he held until 1918) in a close contest with an agrarian radical Unionist, James Woods; his speeches on the land question in this period place him firmly in the realistic and reformist wing of Unionism. Amid the ranks of Conservative and Unionist MPs demoralised and decimated by the Liberal landslide, the energetic Craig found it relatively easy to make a name for himself at Westminster, principally as a vigorous opponent of Home Rule. Devolution for Northern Ireland after 1921 ended this phase of his career. Although, like many other Unionists, Craig was reluctant to accept such a settlement of the Irish question, he rapidly made a virtue of necessity. His political concerns became increasingly parochial and 'little Ulsterist' in outlook and he became more-or-less indifferent to the wider interests of Great Britain and the empire.

As the Free State moved towards the adoption in 1937 of what one of its ministers (Sean McEntee) was happy to describe as 'a Catholic constitution for a Catholic state', Craig was equally happy to talk of 'a Protestant parliament for a Protestant people'. His style of work became increasingly casual; he distributed 'bones' to the 'dogs', as he once described his operation of the spoils system.

Craig in his earlier years enjoyed a promising career outside Ulster. From 1900 to 1902 he served with distinction in South Africa and by 1920 he had become Parliamentary and Financial Secretary to the Admiralty. It is hard to resist the conclusion that the return to Ulster narrowed his horizons. In this he resembled his great local nationalist rival, Joe Devlin, who had, if anything, an even more promising Westminster career between 1900 to 1918 and was equally shrivelled by the devolution experiment which made him little more than a local tribal leader.

William Craig, 1924-

Having been active in the Young Unionist Movement, William Craig was elected as the Stormont MP for Larne in 1960 and became government Chief Whip in 1962. In this position he played a key role in Terence O'Neill's 'emergence' as Brookeborough's successor and was one of O'Neill's close allies in the early years of his premiership. He served as Minister of Home Affairs and then as Minister of Health and Local Government. When O'Neill set up a new Ministry of Development in 1965 Craig was appointed Minister. He returned, unhappily it appears, to Home Affairs in 1966. The onset of the civil rights movement saw the beginning of a clear shift to the right in his political views, and his decision to restrict the route of the 5 October 1968 civil rights march in Derry and the resulting police violence against the marchers made the North internationally newsworthy. Sacked by O'Neill in December 1968 for criticising reformist concessions and supporting an independent Ulster, he emerged as the most active and voluble Unionist Party critic of government 'appeasement' policies. He was expelled from the parliamentary Unionist Party in 1970 for refusing to support the government in a motion of confidence and was decisively defeated when he contested Brian Faulkner for the party leadership in March 1971. Although re-admitted to the parliamentary party, his hints of the use of force and support for independence made him unacceptable in the Cabinet. He founded Vanguard, a Unionist pressure group with paramilitary links, in February 1972. Vanguard organised a two-day province-wide strike in March 1972 against the suspension of Stormont: 200,000 workers responded and industry was brought to a halt. Briefly reconciled with Faulkner, he soon reverted to incendiary addresses to mass rallies and large groups of uniformed men. In a speech to the Monday Club in October 1972 he declared, 'I am prepared to come out and shoot to kill,' and also continued to call for independence or dominion status. Another strike call in February 1973 led to intimidation, gun battles and five deaths. He led the opposition to the 1973 White Paper at the Ulster Unionist Council, and when defeated broke with the Unionist Party and turned Vanguard into the Vanguard Unionist Progressive Party. The VUPP obtained 10.5 per cent of the votes cast and seven of the 78 seats in the election for the Northern Ireland Assembly in 1973; Craig was elected in third place for North Antrim. As one of the leaders of the United Ulster Unionist Council, he entered into the alliance with industrial militants and paramilitaries that destroyed the power-sharing Executive. During the Constitutional Convention he supported the iconoclastic idea of an 'emergency coalition' including the SDLP, thereby misjudging not only the other members of the UUUC but also his own party. He was expelled from the UUUC and nine of the thirteen Vanguard members of the Convention refused to support the idea. This was the turning point in his career. He had been elected to Westminster as MP for East Belfast in February 1974, but his critics, particularly the DUP, accused him of weakening the Loyalist position. Lacking a secure party base, the VUPP ceased to exist in 1978 and Craig lost East Belfast to Peter Robinson of the DUP in 1979. After failing to be elected to Prior's Assembly in 1982, he played no further significant role in Ulster politics.

Eamon de Valera, 1882-1975

Born in New York of a Spanish father and Irish mother; educated at Christian Brothers' school, Charleville, Blackrock College and University College, Dublin. Last commander to surrender in 1916 Rising; President of Sinn Fein 1917-26. At first, an aggressive opponent of Ulster Unionism. In Dublin in June 1917 de Valera declared: 'All the papers shouted out that Sinn Fein wanted to coerce Ulster. He did not believe in mincing matters, and would say that if Ulster stood in the way of Irish freedom, Ulster should be coerced [cheers]. Why should it not?' (*Weekly Irish Times*, 7 July 1917) In September 1917 he went further at Cootehill: 'We say to these planters ... If you continue to be a garrison for the enemy ... We will have to kick you out.' (*Weekly Freeman*, 28 September 1917)

Between 1918 and 1922 de Valera was forced to formulate a more flexible position in relation to the Ulster Unionists than the simple demand that the obstacle blocking the road to Irish self-determination should be removed. His tone became more conciliatory, but he still insisted that Ulster ought to be an integral part of an Irish state. Although elected as President of the Irish Republic in August 1921, de Valera resigned when the Treaty was ratified by the Irish on 15 December 1921. De Valera had advised the Irish delegates that if the Treaty negotiations had to be terminated, they should 'break' on the question of Ulster – interestingly, however, the most notable feature of the lengthy and passionate debate on the Treaty terms in Dail Eireann was the almost complete absence of reference to the issue of partition. In the aftermath of the Civil War de Valera resigned the presidency of Sinn Fein in March 1926 and established Fianna Fail in November 1926. Led the first Fianna Fail governments from 1932 to 1948 and also 1951 to 1954 and 1957 to 1959. President of the Irish Republic 1959-73. As premier, he signed the condolence book in the German embassy after Hitler's death in 1945.

Joe Devlin, 1871-1934

Joseph Devlin was born in Hamill Street, Belfast, educated at Divis Street Christian Brothers' school and began his working life as a barman, but soon became a journalist for the *Irish News*. He emerged rapidly as a leading figure in Belfast nationalist politics; in the early 1900s Devlin pitted his resources against the Belfast Catholic Association, the political machine of the local bishop. This revealed his deep hostility to any form of factionalism – in this case a sectarian one – within nationalism. In an article in the *Leader* (19 February 1910), Francis Cruise O'Brien observed of Devlin's anti-factionalism: 'He confuses adjectives with arguments and consequently there is no weight in what he says ... Ideas to Mr Devlin spell faction. To suggest that his methods are not wise methods and that sometimes they are not creditable methods is to sin the unforgivable sin against Ireland.' After 1902, when he became an MP for Kilkenny, and then from 1906 to 1918 as representative for West Belfast, Devlin was an equally bitter opponent of a rather different figure – the pluralist and conciliatory William O'Brien and his nationalist All for Ireland League of MPs. During the Home Rule crisis of 1912-14 Devlin was a major figure; he used his influence to stop

Redmond from accepting a partitionist settlement, yet by 1916 he himself appears to have been convinced that it would be a mistake to coerce Unionists into a united Ireland. He remained, however, a firm opponent of the establishment of any local parliament. At times Devlin made efforts to work in the Northern Ireland parliament, but always felt that his overtures received a less than generous response from the Unionist elite. His death, however, seemed to provoke a genuine sense of grief in Craig.

Brian Faulkner, 1921-1977

Prime Minister of Northern Ireland. Born in Helen's Bay, County Down. His father owned a linen factory producing shirt collars. A Presbyterian, he was educated from the age of fourteen at St Columba's College, Rathfarnam, an Irish public school with a largely Anglican attendance. Entered the family firm in 1940 and became active in Unionist politics from 1946. Joined the 'bourgeois' Eldon Lodge of the Orange Order in 1946 and was more deeply involved in Orangeism than most of his Unionist Party contemporaries. Elected to Stormont for East Down in 1949, a seat he held until Direct Rule. In 1973 he became the Unionist member for South Down in the Northern Ireland Assembly. His Orange credentials were fortified by his action in 1955 in leading an Orange march of 15,000 along the Longstone Road, a Catholic area near Kilkeel. In 1952 and 1953 the Minister of Home Affairs had banned such marches, but due to populist Protestant pressure the ban was lifted in 1955. He became Chief Whip in 1956 and Minister of Home Affairs in 1959.

When Brookeborough resigned, his successor was chosen in a process of 'consultation' between Brookeborough, the Governor of Northern Ireland and the Chief Whip, William Craig. A more democratic process of consultation with the parliamentary party might well have resulted in a victory for Faulkner, whose populist appeal would have weighed heavily against the detached and aloof O'Neill. Faulkner was offered the congenial and high profile position of Minister of Commerce at which he excelled. As early as 1966 the opposition to O'Neill in the Unionist parliamentary party was looking to him as a possible successor, but he stayed in the Cabinet until January 1969 when he resigned over the decision to appoint the Cameron Commission to inquire into the violence since October 1968. He argued that the commission was a way of avoiding a difficult decision: whether to resist the pressure for reform, particularly that for 'one man one vote' in local government elections, or to 'capitulate' to it. In the election for O'Neill's successor he was defeated by Major James Chichester Clark who had resigned from O'Neill's government over the decision to accede to demands for electoral reform, but despite this was regarded as more moderate than Faulkner, who had supported the decision. Faulkner became Minister of Development and when Chichester-Clark resigned in March 1971 he easily defeated William Craig, who had just been readmitted to the parliamentary party after being expelled a year earlier for disloyalty.

His premiership saw an intensification of IRA violence to which he responded first by offering a new committee system at Stormont with key chairmanships going to members of the opposition and then, as the security situation deteriorated rapidly, with the disastrous decision to introduce internment on 9 August 1971. Although he bitterly criticised the decision to introduce Direct Rule, he soon became a central figure in the attempt to work out a settlement based on power-sharing. His supporters fought the 1973 Assembly elections pledged to support the British government's constitutional proposals and he subsequently became the Chief Executive of the power-sharing government established in November 1973. At the Sunningdale conference in December he was, however, forced to give ground by a united front of the SDLP, Irish ministers and Heath on the role and functions of the Council of Ireland. His famed ability to sell policy to the Unionist grass roots was stretched to breaking point. When the Ulster Unionist Council rejected the Sunningdale Agreement he resigned as leader on 7 January 1974. After the collapse of the executive he launched the Unionist Party of Northern Ireland in September 1974. This had virtually disappeared by the end of the 1970s. Faulkner retired from politics in August 1976 and died in a riding accident in March 1977.

Sean Lemass, 1899-1971

Born in Dublin into a family of Huguenot origins. His father owned a hatter's shop in Capel Street. Educated at the Christian Brothers' O'Connell school. He joined the Irish Volunteers when he was fifteen, participated in the 1916 Rising in the GPO, was imprisoned but released after a few weeks because of his youth. Rejoined the Dublin Volunteers and was active in the War of Independence. Imprisoned in Ballykinlar in December 1920, he was released when the Treaty was signed. He joined the anti-Treatyites in the Four Courts where he was arrested. He escaped and fought in the Civil War during which his elder brother, Noel, was killed by pro-Treaty forces. After the Civil War he was first elected to the Dail for Sinn Fein in a by-election for Dublin South in 1924 and played a crucial role in the birth of Fianna Fail in 1926. He had used his time in prison to study economics and industry and these became his core interests when Fianna Fail won power. As Minister of Industry and Commerce he was responsible for the drive to build up Irish industry behind tariff walls in the 1930s. He was also prominent in the portrayal of Fianna Fail as an economically and socially progressive party with a special vocation to defend the interests of workers. He once defined his role as 'the left wing of Fianna Fail: I have to drive the others'. ('A Pragmatic Man Who Saw an Opportunity in Everything', *Irish Times*, 12 May 1971)

He became Tanaiste (deputy prime minister) in 1945, and in the difficult post-war years struggled to reconstruct Fianna Fail's economic policies as the limitations of protectionism became clear during the major economic crisis of the mid-1950s. He managed the difficult reversal of policy in 1958-59 when the Fianna Fail administration committed itself to getting rid of protectionism and inviting in foreign capital. His willingness to jettison Sinn Fein economics was also apparent in a more flexible attitude towards Northern Ireland. He became leader of Fianna Fail and Taoiseach on De Valera's retirement in 1959. He discouraged the use of the United Nations as a forum for anti-partitionist propaganda and favoured the gradual discontinuance of the pejorative term 'six counties' in favour of 'Northern Ireland'.

While still committed to an ending of partition, he saw

this as most likely to come about through a process of lessening tensions between Unionism and nationalism and looked to the development of north-south economic co-operation as part of this process. Although his initial suggestion of a north-south free trade area was strongly repudiated by Lord Brookeborough in 1959, pressure from the British government and sections of Northern industry had produced a softening of tone even before O'Neill became Prime Minister. (See British government memorandum to Northern Ireland government on Economic Relations with the Irish Republic, PRONI Cab. 4/1115, 2 February 1960.) O'Neill's strong desire to modernise the image of Northern Ireland and establish his flexibility compared to that of his predecessor allowed him to ignore the degree to which Lemass had publicly identified the improvement and deepening of north-south economic links with ending partition and invite him to Stormont in January 1965. The communique issued after the meeting noted that the talks 'did not touch on constitutional or political questions', but critics noted that O'Neill had not consulted or informed his Cabinet colleagues about the visit which Faulkner claimed 'made the whole affair seem furtive and suspect'. (*Memoirs*, p. 39) After his retirement as leader in 1966 he established the All Party Committee on the Constitution which, among other areas, considered the possibility of amending Articles 2 and 3.

Cardinal Joseph MacRory, 1861-1945

Archbishop of Armagh, born Ballygawley, County Tyrone, educated Armagh and Maynooth. Professor at Olton College Birmingham 1887-89 and Maynooth 1889-1915. Bishop of Down and Connor 1915-28; supporter of Michael Collins but opposed Collins's decision to call off the Republican boycott of Belfast goods in January 1922. Represented Northern nationalists at a meeting of the provisional government in Dublin later the same month. Strongly opposed Dublin recognition of Northern Ireland. Cardinal MacRory refused to take in person an honorary degree offered by Queen's University, Belfast, in 1929. In 1931 he declared that the Protestant church in Ireland was 'not even a part of the

Church of Christ'. J.J. Lee, in *Ireland 1912-85*, Cambridge 1989, basing himself on the German archives, shows that the Nazis believed in 1940 that MacRory was in favour of 'possible German action' to end partition. In October 1941 he wrote to the US envoy to Dublin, David Gray: 'The only case in which you can escape making peace with him [Hitler] is if you win out yourselves. But is this likely? When can you hope to be able to invade Germany and defeat the German army on its own soil? And suppose that did ever happen, is there the ghost of a chance of a just peace then?' (Quoted in Dermot Keogh, *Twentieth-Century Ireland*, Dublin 1994, p. 128.) For his view that Northern Catholics were badly treated on educational and other matters, see Mary Harris, 'The Catholic Church, Minority Rights and the Founding of the Northern Irish State' in D. Keogh and M. Haltzel (eds), *Northern Ireland, the Politics of Reconciliation*, Cambridge 1993.

Harry Midgley, 1892-1957

Born in Seaview Street, North Belfast, and educated at Duncairn Gardens National School. At fourteen he became an apprentice joiner in Workman and Clark's shipyard. Active in the Independent Labour Party as a supporter of James Connolly before 1914. Fought in the First World War. Stood as an Independent Labour candidate on an anti-partitionist platform in 1921 election for the Northern Ireland parliament. In 1925 he won a Belfast Council seat in the Dock ward for the NILP. When he won the Dock seat in the Stormont elections in 1933 he was chairman of the NILP and the dominant Labour figure in Northern Ireland. He had dropped his anti-partitionism and became an ardent supporter of progress within the UK. His forthright support for the Republican side in the Spanish Civil War and attacks on the role of the Catholic Church in the conflict were important factors in alienating the substantial Catholic working-class portion of the Dock electorate, and he lost the seat in the 1938 General Election. Growing friction on the left of the NILP and with its anti-partitionist section was exacerbated by the outbreak of the war and the South's neutrality. Having won the predominantly Protestant constituency of Willowfield in 1941, he pushed the NILP to commit itself to support for Northern Ireland's position inside the UK, and when he failed he resigned and formed the Commonwealth Labour Party in 1942. When Basil Brooke became Unionist leader in 1943 Midgley was appointed Minister of Public Security and, although he did not join the Unionist Party and the CLP fought the 1945 elections, his biographer notes, 'Midgley's career began, at this juncture, to slide almost inexorably towards the politics of Protestant exclusivism.' (Graham Walker, *The Politics of Frustration: Harry Midgley and the Failure of Labour in Northern Ireland*, Manchester 1985, p. 218) He resigned from the government in 1945 and retained his seat in the General Election, although none of the other CLP candidates was successful. In 1947 he joined the Unionist Party, the Orange Order and the Black Preceptory and was rewarded with the post of Minister of Labour in 1949. He was Minister of Education from 1950 until his death.

Sir John Milne Barbour, 1868-1951

Educated at Harrow and Brasenose College, Oxford, Milne Barbour, a prominent businessman, became president of the Belfast Chamber of Commerce in 1911 on the eve of the Home Rule crisis. Elected Stormont MP for Antrim in 1921, Milne Barbour was Parliamentary Secretary to the Minister of Finance from 1921 to 1940 and simultaneously Minister of Commerce from 1925 to 1941. From 1941 to 1943 he was Minister of Finance. A synodsman of the Church of Ireland, Milne Barbour was heavily involved both in Freemasonry and the Boy Scout movement. Although a relatively liberal figure, Milne Barbour refused the definition 'Irishman' and insisted that he was a 'Britisher'.

James Molyneaux (Lord Molyneaux of Killead), 1920-

Leader of the Ulster Unionist Party from 1979 to 1995. Although born into a Church of Ireland family, Jim Molyneaux was educated at a Catholic school; later, as a young British soldier, he was one of the liberators of

Belsen. Despite this somewhat unusual background, he was widely regarded as a dour Orangeman in political life. Unfair as it was, this perception had some basis to it – Molyneaux was one of the lower middle-class cadres (secretary of the South Antrim Unionist Association from 1964 to 1970) who took advantage of the flight of the upper classes from Unionist political activity under the twin impacts of the IRA and Paisleyism. Stepping into the breach, Jim Molyneaux was elected MP for Antrim South from 1970 to 1983 and then for Lagan Valley from 1983 to 1997. In both constituencies he had a massive majority. Molyneaux stood for a stolid Unionism, eschewing the demagogy of Paisleyism but never genuinely interested in a devolutionist power-sharing settlement with the SDLP. Devolution, he told his biographer Ann Purdy, was 'not worth the candle'.

Molyneaux was an admirer of Enoch Powell and allowed him to conduct the Unionist Party's 'foreign policy' at Westminster. Powell supposedly understood Mrs Thatcher and the Whitehall system, but in the end this confidence in Powell was misplaced. The Thatcherite imposition of the Anglo-Irish Agreement of 1985 inflicted a blow on Molyneaux's leadership from which it never fully recovered. Stubbornly, however, he held onto the leadership for another decade, losing out in the end only because of his failure to prevent the publication of the Frameworks Documents in 1995. In fact, Molyneaux was far less culpable in this instance; his early management of the 'peace process', including his handling of the Downing Street Declaration of 1993, was quite impressive. Having lost the leadership, Molyneaux did not retire from political life; rather, from behind the scenes he remained a formidable opponent of the new leader of the Ulster Unionist Party, David Trimble.

Terence O'Neill (Lord O'Neill of the Maine), 1914-1992

Prime Minister of Northern Ireland. Son of Orange Conservative MP Arthur Bruce O'Neill, the first Westminster MP to die at the front in the First World War, O'Neill was brought up largely in his mother's Liberal circle, she being the daughter of the Earl of Crewe, a member of Asquith's Cabinet. Educated at Eton, he drifted through various stock exchange jobs before military service in the Second World War. Then, rather like Parnell, O'Neill returned home to pick up the inheritance of a famous political family. Minister of Finance at Stormont from 1956 to 1963, he was appointed Prime Minister largely, his critics alleged, because of his aristocratic connections rather than on account of the possession of any particular political skill. In his early years in office he was concerned primarily to strengthen his position by winning back Protestant support which the Unionist Party had lost to the Northern Ireland Labour Party in the period after 1958. 'Stealing Labour's thunder' (to use O'Neill's own term), rather than allaying Catholic resentments, was his main preoccupation. While capable of the occasional conciliatory grand gesture – such as a famous visit to a Catholic school – O'Neill espoused a rhetoric of planning and modernisation by which nationalist grievances would be dissolved by a shared participation in the benefits of economic growth. He saw no role for structural reform.

The emergence of the civil rights movement presented O'Neill with an excruciating dilemma. On the one hand, placating the reformers was likely to mean consolidation of the Unionist internal opposition. On the other, failing to do so would probably lead – in his eyes at least – to British intervention and a complete collapse of local autonomy. O'Neill's legacy is an ambiguous one; even the reputation of his path-breaking talks with the Irish premier, Sean Lemass, suffered from later claims by Lemass's widow (bitterly repudiated by O'Neill) that they had been about 'Irish unity'.

Hugh MacDonald Pollock, 1852-1937

Stormont MP for South Belfast 192 1-29 and Belfast Windsor 1929-37; Minister of Finance in the Northern Ireland government 192 1-37. Described by Sir Robert Kennedy in 1937 as a 'good financial accountant for all local purposes but he is old, cranky and tactless' (P. Bew, K. Darwin and G. Gillespie (eds), *Passion and Prejudice*, Belfast, 1993, p. 4).

Wilfrid Bliss Spender, 1876-1960

Born into a Plymouth family and educated at Winchester and the Staff College, Camberley, Spender came from a journalistic and literary background. His cousin J.A. Spender was a well-known liberal commentator. Wilfrid Spender at first pursued what appeared to be a highly promising military career, but resigned from the General Staff over the Ulster question in 1913. An Ulster Volunteer Force officer in 19 13-14, he returned to the General Staff in 1914 and was awarded the DSO and MC in 1918. Commanded the UVF in 1919 and inaugurated the B Specials in 1920; CBE 1921; First Secretary to Northern Ireland Cabinet, 192 1-25; Permanent Secretary to the Minister of Finance and head of the Northern Ireland Civil Service, 1925-44; member of the Joint Exchequer Board, 1933-54. Coined the phrase 'factory of grievances' to describe the devolved Stormont system of government. On 12 June 1937 Spender voiced his personal credo in a private letter: 'Why, oh why, will every Irishman dig up the musty pages of history instead of dealing practically with the present and future. If I were Minister of Education, I would allow ancient Greek history to be taught as I think it has a wonderful broadening effect on the mind, and only the broad outlines of English and Irish history. That and bible history properly taught would be far better instruction than the pointless and ghoulish digging up of the results of British policy ... You can take it from me that British governments since 1922 have been more generous to Ulster than the Free State government could afford to be. Here is a practical question: 'Would you [lose] full rates on agricultural land in order to placate the South? You might but very few of your neighbours [would] of either creed.' (PRONI D2661/C/1/5)

Appendix

Note on the Construction of Table 3

The section of this table referring to 1971 is reproduced from Aunger's article 'Religion and Occupational Class in Northern Ireland', *Economic and Social Review*, 7 (1975). The section referring to 1911 was constructed from the 1911 Census of Ireland for the counties of Armagh, Antrim, Down, Fermanagh, Londonderry and Tyrone and the cities of Belfast and Londonderry. To assist comparability the principles used in its construction followed as far as possible those used by Aunger. Economically active males and females were first divided, by occupation, into seven strata: 1) professionally qualified and higher administrative; 2) managerial and executive; 3) inspectorial, supervisory and other non-manual (higher grade); 4) ibid (lower grade); 5a) routine non-manual; 5b) skilled manual; 6) semi-skilled manual; 7) routine manual. The criterion for this division used by both Aunger and ourselves is an adapted form of the Hall-Jones scale of occupational prestige. For details of this scale, see J. Hall and D.C. Jones, 'Social Grading of Occupations', *British Journal of Sociology*, Vol. 1 No. 1, 1950. A chart indicating the position of specific occupations is given in A.N. Oppenheim, *Questionnaire Design and Attitude Measurement*, London 1966, pp. 275-84. As in Aunger's table, persons with the following occupations were excluded from the classification for 1911, as their occupational descriptions provided insufficient information for grading: farmers, farmers' relatives, 'others concerned with agriculture', 'others', members of the armed forces and students. A number of conventional decisions on categorisation of occupations not on the Hall-Jones scale had to be made. It seems probable that Aunger had to make similar decisions.

Since there is probably a degree of inconsistency between these decisions, comparison between 1911 and 1971 cannot be said to be completely valid.

The arrangements described gave the following results for 1911 (the very small number of Jews being included in the figures for Protestants).

Class	Protestant	Catholic
1	6,596	1,819
2	3,754	902
3	11,774	4,122
4	1,911	2,728
5a	49,457	30,256
5b	94,596	35,382
6	62,209	40,666
7	48,798	28,537
Total	279,086	144,412

(The decline of the agrarian population is, of course, the main factor in the enormous intercensal growth of what is counted here as the economically active population.)

To produce the scale in the main text, grades 1, 2 and 3 were taken together to give 'Professional, managerial' (I); grades 4 and 5a were taken together to give 'Lower-grade non-manual' (II), and grades 5b, 6 and 7 were renumbered III, IV and V respectively.

Index

THE POLITICS OF ILLUSION
A POLITICAL HISTORY OF THE IRA

Henry Patterson

This is the first comprehensive study of the IRA's attempts to create a 'social republicanism', a marriage between militant nationalism and the politics of the left. From agitation amongst the peasantry in the 1920s to efforts in the 1990s to add a political dimension to purist nationalism in the form of Sinn Fein's 'peace process', Henry Patterson analyses the various failed attempts to marry two fundamentally incompatible ideologies.

In this highly praised work the author steers us through the complex, schismatic and inevitably secretive history of both the Provisional and the Official IRA, Sinn Fein and the various organisations with which they have been associated. He teases out the meaning and significance of the twists and turns in republican policy, which at different periods have involved working with trade unions, collaboration with Nazi Germany, hunger strikes and, of course, both urban and rural guerrilla warfare.

This fully revised and updated new edition takes the history of Irish republicanism beyond Sinn Fein's best ever performance in the 1997 Westminster and Dail elections to the IRA's renewed ceasefire. Henry Patterson's conclusion is that 'physical force' or militarist nationalism and the politics of the left make uneasy and, when the rhetoric is cleared away, self-deluding and illusory bed-fellows.

'Subtle and authoritative'
Fintan O'Toole, *New York Review of Books*

'Of immense value"
Michael D. Higgins, *The Irish Times*

Henry Patterson is Professor of Politics at the University of Ulster and the author of numerous books and articles on Irish history, including *Class Conflict and Sectarianism*.

paperback

also published by Serif

THE NORTHERN IRELAND PEACE PROCESS, 1993–1996
A CHRONOLOGY

Paul Bew and Gordon Gillespie

For those who knew how to read them, interesting smoke signals emerged from Northern Ireland during the summer of 1993: there were moves afoot to bring an end to the violence which had plagued the province for a quarter of a century.

In August 1994 the IRA announced a ceasefire and for almost eighteen months headlines were dominated by negotiations in Dublin, handshakes in Washington and talks between Sinn Fein and the British government. Peace had broken out. There followed a complex series of discussions which eventually foundered on the rock of decommissioning paramilitary arms. Then in February 1996 bombs in Docklands and elsewhere in London brought the peace process to a sudden and bloody end.

The Northern Ireland Peace Process 1993–1996 records these developments, charting official talks, apparently minor incidents whose significance became apparent months later, and major political shifts and turns. Explanatory essays about the major turning-points in the peace process are woven into a political diary which will be essential reading for anyone interested in Irish affairs.

'Meticulous'
Dick Walsh, *The Irish Times*

paperback

THE STRANGE DEATH OF LIBERAL ENGLAND

George Dangerfield

At the beginning of the twentieth century Britain's empire spanned the globe, her economy was strong and the political system seemed to be immune to the ills which afflicted so many other countries. After a resounding electoral triumph in 1906 the Liberals formed the government of the most powerful nation on earth, yet within a few years the army had mutinied, industrial unrest was rife, civil war loomed in Ireland and the proceedings of 'the mother of parliaments' were reduced to little more than farce.

The Strange Death of Liberal England is the classic study of this rapid collapse of a self-confident body politic. Three factors combined to bring Liberal England to its knees. The Home Rule crisis brought Ireland to the brink of civil war and led to the mutiny at the Curragh, while the campaign for women's suffrage created widespread civil disorder and discredited the legal and penal systems, and an unprecedented strike wave swept the land.

The years before the First World War are often presented as a golden age, but this stylish and witty history shows the turbulence of an alleged *belle époque* to have been the writing on the wall for a nation which had for too long thought of itself as all-powerful

'A classic both of popular history, in the best sense of that phrase, and of good and interesting writing.'
The Irish Times

George Dangerfield was a Fellow of Princeton University and winner of the Pulitzer Prize for American History; his books include *The Damnable Question: A Study in Anglo-Irish Relations* and *The Awakening of American Nationalism*.

paperback

PLEASANT THE SCHOLAR'S LIFE
IRISH INTELLECTUALS AND THE CONSTRUCTION OF THE NATION STATE

Maurice Goldring

As Europe witnesses new states being born and clothing themselves in the symbolic apparel of nationhood, Maurice Goldring's exploration of the conscious creation of national 'traditions' could scarcely be more timely.

In this innovative survey of the interplay of literature and folklore in the building of cultural identity, Maurice Goldring makes a major contribution to our understanding of nationalism. In a penetrating and readable study of the cultural origins of Irish nationalism, he shows how Dublin intellectuals promoted the use of Galeic and concentrated their energies on idealising the life of the peasantry in the West of the country. At the same time, the Catholic clergy expanded its authority in the countryside and the power vacuum in the towns was filled by an inward-looking lower middle class. The alliance between the church and the intelligentsia which followed laid the basis for a social and moral conservatism that was used to manipulate the world-view of ordinary citizens and is only now being shaken off.

'Subtle and penetrating . . . Good social criticism, and good literary criticism too'
Conor Cruise O'Brien

'Carefully wrought, subtle and intelligent'
John McGahern, *The Irish Times*

Maurice Goldring is Professor of Irish Studies at the University of Paris and author of a number of books including *Belfast: From Loyalty to Rebellion*

paperback

THE CROWD IN HISTORY
A STUDY OF POPULAR
DISTURBANCES IN FRANCE AND
ENGLAND, 1730–1848

George Rudé

Who took part in the widespread disturbances which periodically shook eighteenth-century London? What really motivated the food rioters who helped to spark off the French Revolution? How did the movement of agricultural labourers destroying new machinery spread from one village to another in the English countryside? How did the *sans-culottes* organise in revolutionary Paris?

George Rudé was the first historian to ask such questions and in doing so he identified 'the faces in the crowd' in some of the crucial episodes in modern European history. An established classic of 'history from below', **The Crowd in History** is remarkable above all for the clarity with which it deals with the full sweep of complex historical events. Whether in Berlin, Beijing or Soweto, crowds continue to make history, and Rudé's work retains all its freshness and relevance for students of history and politics and the general reader alike.

'It may seem incredible that nobody tried before to discover what sort of people actually stormed the Bastille, but Rudé is the first to have done so ... Like all his work this book is concentrated, simple and clear, and admirably suited to the non-specialist reader.'
Eric Hobsbawm, *New York Review of Books*

George Rudé's numerous books include *Wilkes and Liberty, The Crowd in the French Revolution* and, with Eric Hobsbawm, *Captain Swing*. One of the most innovative social historians of the twentieth century, he died in 1993.

paperback